(THE HOPE)

The values change every time the universe changes.

And that's every time we redefine a big enough bit of it, which we do all the time, through the process of discovery that isn't discovery, just the invention of another version of how things are.

And yet, in spite of that, we still go on believing that today's version of things is the only right one, because as you've learned from this series, we can only handle one way of seeing things at a time.

We've never had systems that would let us do more than that.

So we've always had to have conformity with the current view.

Disagree with the Church, and you were punished as a heretic; with the political system, as a revolutionary. With the scientific establishment, as a charlatan. With the educational system, as a failure.

If you didn't fit the mold, you were rejected.

But, ironically, the latest product of that way of doing things is a new instrument, a new system, that while it could make conformity more rigid, more totalitarian, than ever before in history, could also blow everything wide open.

Because with it, we could operate on the basis that values and standards and ethics and facts and truth all depend on what your view of the world is; and that there may be as many views of *that* as there are people.

And with this capability of keeping a tally on those millions of opinions, voiced electronically, we might be able to lift the limitations of conforming to any centralized representational form of government (originally invented because there was no way for everybody's voice to be heard).

You might be able to give everybody unhindered, untested access to knowledge. Because the computer would do the day-to-day work for which we once qualified the select few in an educational system originally designed for a world where only the few could be taught.

You might end the regimentation of people living and working in vast, unmanageable cities, uniting them instead in an electronic community, where the Himalayas and Manhattan were only a split second apart.

You might with that and much more break the mold that has held us back since the beginning, in a future world that we would describe as balanced anarchy, and *they* will describe as an open society, tolerant of every view, aware that there is no single privileged way of doing things; above all, able to do away with the greatest tragedy of our era, the centuries-old waste of human talent that we couldn't--or wouldn't--use.

Utopia? Why?

If, as I've said all along, the universe is at any time what you say it is--then say!

James Burke,
The Day the Universe Changed
(BBC-TV series), his final speech.

(THE DARING PROPOSAL)

Next, meet Mr Ted Nelson, gadfly, prophet and self-confessed computer crackpot, with a lifetime's obsession wrapped up in an enormous program called (after Coleridge's unfinished poem) Xanadu. Boon or boondoggle, nobody is quite sure. But the giant piece of software for steering one's own thought processes (including alternative paths, mental backtracks and intellectual leaps) is hardly lacking in ambition or vision.

Conceived originally by Mr Nelson while a student at Harvard as simply a note-keeping program for preserving his every thought, Xanadu has evolved into a total literary process: creating ideas; organising the thoughts, with traces showing backtracks, alternative versions and jumps to cross-referenced documents; manipulating the text; publishing the results; and logging a share of the royalties to every other author cited.

Every document in Xanadu's database has links to its intellectual antecedents and to others covering related topics. The linked references work like footnotes, except that Xanadu offers an electronic "window" through which they can be accessed there and then. Because the whole process works in a non-sequential way, the inventor calls the output "hypertext."

Mr Nelson looks forward to the day when anybody can create what he or she wants--from recipes to research papers, sonnets to songs--and put it into Xanadu's database and quote or cite anybody else. Royalties and subroyalties, monitored automatically by the host computer, would be paid according to the amount of time a user was on-line and reading a specific document. It sounds pretty wild at the moment, but hypertext could be commonplace before the century is out.

The Economist
(London), 23 Aug 86

LITERARY

Edition 87.1

THE REPORT ON, AND OF, PROJECT XANADU
CONCERNING
WORD PROCESSING, ELECTRONIC PUBLISHING,
HYPERTEXT, THINKERTOYS,
TOMORROW'S INTELLECTUAL REVOLUTION,
AND CERTAIN OTHER TOPICS
INCLUDING
KNOWLEDGE, EDUCATION AND FREEDOM.

MACHINES

THEODOR HOLM NELSON

COMPUTER BOOKS BY TED NELSON

Computer Lib, published by the author, 1974; second edition from Microsoft Press, fall 1987.

The Home Computer Revolution, published by the author, 1977.

Literary Machines, published by the author, 1981; various revisions from year to year; this is edition 87.1, being published by the author, 1987. Simultaneous mass-market edition being published by special arrangement by The Distributors, 702 South Michigan, South Bend IN 46618; simultaneous Macintosh hypertext edition in GUIDE being published by Owl International, Inc., 14218 NE 21st Street, Bellevue WA 98007.

VIDEOTAPES ABOUT THE XANADU SYSTEM

"Technical Overview of the Xanadu(tm) Hypertext System." VHS extended play, 2 hours 40 minutes. A whiteboard talk by Ted Nelson. $50 postpaid (foreign orders add $5 for airmail, purchase orders add $5 carrying charge.) Project Xanadu, 8480 Fredericksburg #138, San Antonio TX 78229.

"The Posterity Machine." Talk by Ted Nelson at Vassar College, 1986. VHS, two hours. $30 postpaid (foreign orders add $5 for airmail, purchase orders add $5 carrying charge.) Project Xanadu, 8480 Fredericksburg #138, San Antonio TX 78229.

DONATIONS TO THE CAUSE

Money sent to Project Xanadu is probably not tax-deductible.

User-names on the network (Xandles) may be reserved for $100, subject to various arbitrary restrictions and arbitrary cancellation. Consider it a donation.

EDITION 87.1. This book is mostly about Project Xanadu and its offspring, the Xanadu(tm) hypertext system--a certain kind of computer program--and its implications for the future. This is a form of storage, a new form of literature, and a network that might just revitalize human life. It is embodied in an existing piece of software, which we are trying to promote, sell, and explain. We think that anyone who actually *understands the problems* will recognize ours as the unique solution.

The original *Literary Machines*, written hastily in King of Prussia, Pennsylvania, in the early months of 1981, expanded on my paper "Replacing the Printed Word" from the 1980 World Computer Conference. It is not the book I would have written in leisure, and has been changed in various ways from time to time, but remained badly typed and sloppily illustrated until now. It should have been completely rewritten, of course, but various people have grown to love its old organization, so I have grafted this edition's changes onto the old structure.

This edition is being published simultaneously by the author; in a mass market edition by the Distributors, of South Bend, Indiana; and as a hypertext on disk for the Macintosh by Owl International, Inc., of Bellevue, WA, using their GUIDE program.

To get on the mailing list of Project Xanadu, please send a donation of at least $2 to Project Xanadu, 8480 Fredericksburg #138, San Antonio TX 78229.

This book is a hypertext, or non-sequential piece of writing.

It is partly *about* hypertext, or non-sequential writing, and using a hypertext form will, I hope, help communicate some of the benefits of such writing.

One   **Two**   **Three**

PLAN OF THIS BOOK

There is a Chapter Zero, several Chapters One, one Chapter Two, and several Chapters Three.

It is suggested that you read Chapter Zero first; then any of the introductory Chapters One; and then Chapter Two, which is the heart of the book. (Because Chapter Two is long and sequential, its parts are numbered. Other sections of the book are not numbered because they are not, in principle, sequential.) You may or may not feel that you understand it fully.

It is suggested that you then read one of the closing chapters. This will help you see what the future of the system is supposed to be about.

At this point it is suggested that you read another of the introductory Chapters One, and look over Chapter Two again. You will almost certainly understand it better.

Continue in this vein, passing repeatedly through Chapter Two, until you understand this book.

Pretzel or infinity. It's up to you.

There are also several Chapters Four, which deal with certain technical aspects of the system, and several Chapters Five, which deal with certain business aspects. No instruction for reading these chapters is provided.

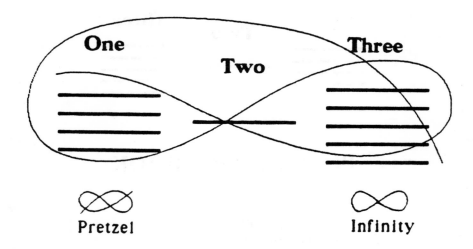

Whenever a work's structure is intentionally one of its own themes, another of its themes is art.

Annie Dillard

1981 DEDICATION

This book, and the system it foretells, are dedicated to

Eric Blair (1903-1950)

better known by his pen-name

"GEORGE ORWELL;"

an acute, sad and bitter observer and prognosticator
who understood tyranny perhaps better than any tyrant,
who understood information control
long ahead of the rest of us;
and who left us cunning, elegant and timely warmings.

Somehow many take his name to stand for
all that he despised;
so that the word "Orwellian,"
meaning tyrannical, oppressive, mind-controlling,
and futuristically threatening,
is itself the perfect example of the twisted Newspeak he foresaw.

**May his simple, honest, angry devotion
to truth and human freedom
live forever.**

1987 DEDICATION

This book in its present version is dedicated to

DOUGLAS C. ENGELBART,

visionary of what he calls
The Augmentation of Human Intellect by Computer;
and, as part of that, the inventor of what we now call
"Word Processing,"
"Outline Processing,"
"Screen Windows,"
the mouse;
and (what this book is largely about)
THE TEXT LINK;
a man whose warmth and gentle determination
are an inspiration to all who know him.

**May his simple, honest, saintly devotion
to the uplift and empowerment of the human mind
live forever.**

Posterity is the religion of the intellectuals.

Woody Allen

Words without thoughts
never to Heaven go.

Hamlet

Litera scripta manet.
(The written word remains.)

Horace

Extremism in the defense of liberty
is no vice.

Barry Goldwater

Give me a lever long enough
and I will move the world.

Archimedes,
as generally misquoted

Toto, something tells me
we're not in Kansas anymore.

Dorothy
(*The Wizard of Oz*,
  MGM version)

CONTENTS

TECHNICAL CHAPTERS FOUR

BUSINESS CHAPTERS FIVE

AFTERCHUNKS

HYPERWORLD

All men dream, but not equally.
Those who dream by night,
in the dusty recesses of their minds,
wake in the day to find that it was vanity.
But the dreamers of the day are dangerous men,
for they may act their dreams with open eyes
to make it possible.
T. E. Lawrence

LITERARY 0/1 MACHINES

HYPERMEDIA AT LARGE

Suddenly, everyone is talking about hypertext. You hear the word on every side. At a conference in March 1987 I overheard the word nine times walking through the lounge.

Similarly, in the new area we may call Interactive Show Biz--where they are now creating branching videodiscs and other interactive productions--the word of the hour seems to be "hypermedia."

I am bemused by this, and find it somewhat ironic. I coined the term "hypertext" over twenty years ago, and in the ensuing decades have given many speeches and written numerous articles preaching the hypertext revolution: telling people hypertext would be the wave of the future, the next stage of civilization, the next stage of literature and a clarifying force in education and the technical fields, as well as art and culture. Same for "hypermedia" (a term first published somewhat later).

For years I got the impression that no one had heard or read any of this at all. And now, abruptly, it seems that many people did indeed hear, and many have begun to agree. (The first hypertext conference not my own doing is scheduled for November 1987.) The strange thing is that all this took so long and then happened so suddenly.

But what is it all about?

Well, by "hypertext" I mean *non-sequential writing*--text that branches and allows choices to the reader, best read at an interactive screen.

As popularly conceived, this is a series of text chunks connected by links which offer the reader different pathways.*

"ORDINARY" HYPERTEXT

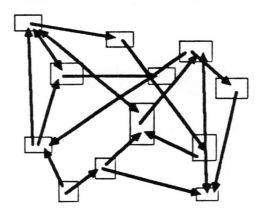

---

*This is the structure, for example, of the "Notecards" system, programmed by Frank Halasz and Randy Trigg at Xerox Palo Alto Research Center and offered by Xerox on its D-class computers. It is also the structure offered on the Hypertext Abstract Machine under development at Tektronix by Mayer Schwartz and Norm Delisle.

LITERARY 0/2 MACHINES

I will not argue with this definition here, but I hope it will become clear throughout the book how much more I think hypertext can be.

MOST GENERAL WRITING

Hypertext can include sequential text, and is thus the most general form of writing.* Unrestricted by sequence, in hypertext we may create new forms of writing which better reflect the structure of what we are writing *about*; and readers, choosing a pathway, may follow their interests or current line of thought in a way heretofore considered impossible.

This generality is a vital aspect of the idea. Because computer text systems are in a calamitous state.

The world of paper is at least unified and compatible. Objects can be easily mixed and matched. Books, manuscripts and notes can be stored on the same shelf, opened on the same desk. You need not start up, initialize or insert a disk before opening a magazine.

But now enter the world of computer text systems. There is "word processing" and "outline processing," "teleconferencing," "networks," bulletin boards, "videotext" (in whose name true atrocities have been proposed), electronic mail, version control

---

*In one direction of generalization, it is also the most general form of language.

systems, pop-up note pads, electronic sticky notes, and now various systems called "hypertext."

Even among nonlinear text systems, quite a variety are now available for the desktop computer. They variously offer jumps around text, outlining and text expansion; the ability for different users to put separate notes onto linear documents; the categorization of messages according to social-strategic type (inquiries, commitments, fulfillments).

This variety of innovations is laudable. The dark side, however, is the general incompatibility of it all. These colorful and varied facilities cannot be combined or used at the same time, let alone have their contents easily shared and combined and displayed side-by-side. No longer on the same shelf, these things must be turned on differently, at different times, used on different computers and stored on different disks--and the user typically must *keep paper notes* as to their particulars. Not only the different kinds of disks must be saved, and directions as to their use, but also *papers to tie them all together*.

At least there is a background sense of openness and pluralism. Though incompatible, the different text systems have a point of view in common: that the different contributions of different users are important, and so they offer new pluralistic styles based on many people adding to the body of writing. The initiatives and contributions of many peole are assumed to be worthwhile.

LITERARY 0/3 MACHINES

But there is at present no way to gather, and save, and publish, the many documents and scraps that people are writing on screens and sharing through an immense variety of incompatible systems.

Such incompatibilities are only one aspect of the dismal state of the computer field.* The computer, and now the personal computer, have opened whole new realms of disorder, difficulty and complication for humanity. With so-called "computer basics" and so-called "computer literacy," beginners are taught a world of prevailing but unnecessary complication. Nearly everything has to be fitted into oppressive and inane hierarchical structure and coded into other people's conceptual frameworks, often seeming rigid and highly inappropriate to the user's own concerns. The files in which we must keep things on conventional computer systems are detached from their relationships and history, and (for many if not all users) entwine like wire coathangers in a tangle of unknown relationships and increasing disorder.

MORE GENERAL HYPERMEDIA

In the realm of the more high-bandwith hypermedia--interactive movies, graphics, sound and music--even more confusion reigns. There is great momentum behind interactive videodisc, especially things called CD-ROM, CDI and DVI. These have not caught on or even been seen, but they are being pushed by Big Corporations with Big Track Records.

Supposedly when they come out these media will be mass-marketed disks, sold only in a final form, and thus, like phonograph records, delivered by the Information Lords to the Information Peons. This is rather unlike the prevailing thought among computer-text-system people, where everyone's contribution is thought to be valued.

Some people like all this incompatibility and complication, and say it is the new world we must learn to live in. Others, already hating computers, correctly dread these matters and hope vainly to stop the computer tide. I propose a third approach: to unify and organize in the *right* way, so as to clarify and simplify our computer and working lives, and indeed to bring literature, science, art and civilization to new heights of understanding, through hypertext.

As the most general form of writing, hypertext will not be "another type" of obscure structure, but a framework of reunification. (Note that in the original hypertext system of Douglas Engelbart, who invented electronic text systems, it *was* all together; it is the others who have torn it all apart into incompatible pieces.)

---

*For continuing remarks in this vein, see my book *Computer Lib*, second edition from Microsoft Press, fall of 1987; especially the early chapter, "A Field of Rubble."

LITERARY 0/4 MACHINES

For I believe that the potential for a new Golden Age, through such a unification of electronic text systems, lies before us, and just in time, too.

PROJECT XANADU

Project Xanadu, which this book is about, has been a long-term venture to develop a hypertext system to support all the features of these other systems, and many more. Project Xanadu began in the fall of 1960,* and put a prototype on line for experimentation in January of 1987. We hope to offer a commercial version in 1988, at three levels: a single-user version; a network server for offices; and a public-access system to be franchised like hamburger stands. All this will be discussed later.

The reason it has taken so long is that *all* of its ultimate features are part of the design. Others begin by designing systems to do less, and then add features; we have designed this as a unified structure to handle it all. This takes much longer but leads to clean design.

The problem is not hardware. It is *generalized, clean software design.* And when the problems above, in their generality, become clear to others, we think they will see that it makes much more sense to adopt an existing, unified solution than to keep nailing features where they weren't originally planned.

THE STRUCTURE

The Xanadu system is a unique form of storage for text and other computer data. The system is based upon one pool of storage, which can be shared and simultaneously organized in many different ways. This makes it possible easily to *make new things out of old,* sharing material between units. Described simply:

> all materials are in a shared pool of units, but every element has a unit in which it originated;

> new units can be built from material in previous units, in addition to new material;

---

*This is the first hypertext system to be so called (though Engelbart's NLS system at Stanford Research Institute was *really* the first hypertext system).

After approximately fifty man-years of effort, the Xanadu program is operational in prototype and available for experimentation at the end of a phone line. The back-end program presently runs on a Sun Workstation under Unix. It is written in C and presently (May 87) compiles to about 137K of 68000 native code on the Sun. This does not include buffer space, of which the more the merrier (1 megabyte and up recommended).

Front-end programs should include our protocol manager, a module which handles sending and receiving in the FEBE(tm) Front End-Back End protocol. It presently compiles to about 30K on the Sun.

LITERARY 0/5 MACHINES

there can be arbitrary links betwen arbitrary sections of units.

We call this "xanalogical storage" (not a trademark).*

XANALOGICAL STORAGE

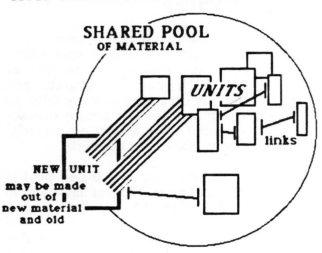

SHARED POOL OF MATERIAL

UNITS

links

NEW UNIT may be made out of new material and old

There are three basic relationships in xanalogical storage: *origin*, the parts where elements begin; *commonality*, the sharing of elements between units; and *links*, which mark, annotate and connect portions of units.

Explaining and exploring this, and our particular methods, will take the rest of the book, especially Chapter Two and the Chapters Four.

THE ASPIRATION

The Xanadu system, designed to address many forms of text structure, has grown into a design for the universal storage of all interactive media, and, indeed, all data; and for a growing network of storage stations which can, in principle, safely preserve much of the human heritage and at the same time make it far more accessible than it could have been before.

From this you might get the idea that the Xanadu program is an enormous piece of software. On the contrary: it is one relatively small computer program, set up to run in each storage machine of an ever-growing network.

And rather than having to be run by the government, or some other large untrustworthy corporation, it can be dispersed under local ownership to serve entire nations and eventually the world.

---

*Just as Xerox Corporation created the term "xerography" as a generic term for its new type of copying, we propose this as a generic for our new conceptual structure of storage. The *particular* way we do xanalogical storage will be discussed in excruciating detail later.

LITERARY 0/6 MACHINES

A SINGLE PROGRAM, RUNNING THROUGHOUT A NETWORK

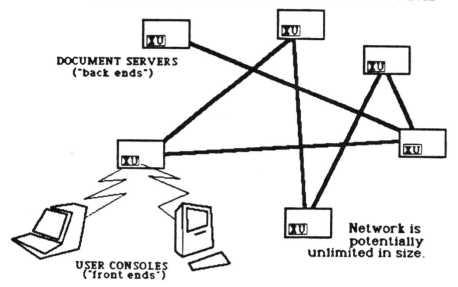

DOCUMENT SERVERS
("back ends")

USER CONSOLES
("front ends")

Network is potentially unlimited in size.

THE SMALL IMPORTANT USES

The sweeping character of Project Xanadu has sown confusion: because of its long-term ideals, its immediate uses in miniature have not been noticed by many people.

Because the system is based upon one pool of storage which can be shared and organized in many ways, materials can be reorganized constantly without losing their *previous* organiztion.

LITERARY 0/7 MACHINES

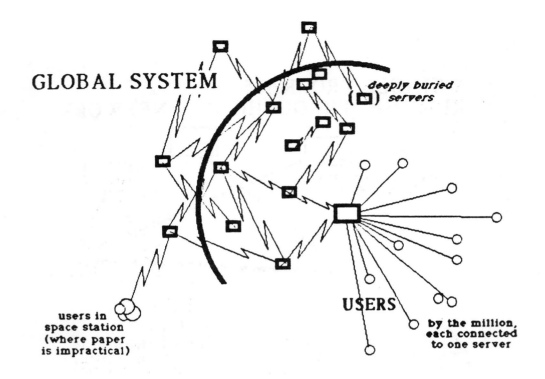

GLOBAL SYSTEM

deeply buried
( ) *servers*

USERS

users in
space station
(where paper
is impractical)

by the million,
each connected
to one server

This means that all materials--whether they are bodies of writing, computer files, company records--can become better and better organized, in ways which better and better reflect their true structure. Thus order becomes *cumulative*--unlike most computer systems, in which *dis*order easily becomes cumulative.

REORGANIZATION
IN PLACE

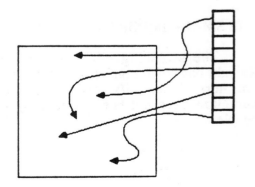

LITERARY 0/8 MACHINES

For a single computer user or office, this new form of storage creates a unified storage structure for all text and numerical information, without the proliferation and scattering of detached files whose origin and meaning become lost.

THE STRUCTURE EXPLAINED

And it is this same structure of continually reorganizable materials, in a stored pool, that we propose as a public utility for the storage of personal and

IMPROVED ORGANIZATION
FOR SINGLE USER OR OFFICE

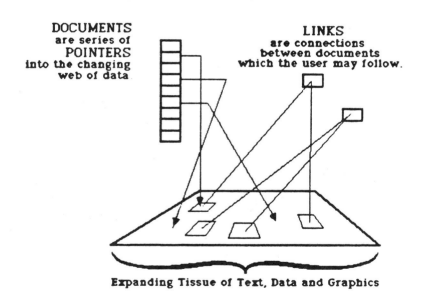

DOCUMENTS
are series of
POINTERS
into the changing
web of data

LINKS
are connections
between documents
which the user may follow.

Expanding Tissue of Text, Data and Graphics

LITERARY 0/9 MACHINES

company information. Why should any individual have to worry about the safety of all those floppy disks--let alone lose precious family photographs--when they can be safely stored in a public utility? Just as the "Mini Self-Storage" facility now proliferates across the country, this will be a public-access facility for recordings, writings, pictures, audio and video and movies, and whatever other data people want to use it for.

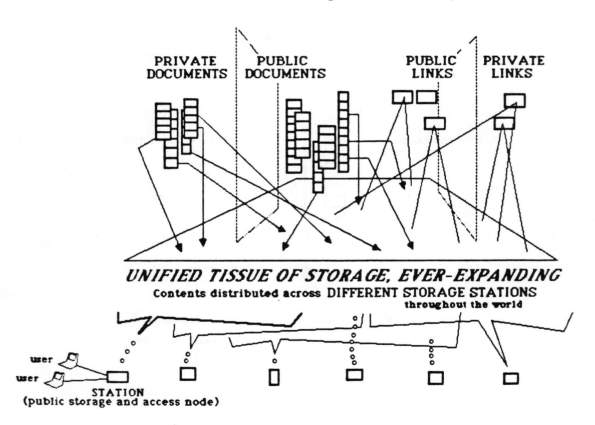

PUBLIC REPOSITORY SYSTEM WITH PLURALISTIC RE-USE,
publication by users

PRIVATE DOCUMENTS

PUBLIC DOCUMENTS

PUBLIC LINKS

PRIVATE LINKS

UNIFIED TISSUE OF STORAGE, EVER-EXPANDING
Contents distributed across DIFFERENT STORAGE STATIONS
throughout the world

user

user

STATION
(public storage and access node)

LITERARY 0/10 MACHINES

Just as the small system promotes cumulative order, the larger system promotes the coexistence and resolution of many viewpoints, through the sharing of private documents and comments, and the publication of hypertext complexes *whose interrelationships remain orderly.*

"THE FUTURE IS NOT WHAT IT USED TO BE"

Envision the world of the future (say, the year 2020, a convenient time when talking about vision). It is not a pretty place.

There is every reason to suppose that even if humanity survives the next century, it will be in ever-more horrific circumstances, a dungheap, more and more filled with spreading slums--the *favelas* of Brazil, the *barrios* of Mexico, the South Bronx of New York; the natural world in retreat, the jungles turning to desert and today's deserts growing, the waters poisoned and growing areas of land turned unsafe by chemicals.

None of this can be stopped. But there is some hope in the realm of human mental affairs, upon which the survival of humanity, and the better parts of human culture, depend.

For facilities to aid the mind, and share its products, have reached a new richness. But they must become unified and available to all, quickly.

THE CRYSTAL PALACE

We stand at the brink of a new age, a new time, when the handling of the written word will change very deeply, and civiilization will change accordingly.

Electronic networking and publishing already come in many flavors, but in a chaotic and Balkanized fashion. A universal repository hypertext network will change that: it will make stored text and graphics, called on demand from anywhere, an elemental commodity, like water, telephone service, radio and television.

Offices will be paperless, as soon as people figure out what this means. (Hint: new ways of structuring to map the *true* connections of documents.)

Education, now pressing in new and uncertain directions, can leap forward into new curricular structures that eliminate sequence and promote initiative and understanding.

And publishing--ah, consider what publishing will become.

Paper printing will soon be prohibitive: not only the cost of the paper, but the increasing cost of its transportation (from forest to mill to printer to warehouse to the bookstore/newsstand to consumer), spell the phasing out of print. But electronic repository publishing can replace that.

LITERARY 0/11 MACHINES

A NEW UNIVERSAL MEDIUM

There is an alternative. That is to create a system that unifies the others, providing both a form of storage and an indexing system for storage that is now in place--and a new layer of user ease. An open hypertext network. (For the meaning of "open hypertext," see "The Problems of Hypertext," a Chapter Three.)

As a new layer able to create compatibilities between existing sytems, it will tear down the walls (many of which were put there intentionally by certain companies). It can recombine what should never have been separate: "word processing," "outline processing," teleconferencing, "electronic mail," electronic publishing, archiving.

Such a system will represent at last the true structure of information (rather than Procrustean mappings of it), with all its intrinsic complexity and controversy, and provide a universal archival standard worthy of our heritage of freedom and pluralism.

Publishing in the new medium will be the storage of text (and other material) in repositories. Readers will call what they want to their screens as easily as turning pages.

And such a simplification is what everyone is yearning for.

Actually, the best comparison is the phone system--in its simplicity, universality, clarity and fundamental character.

What will happen to existing institutions is by no means clear; libraries, the schools, publishers, advertising, broadcast networks, government, may all try to fight these developments; which could impede progress for a while, but not indefinitely. Or they may recognize in them the new shape of their proper work.

THE 2020 VISION

Forty years from now (if the human species survives), there will be hundreds of thousands of file servers--machines storing and dishing out materials. And there will be hundreds of millions of simultaneous users, able to read from billions of stored documents, with trillions of links among them.

All of this is manifest destiny. There is no point in arguing it; either you see it or you don't. Many readers will choke and fling down the book, only to have the thought gnaw gradually until they see its inevitability.

The system proposed in this book may or may not work technically on such a scale. But some system of this type will, and can bring a new Golden Age to the human mind.

WE NEED YOU

The Xanadu group still needs brilliant people looking for adventure and a challenge,

LITERARY 0/12 MACHINES

long hours, low pay, accidental food, and a small chance of fame and fortune. We have to save mankind from an almost certain and immediately approaching doom through the application, expansion and dissemination of intelligence. Not artificial, but the human kind. To humankind.

LITERARY 0/13 MACHINES

CHAPTERS ONE

LITERARY 1/1 MACHINES

AN OBVIOUS VISION

A computer is essentially a trained squirrel: acting on reflex, thoughtlessly running back and forth and storing away nuts until some other stimulus makes it do something else. A perfectly versatile enactor; by rigmaroles and enchantments (called Programs) we make the computer do our bidding.

But then what things should we have it Enact? How can it improve our lives? This is the important issue. That there is a technological imperative, some way it "has to" be done, based on the computer's nature, is a myth and a fabrication. People get cowed, put in their place, when the technoids start enumerating the world as *they* see it.

TWO HOPES

Here then are two reasonable hopes, which I offer to persons of good will.

HOPE 1. To have our everyday lives made simple and flexible by the computer as a personal information tool.

HOPE 2. To be able to read, on computer screens, from vast libraries easily, the things we choose being clearly and instantly available to us, in a great interconnected web of writings and ideas.

Neither of these is happening.

TOMORROW'S WORLD OF TEXT ON SCREENS

Computer screens can bring words and pictures right away, at the user's choice. Businesses know it; there are now tens of millions of computer screens active in the country in business environments, and millions more sold every year.

And now that millions of people have personal computers, many of them, too, begin to see what text on interactive screens can be like. But the immensity of the coming revolution is not clear yet.

The personal-computer avalanche is well along, and many are independently imagining how things might and ought to be. (Though the inexpensive computers have been called *micro*computers so that newcomers will somehow think they're different from the old ones, and subtly inferior. The word "microcomputer" leads people into thinking that the new dinky computers are in some way not as good. Thus the word is like the word *nigger*-- suggesting unspoken inferiorities without having to name any.)

Most, or "all," of our reading and writing can or will, in this century, be at instant-access screens. The question is not *can* we do everything on screens, but *when* will we, *how* will we, and how can we make it *great?*

LITERARY 1/2 MACHINES

To me this is an article of faith; its simple obviousness defies argument. If you don't get it there is no persuading you; if you get it you don't need to be persuaded.

What I don't understand is the apathy about this in the computer field. There is no sense of urgency; there is no unifying vision of uplift for humanity as soon as *every person gets a screen.*

Oh, the woods are abuzz with supposedly great new computer services that will supposedly be offered to the public. Many computer people are "working in these areas." Yet what they give us time and again is complication, complication, because nobody has taught them how to *design simplicity.* No computer school teaches simplicity. Is it beneath them? Or do they simply not imagine it, believing that to teach Complication is their job?

Yet I say simplicity is possible. But simplicity does not come in pieces; you can't buy it in sections or add it in parts, on weekends. A thing is unified and clear and simple because it is designed that way, or it is not unified and clear and simple. Making things clear and simple is *hard.**

------

*Biological unity, a tempting analogy, is another matter-- it takes a long time and millions of mistakes, and does not necessarily act in our particular interests.

Pragmatism and the desire to get along in the world lead people to put up with what should not be put up with. But nothing really stops anyone from creating the good and the elegant except habit, inertia and desuetude-- and the fact that doing right is much harder than not doing right.

The starting point in designing a computer system must be the creation of the conceptual and psychological environment, the seeming of the system-- what I and my associates call the *virtuality.* You begin by designing a conceptual structure and how it should feel, then work back into the mechanics. You decide how it *ought* to be, and then make that vision happen; you don't just patch and splice and add and adapt.

As soon as you understand computers, all this should become obvious. Yet most people have not understood computers-- partly because some computer people didn't want them to-- and so the benefits to our lives have been put off and put off.

And what of the two hopes of which I spoke earlier?

HOPE 1. SIMPLIFYING OUR LIVES

Unfortunately, to the best of my knowledge, no one's personal life has yet been simplified by a computer, and that is the next major threshold in software design. The two words that characterize today's tense life at computer screens are BINGO and OOPS-- Bingo because things come the instant you

LITERARY 1/3 MACHINES

call them, and Oops when you did what you didn't intend-- which in bad computer systems, *most* computer systems, is hard to undo. Oops is the watchword.

Computers should bring simplification, rather than complication, to our lives: they should handle the minutiae, the snibbety details of day-to-day existence. Computer screens should bring us the everyday data of our lives-- whatever memoranda we use-- effortlessly so we no longer have to deal with myriad scribbles on paper. What you write down for your own use should be *always available from a screen*, not randomly lost and buried. Birthdays; appointments; possibilities to be kept track of; the blizzard of everyday natter; the scheduling of our lives (which is very complicated in principle, and which we blunder through, sometimes with great difficulty); the trivia of bookkeeping (which most people make into a yearly chore in relation to the IRS); the cross-indexing and storage management of the things we keep (conventional wisdom says we should keep less-- actually a reflection, I believe, of the fact that our systems are lousy and therefore very inconvenient).

So we need *unified* personal systems for a variety of purposes, tying these objectives together. Now, most computer people are under the impression that this implies a vast amount of *programming*. I say no: what it requires is a lot of *good design*, and the creation of some very simple building blocks. There are a few clean and simple designs we can point to that give a faint hint as to what interactive simplicity is. Two I will point to are the electronic spreadsheet (especially Bricklin and Frankston's original VisiCalc), and Mark Cutter's MacDraw, a graphics and text program for the Macintosh which is an adaptation of Ivan Sutherland's original, great Sketchpad program.

HOPE 2. ACCESS TO IDEAS

The second hope I mentioned earlier was that we could read from and write on screens with new freedom. Remember those ideals that made our country great, such as liberty and pluralism and the accessibility of ideas? Some of us still do.

Imagine a new accessibility and excitement that can unseat the video narcosis that now sits on our land like a fog. Imagine a new libertarian literature with alternative explanations so anyone can choose the pathway or approach that best suits him or her; with ideas accessible and interesting to everyone, so that a new richness and freedom can come to the human experience; imagine a rebirth of literacy. All that is what this book is about.

Yet dammit, what's worst is everybody lacking a sense of urgency. This is the eleventh hour of the human race, and there is a deadly urgency about everything we do.

These two hopes-- the simplification of our lives, the cornucopia of ideas and writings and pictures-- are the focus of my

LITERARY 1/4 MACHINES

own work. Twenty-six years ago, in graduate school, the two hopes I have mentioned came to me, as I hope they have come to you one way or another. I have put a lot of time into trying to make these things happen in ways I consider right, which I used to think were obvious to anyone but apparently aren't.

In future writings I will deal further with the design of simplicity. (Meanwhile my two-part piece, "Interactive Systems and the Design of Virtuality," in the November and December 1980 issues of *Creative Computing*, represents only a part.)

In this book, however, I will deal simply with reading and writing from screens, and the universe that I think is out there to create-- and then explore and live in. Vannevar Bush told us about it in 1945 and called it the memex ("As We May Think," *Atlantic Monthly*, July 1945, 101-8), but the idea has been dropped by most people. Too blue-sky. Too *simple*, perhaps.

The memex was a publishing system that would hold everything that is written, and allow each new user to add connections-- Bush called them *trails*-- to connect and clarify the material that's already stored.

I say Bush was right, and so this book describes a new electronic form of the memex, and offers it to the world.

Bush wrote in 1945. A dozen years later, a young electrical engineer had a similar vision: of computers helping the human mind-- or, as he called it, the augmentation of human intellect. His name was Douglas Engelbart. Working tirelessly at Stanford Research Institute, he built a powerful and intricate system to embody his ideals (now marketed by Tym-Share, Inc. under the name AUGMENT). Inventor of word processing (and incidentally of the mouse, now the pointing tool of the Macintosh), Engelbart is a saintly and inspiring individual. He continues today at Tym-Share, and because of his gentle and retiring qualities has not gotten nearly the recognition he deserves as a man who has so greatly changed the world.

Engelbart is now credited with the invention of "word processing" and "outline processing." But these terms are the most trivial way of describing his work and do not do justice to his vision. He foresaw a world of instant text access on screens, interconnections we can make and share, a new style of shared work among colleagues, and the enhancement of everyone's working imagination.

The system described in this book builds on and fuses these two great visions. It is very close to Bush's original memex, but now computerized; and its purpose is the augmentation of human intellect, as Doug Engelbart foresaw; it is intended to be especially simple for beginning users but easily extended to applications of great complexity; and it is constructed for orderly and sweeping growth as a universal archive and publishing system.

LITERARY 1/5 MACHINES

THE SENSE OF WONDERFUL DEVELOPMENTS

No alert person, drubbed by popular magazines and TV news, can fail to have heard that we are on the threshold of some sort of new era in the use of information. Soon, we hear, we will be able to get at the Library of Congress stored on a disk, or movies in a pinky ring, and information that we want only vaguely may come at us without our even having to ask.

A hundred jarring systems are confuting. Many media moguls-- "smart money"-- think they have it all worked out, although in different directions. Corporations are being formed. The hearts of investors are palpitating. Foundations and federal agencies are continuing to put out money for breakthrough showcase projects. Yet, in my estimation, we have not a state of progress but a state of virtually total confusion. Never before have so many accepted the unrefined technical fantasies of so few. Never before has so much been spent for what has been so little understood or thought out.

Unfortunately, the public little comprehends the varieties of possibilities, the vast range of options. They will believe anything they are told except the whole picture, which nobody tells them. Laymen have no longer the slightest idea of what is going on, and the gap widens continually.

This sort of thing happens easily in any field. Technical people create catchphrases, and people from outside, eager to be up-to-date, seize on the catchphrases as received wisdom, ideas that seem to span and comprehend all the possibilities, expanding to blot out the sky. Those outsiders in turn spread the gospel of the catchphrase to their own corners of the world, never quite sensing what an arbitrary selection has been made for them; failing to ask pointed questions, they in turn become opinion leaders for other outsiders who are even more afraid to ask. To mix parables, it is as if the blind men, after evaluating their corners of the elephant, then each lead other blind men in their own respective directions.

A variety of people are proposing arrangements by which *other* people, meaning we the public, should handle information in the future. A phrase often heard is, "anything you want, instantly." On closer investigation, however, it turns out that there is much disagreement as to what you want, as well as considerable disagreement as to what *instantly* means, and *want*, and *you*. Accordingly, the public ought not submit with docility to just whatever may result spottily by chance.

LITERARY 1/6 MACHINES

Here are some things that you might want to know about.

VIDEOTEXT

In England, France and other countries, so-called "videotex" and "teletext" systems are already in operation, offering a variety of limited searchable information to the home user, with a so-called "adapter" (a disguised computer) handling the interaction and display. Videotext enthusiasts think it could revolutionize the world. Unfortunately this uses a retrograde system of numerical lookup (you have to punch in *numbers* to get anything!) and is locked into low-quality graphics. For this to have originated in the land of Shakespeare was a sorry development.

Fortunately the Canadians fixed it all up. A Canadian system, Telidon, posed as a mere upgrade to these systems, but in fact did an excellent and different thing: it dismissed the Neanderthal retrieval and storage methods and simply offered an improved transmission code for interactive graphics. This solved both evils of videotext at once: by getting rid of the hierarchical numerical controls, it reopened the possibilities to any sort of indexing people might want, and it greatly improved the graphic output. Telidon was really a sort of super ASCII, an upgrade to the way text is already stored and sent between computers; in addition it is a brilliant political maneuver that got rid of the worst imaginable features of continental videotext by an old comic-strip gag-- "Look over there!"-- and snatching the bad stuff away.

Telidon was then adopted by the Bell network (before it was broken up by antitrust) with a few modifications, under the name of NAPLPS. The current state of this standard is one of largely suspended animation, however. The wide acceptance of NAPLPS awaits broad-based consumer uses of computer feed services, which still seem a way from materializing.

THE CABLE BABEL

Videocable operators for a time thought the public was ripe for about anything they offered. However, after some well-publicized videotext experiments offering computer services on videocable (notably by the Knight-Ridder newspaper chain), it became clear that they couldn't decree public use. These experiments were a well-publicized failure, and have been interpreted by shallow commentators to mean that the public was not ready for anything so "sophisticated" as what was being offered. What the experiments really showed was that shallow services meant to appeal to the lowest denominator of public interest did not have public appeal. (For people in big offices to decree dumb services *to be offered to others* is the height of stupidity. Let those who really *want* a thing build it, and you may get something worthwhile.)

LITERARY 1/7 MACHINES

"THE OFFICE OF THE FUTURE"

The phrase "office of the future" has been kicking around for some time now, but nobody agrees as to what it is. Companies that make chairs and filing cabinets think chairs and filing cabinets will be the main part.

Many think the office of the future will consist of souped-up "workstation" computers on one big cable, but with the same kinds of programs and complexities users must deal with now.

The position taken in this book, as you will see, is that the equipment hardly matters at all, but certain kinds of software are absolutely necessary, and that today's complications must vanish like the morning mist.

SHARED-TEXT SYSTEMS

Computerized text communities are springing up. Offices find they can tie their "word processors" together, speeding information between executives.

Various shared-text utilities are also available to the public, to which you connect via personal computer.

Computer Bulletin Boards, "Community Information Systems," teleconferencing systems, all are creating new communities that share text via computers. The armed forces, too, have complex text systems (where commanders at each level can read all messages of those below them, but not those above.)

So-called "electronic mail" means different things in different places. The U.S. post office jumped into "electronic mail" with both feet, assuming that if it was "mail" they owned it; but its ECOM service, intended to take over the electronic mail business, died ignominiously after a year or so of service.

The term "network" means all sorts of different things. Various large-scale systems now exist. Key examples are ARPANET and USENET. ARPANET connects university and military computers all over the country. Originally created for the remote use of military research computers, its main function has become the storing and sending text messages among its users.

USENET is a system for transmitting messages among companies and individuals who use the Unix system; different Unix computers pass along messages in a great decentralized transmitting net. (It's sometimes startling, when you're in a Unix household, to hear the computer answering the phone in the middle of the night to get your Usenet messages.)

The Source, Compu-Serve and Murray Turoff's EIES all have popular systems for sharing text and sending messages. Even the folks who brought you the Whole Earth Catalog have their own conferencing system, The Well.

LITERARY 1/8 MACHINES

BALKANIZATION

Unfortunately all of these systems and approaches have their complications, intricacies, shortcomings and incompatibilities. It is possible to publish with royalty on some of them, but only in the clumsiest fashion. The conferencing nets often deliberately throw away the material after a stated period-- ignoring its potential archival value. There is little consistency, great complication, and little hope for unity-- unless a wider method can be found to which all may be cleanly mapped.

ELECTRONIC PUBLISHING

For some five hundred years the educated public has been reading from books and magazines of paper. Now all of that may change.

Electronic publishing is coming, this much all agree on. Just what it will be is not so clear.

As screens become more and more available, there is less and less reason for printing on paper. The costs of wood pulp and gasoline (to move the paper to and from the printer), the long lead times of paper editorship and production, the increasing divergence of specialized interests, the lowering cost of computers with screens, of disk storage and digital communications; all suggest this.

Beginning thinkers in this area often suppose that what will be offered to the screen reader will be merely individual stored documents, available on line quickly, but based somehow on conventional documents nestling in conventional computer files.

Our point of view is different.

Many approaches to electronic publishing are very complicated. But that can't work on a broad scale; "publishing" suggests use by the public. Meaning simplicity.

WHITHER?

All these approaches are different. They *seem* to be converging, but are they? The existing systems do not combine well; hooking them together creates something like the New York subway system.

I say we need unified design. It has to be simple. It has to be powerful. It doesn't have to be complicated; in fact, *can't* be complicated. I believe, indeed, that the design we need will derive simply from what we have known in the past.

The future of the written word can and will be built on an electronic version of its past, losing nothing of its heritage, but totally changing its nature by instantaneous accessibility.

LITERARY 1/9 MACHINES

And this world, this new literature, will be built from the "document" as we have long known it, the "author" as we have long known him or her, and an extended form of "writing" as we have long done it and read it-- rather than what some people, such as McLuhan and the video freaks and the CAI folk, have been telling us would be anonymous, collective, scrambled, psycho-metric, and/or Boolean.

I believe there exists a clean, complete and thorough solution. And that is what will be described here.

LITERARY 1/10 MACHINES

TWO CULTURES FACE THE FUTURE

C.P. Snow pointed out long ago that there are two educated cultures, the culture of technology and the culture of the humanities, and they don't talk to each other. That was twenty-five years ago, but it's still true.

Not only is it still true, but the two cultures have united on a *false, agreed-upon definition of what computers are*. In this polite conspiracy the members of the two cultures, technical and literary-- who rarely talk to each other-- have it all figured out, quite wrongly.

Their shared false notion of computers is that they are Inhuman, Oppressive, Cold, Relentless; and that they somehow Reduce Everything to Mathematics.

One camp says "yessir, and I run 'em," and the other camp says, "I want no part of it."

This view, in its two variations, is a strange fact of our culture and psychology. But it has virtually nothing to do with computers. What computers *really* are is irrelevant to this curious compact.

To throw things in a sharper light, let me refer to the technical types as the *Technoids* (or Noids for short), and I will refer to those with a humanistic background, in literature, history, the arts, etc., as the *Fluffies*.

THE NOIDS

The Technoids have an exaggerated and caricatured notion of what constitutes clear-minded thinking, and never miss a chance to denounce other cognitive styles as "illogical." (For some reason a rigid and punitive notion of "logic" is important to such people.)

My favorite example is the typical Technoid insistence that you can't type a number into a computer using the letter Oh, you have to use the numeral Zero, because otherwise it isn't Logical. This despite the fact that a computer can easily be programmed to recognize that when you type Oh in the middle of a number you mean Zero, just the way a program can distinguish between a decimal point and a period, or a hyphen and a minus-- contextually.

But that overlooks what the Technoids' notion of Logic is about: rigidity and the chance to be boss.

Despite the way they oversimplify logic, the Technoids are also Lords of Complication: they enjoy keeping track of intricacies and memorizing numerous buttons. And they shower contempt on people who have difficulty learning the complicated systems that they, the Technoids, dream up.

LITERARY 1/11 MACHINES

NOIDS' OUTLOOK

The Technoids are usually hired guns, interested in the next complex problem they can get into. They generally have an obsession with favorite methods, and a negligible concern for history, art, literature or human freedom. Indeed, some of them really *like* to oppress other people (and some of this type get to head computer centers eventually).

In a famous experiment, psychologist Stanley Milgram, wearing a white coat, instructed unsuspecting subjects, who thought they were merely paid assistants, to push buttons that they were told would inflict terrible pain on others. To Milgram's chagrin, nearly everyone followed instructions without a qualm.

This in a way characterizes the Technoid mentality. If the government solicits bids on a Deterrent Weapons System that will selectively barbecue only the small children of an Aggressor Nation, the Technoid will probably say Yes Sir, Can Do, What Color Do You Want the Corpses? While the Fluffy who has read Sophocles and/or Tocqueville may be *slightly* more likely to say, Wait a Minute...

THE FLUFFIES

The Fluffy cognitive style leans toward vagueness and the reduction of issues to vague idealistic terms (they being unused to specifics except for Metaphors and Objective Correlatives). Their disposition is always to get away from specifics as being mundane and/or Sociological.

And they do not like computers or the idea of screens. "I love books," "I hate computers," "It sounds so cold," "I can't see cuddling up with a CRT in bed," "I can't take it on the train (in a hammock, into the woods)," etc. They have no conception of the importance and immediacy of creating an electronic literature that embodies what they believe in.

(I have experienced many levels of Fluffy negativism to computer ideas, which we may call Fluffy-Indifferent, Fluffy-Resistive, Fluffy-Hostile and Fluffy-Aggressive. You will encounter them all in the publishing industry and in Library Science.)

LITTLE CORNERS

About the only thing the groups have in common is their shared view of computers. Their views of each other are mutually derogatory, roughly on the level of "*You're* the one who eats strange food, not me!"

But one interesting aspect of the two cultures is their view of each other in the world. Each sees the other group as "those people in their little corner, unaware of the big wide world."

LITERARY 1/12 MACHINES

To the Fluffies this real world is history, art, literature, and the little corner is "technical things." To the Technoids the real world is that of Technical Questions and Ideas, and the little corner is the artsy-craftsy nook of bygone concerns.

SYSTEMS HUMANISTS

As you may have suspected, I see another point of view. As far as I am concerned both the Technoids and the Fluffies are in their own little corners. In the broader view, the goals of tomorrow's text systems will be the long ones of civilization-- education, understanding, human happiness, the preservation of humane traditions-- but we must use today's and tomorrow's technologies. We who believe this are *systems humanists*, striving to further the ideals of the humanist perspective by the best available means. This means finding the ways that human literature, art and thought-- including science, of course-- may best be facilitated, preserved, and disseminated.

Consider the analogy of water. Civilization as we now know it is based in part on running water-- supplying it, distributing it, and turning it off and on where you need it. That overall system had to be thought out. Similarly, someone now must design waterworks for the mind.

The literature we envision, described in this book, is meant to be a utility, a commodity, a waterworks for the mind; your computer screen will be the spigot-- or shower nozzle-- that dispenses what you need when you turn the handle. But that system must be based on the fluidity of thought-- not just its crystallized and static form, which, like water's, is hard and cold and goes nowhere.

LITERARY 1/13 MACHINES

HYPERTEXT

Spoken language is a series of words, and so is conventional writing. We are used to sequential writing, and so we come easily to suppose that writing is intrinsically sequential. It need not be and should not be.

There are two outstanding arguments for breaking away from sequential presentation. One is that *it spoils the unity and structure of interconnection.* The other is that *it forces a single sequence for all readers which may be appropriate for none.*

1. *Spoiling the Unity and Structure*

The sequentiality of text is based on the sequentiality of language and the sequentiality of printing and binding. These two simple and everyday facts have led us to thinking that text is intrinsically sequential. This has led to the fallacy that presentation *should* be intrinsically sequential. Marshall McLuhan even put this fallacy at the center of European thought, and perhaps he was right, perhaps it is.

But sequentiality is not necessary. A structure of thought is not itself sequential. It is an interwoven system of ideas (what I like to call a *structangle*). None of the ideas necessarily comes first; and breaking up these ideas into a presentational sequence is an arbitrary and complex process. It is often also a destructive process, since in taking apart the whole system of connection to present it sequentially, we can scarcely avoid breaking-- that is, leaving out-- some of the connections that are a part of the whole.

Of course, we do this kind of simplifying sequential breakdown all the time, but that doesn't mean we *should*, it just means we *have to*.

(Some thinkers, of course, really *do* believe that certain of their ideas are primary and that the rest follow from them, and that's fine. I criticize merely the presumption that all systems of thought have an intrinsic sequence, or should be made to.)

2. *Forcing Simple Sequence Inappropriate for All Readers*

People have different backgrounds and styles (as I said of the Noids and Fluffies in Chapter 1.3). Yet sequential text, to which we are funneled by tradition and technology, forces us to write the same sequences for everyone, which may be appropriate for some readers and leave others out in the cold, or which may be appropriate for nobody. (This book, too, is hardly everybody's cup of tea, since there is not very much *choice* among its sequences.)

Thus it would be greatly preferable if we could easily create different pathways for different readers, based upon background, taste and probably understanding. Now, in normal circumstances this is handled by writing different articles (and books) about the same subject, and publishing them in different places (or ways) for different audiences. This will give readers many choices in approaching the same work.

In the computer world this will change, especially if-- as I foresee-- there will be one great repository, and everything will be equally accessible. This means that "different" articles and books will more likely be *different versions of the same work*, and *different pathways through it for different readers.*

THE ALTERNATIVE: NONSEQUENCE

Nonsequential writing on paper can be all sorts of things-- magazine layouts, funny arrangements of poetry, pieces of writing connected by lines, or many other things.

As we go in this century from paper to the computer screen-- and tomorrow's computer screens will have the richness and resolution of paper-- all these nonsequential forms, and more, are possible. And we must discover and invent them.

Some are obvious. The most obvious is that which simply connects chunks of text by alternative choices-- we may call these *links*, of which more later-- presented to the user. I call this simply *chunk style hypertext*. The user, or reader, moves through it by reading one chunk, then choosing the next.*

CHUNK STYLE HYPERTEXT

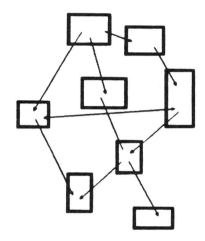

Another form of text that is becoming increasingly important is *compound text*, where materials are viewed and combined with others. (This term too has recently become common.) A good way of visualizing this is as a set of windows to original materials from the compound texts themselves. Thus I prefer to call this *windowing* text.

---

*Note that if the connections to be followed are given different types, we may call these *colored links*.

(This is the mathematical usage, where connections are called "colored" if they are of different types.)

LITERARY 1/15 MACHINES

WINDOWING OR COMPOUND TEXT

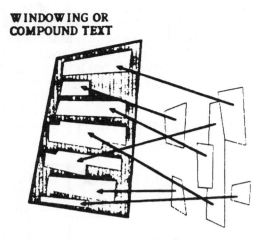

Extending the notion slightly, we get *windowing hypertext*-- where nonsequential writings-- hypertexts-- window to other stored materials.

COMPOUND HYPERTEXT

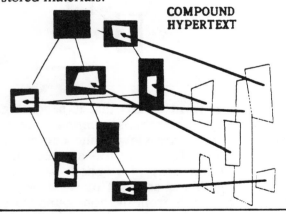

It is this notion, then, of windowing or compound hypertext-- which we foresee as the vital and basic new information system of the future-- that has charged and inspired the present work.

Unfortunately, for thousands of years the idea of sequence has been too much with us,* because nothing else has been practical; and indeed, creating a system subtle and profound enough to meet our real needs has proven to be an extensive task indeed.

The structure of ideas is never sequential; and indeed, our thought processes are not very sequential either. True, only a few thoughts at a time pass across the central screen of the mind; but as you consider a thing, your thoughts crisscross it constantly, reviewing first one connection, then another. Each new idea is compared with many parts of the whole picture, or with some mental visualization of the whole picture itself.

It is the representation of whole structures of ideas, and placing them on the page for others to understand, that we call *writing*. Writing is the representation and the presentation of thought.

(So are pictures and diagrams; but they are intrinsically nonsequential, and so not relevant to the present argument.)

---

*Except for the Talmud. This is an extraordinary hypertext, a body of accumulated comment and controversy, mostly on the Torah (the Hebrew Old Testament) and on life in general, by Jewish scholars of old. It has been accreted over centuries with commentaries on commentaries. This hypertext is a fundamental document of Jewish religion and culture, and the Talmudic scholar is one who knows many of its pathways.

LITERARY 1/16 MACHINES

HYPERTEXT DEFINED

By hypertext I simply mean non-sequential writing. A magazine layout, with sequential text and inset illustrations and boxes, is thus hypertext. So is the front page of a newspaper, and so are various programmed books now seen on the drugstore stands (where you make a choice at the end of a page, and are directed to other specific pages).

Computers are not intrinsically involved with the hypertext concept. But computers *will* be involved with hypertext in every way, and in systems of every style. (Ideally, you the reader shall be free to choose the next thing to look at-- though repressive forms of hypertext do turn up.)

Many people consider these forms of writing to be new and drastic and threatening. However, I would like to take the position that hypertext is fundamentally traditional and in the mainstream of literature.

Customary writing chooses one expository sequence from among the possible myriad; hypertext allows many, all available to the reader.

In fact, however, we constantly depart from sequence, citing things ahead and behind in the text. Phrases like "as we have already said" and "as we will see" are really implicit pointers to contents elsewhere in the sequence.

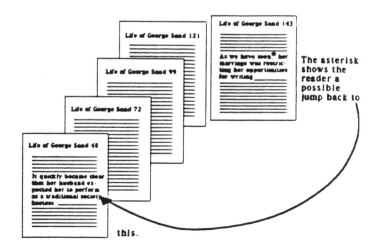

LITERARY 1/17 MACHINES

WHAT'S HARD ABOUT WRITING

There are basically two difficulties in writing sequential text: deciding on sequence-- there are so many possible connections!-- and deciding what's in and out. Both of these problems go away with hypertext. You no longer have to decide on sequence, but on *interconnective structure*, which provides much greater flexibility. You no longer have to decide what's in or out, but simply where to put things in the searchable maze.

WHAT'S TRICKY ABOUT READING

In reading works of non-fiction, the active reader often skips ahead, jumps around, ponders about background material. These initiatives are useful and important; if we provide pathways to help active reading, it will be possible to enhance initiative and speed comprehension.

TWO STYLES OF HYPERTEXT ORGANIZATION

1. *Presentation and Effect*

One style of hypertext organization is based on its possible effect on the reader. The connective structure is a system of *planned presentations* which the reader may traverse. Variant sequences and alternative jumps will be contrived for how they look, feel and get ideas across.

2. *Lines of Sructure*

The other style of hypertext organization is based on simply representing the structure of the subject, with possible directions of travel mapping the relations in the network of ideas being presented. The internal relations of the subject are thus represented in the connective relations of the hypertext. This is simpler than calculating the effect on the reader, since the author is only concerned with analyzing and representing what the structure really *is*, and the reader is exploring the structure as he or she explores the text.

Actually, both styles of organization will probably blend, since the ideal presentation will follow lines of structure, and the mere representation of structure will presumably need enhancement by showmanship.

THE PROBLEM OF ORIENTATION

There are tricky problems here. One of the greatest is how to make the reader feel comfortable and oriented. In books and magazines there are lots of ways the reader can see where he is (and recognize what he has read before): the thickness of a book, the recalled position of a paragraph on the left or right page, and whether it was at the bottom or the top. These incidental cues are important to knowing what you are doing. New ones must be created to take their place. How these will relate to the visuals of tomorrow's hot screens is anybody's guess, but it is imperative to create now a system on which they may be built.

LITERARY 1/18 MACHINES

THE IMPROVED REPRESENTATION OF THOUGHT

It is my belief that this new ability to represent ideas in the fullness of their interconnections will lead to easier and better writing, easier and better learning, and a far greater ability to share and communicate the interconnections among tomorrow's ideas and problems. Hypertext can represent *all* the interconnections an author can think of; and compound hypertext can represent all the interconnections *many* authors can think of, as we shall see.

THINKERTOYS

This work began in 1960 with the problem of intercomparing complex alternatives-- of looking at two alternative structures, paragraphs or arrangements on the screen side by side, and noting in detail their differences and advantages.

Such intercomparison systems, I still believe, will become a vital aspect of our working lives-- once they are easy to use. I do not know of anything on the market yet that does this.

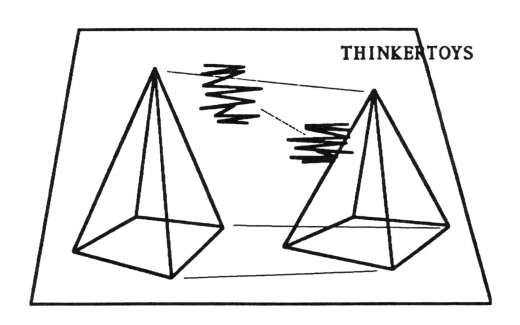

THINKERTOYS

LITERARY 1/19 MACHINES

THE SCHOOL PROBLEM

Most people consider school to be a grim necessity to be accepted, endured and survived. School, as nearly everyone freely admits, is dull, unpleasant, and designed to build mediocrity. It is a mapping of the world of ideas into a sequential bureaucratic presentational system, with generally awful results.

1. The Curriculum

The very system of curriculum, where the world's subjects are hacked to fit a schedule of time-slots, at once transforms the world of ideas into a *schedule*. ("Curriculum" means "little racetrack" in Latin.)

A curriculum promotes a false simplification of any subject, cutting the subject's many interconnections and leaving a skeleton of sequence which is only a caricature of its richness and intrinsic fascination.

2. Teacher as Feudal Lord

The world of ideas is carved into territories, and assigned as fiefdoms to individuals who represent these territories (called Subjects); these lords and ladies in turn impose their own style and personality on them. The pupil must pay homage to the Duchess of History, the Count of Mathematics; and if you and these individuals do not like each other, you will almost surely dislike the subjects they control, which take on their stamp and personality. Each feudal lord has absolute power to bore, offend, and sever access.

The teacher controls access to the subject under his or her own viewpoint. If you find this viewpoint unfriendly, unpleasant or confusing, that subject becomes closed to you forever.

These two principles-- the crushing of living subjects into curricular caricatures, and their bestowal to feudal overlords-- effectively guarantee that whatever is taken in school becomes and remains uninteresting. Everything is intrinsically interesting, but is drained of its interest by these processes.

Thus follow both the dreariness of education and the crippling of the mind as we see it everywhere today. Education is typically the process of successively ruining subjects for you, and the last subject to be ruined determines your profession. An educated person is someone who says, "I don't know anything about that, I never took it." Whereas a free-minded person can become excited about a new idea, in any subject, whether or not he or she ever heard about the idea or the subject before.

LITERARY 1/20 MACHINES

What is perhaps even worse, this system imbues in everyone the attitude that the world is divided into "subjects;" that these subjects are well-defined and well-understood; and that there are "basics," that is, a hierarchy of understandings which must necessarily underpin a further hierarchy of "advanced ideas," which are to be learned *afterward*.

This outlook could not have been better designed to crush people's mental spirits, to keep them from becoming involved with ideas, from thinking, exploring, conjecturing, taking interest.

LITERARY 1/21 MACHINES

A BRIEF HISTORY OF
THE XANADU CAPER

Eagles don't flock.
You have to find them one by one.
H. Ross Perot

RETROSPECT

Complicated ideas evolve slowly. People who do not work endlessly with ideas may not easily imagine how many are the steps that intensive work with ideas entails; how many are the guesses, postulations, reconsiderations, shifts of thought, confusions, resyntheses, reintegrations; how much is the rework of dearly-held insights in clouds of confusion. The swirl of needed changes never seems to end.

Whereas expeditions and projects by their nature have a beginning and a goal-- if not always an end. And even when they end, expeditions and projects do not end in the spirit they began in. Project Xanadu, as it is now called, has been a swirl of changing ideas, a project *and* an expedition. What it has become little resembles how it started. It began as a one-man dream, incubated through long walks in Cambridge, and has gone through many stages. It has been an ordeal of many sorts for many people. It is at last an unusual computer program with its own philosophy and sweeping implications, which we believe are revolutionary.

"ON THE SHOULDERS OF GIANTS"

I started this thing long ago thinking I could do it alone. I have always far preferred to work alone on complex ideas, usually finding people's suggestions diversionary, obtrusive and irrelevant. Thus I did not imagine at the outset that I would come to shepherd a group of people smarter than I who would actually change the design, make it much bigger than I had conceived (and overrule several of my assumptions), actually get the thing *done*, and get it done *right*.

The project has from the first been carried out in a conspiratorial atmosphere on the assumption that I (later we) understood something others did not understand, and has reached for ideals others were not yet ready to comprehend. This has been largely true, but has deprived us of the companionship and inspiration of outside colleagues. On the other hand, we have been confronting

LITERARY 1/22 MACHINES

large-scale, indeed cosmic, social and political issues that many computer people want not to think of.

It would have been nice to get advice from Jefferson and DaVinci and some other heavies. (Just a "nice going" now and then would have helped a lot.) Unfortunately they weren't around, so we had to wing it. And the scholars and humanists who are the usual heirs and guardians of their tradition weren't available for comment. So we have been thrown on our own resources.

MYSTERIES OF THE PROJECT

In retrospect it is baffling. I know now that there was no reason to expect to find the technical methods-- they just happened to be where no one else was looking; there was no reason to expect a collection of eccentric geniuses devotedly to work the thing through without salary, but they did; there was no reason to expect we could advance to this point while retaining enough control to assure that it will be done *right*. But we have. Strange forces are at work, and we will try to stay tuned.

Through all of it we applied a relentless pressure for consistency and simplicity, and the thing cooked down remarkably. The amazing fact is that it has worked, that the hard technicalities could be pushed to fit soft ideals. But only by intricate search. This *could not have been done with schedules and deadlines*. When a project requires both exhaustive exploration and unusual inspiration, it is going to take however long it takes.

The Xanadu system has been created because I and my collaborators *wanted to use it*.

We who made it want to be ordinary users of the system. The group is not, as a rule, particularly modest or retiring; yet we have created a large-scale system on which we desire no more than to be *ordinary users*, not kings or censors or "gatekeepers." We have designed this network with no positions of superiority, rather in the way that the Constitution ruled out positions of nobility. It is not that our wants are modest, but rather that we want to put an emperor's resources at the fingertips of all users, especially children and scientists and poets. ("At last I can live like a human being!"-- Nero, on completion of his palace.)

HOW AND WHY IT BEGAN

From earliest youth I was supicious of categories and hierarchies. They were always interesting and alluring; they were usually spurious. I instinctively distrusted people's categorizations as oversimplifying, and hierarchies as often seemed to be trickery as descriptions of the world.

When I was in junior high, the eccentric philosopher Korzybski got a big play in *Astounding Science Fiction*; he denounced categories, models and descriptions as shallow and misleading. This seemed to me just right.

LITERARY 1/23 MACHINES

I mention my mistrust of categories and hierarchies, not for its metaphysical value (if any), but because it provides a *fine orientation for building information systems.* Because if you are not falsely expecting a permanent system of categories or a permanent stable hierarchy, you realize your information system must then deal with an ever-changing flux of new categories, hierarchies and other arrangements which all have to *coexist*; it must be a tolerant system which allows them to cohabit comfortably, helps track their variations and disparities, and is forever ready to accommodate new arrangements on top of those already present.

SCHOOL

When I was twelve, my heroes were Bucky Fuller, Bertrand Russell and H.L. Mencken, as I recall. Also Walt Disney, of course, and Orson Welles. I grew up hanging out in bookstores and stockpiling magazines, fascinated with almost every idea I encountered. Whereas I found school a rather dismal place, a forced march through narrow corridors under conditions of maximum unpleasantness, into which only a few ideas were allowed to penetrate.

School and I were very unhappy with each other. My real education took place in bookstores, to which I would sneak when avoiding sports; in movie theaters (I lived where you could see a lot of English films); from conversations with my grandparents and great-grandparents; and from magazines in heaps.

School did not cover the interesting stuff, or made it dreary when it did; the slow pace and classroom "discussions" were unendurable. I dropped out of seventh grade-- a searing experience-- but was somehow pushed back into school, and through high school, and into college.

But college was another story. Ideas were important and welcome there. Things were still hacked into strange and traditional categories; but I wandered through an eclectic interdisciplinary program, trying to pull together philosophy and the social sciences at various levels. (But then graduate school was like grade school again.)

SYSTEMS

In high school, when I got serious about writing, I was continually trying different systems for organizing ideas. File cards (around which there was a mystique) were clearly hopeless. I tried index tabbing, needlesort cards, making multiple carbons and cutting them up. None of these solved the basic problem: an idea needed to be in several places at once. (And at that point I had not consciously begun to question the tradition that writing should be in sequence.)

When I read that Haloid Corporation had a new copier that would make copies for a nickel, I trudged all over Manhattan trying to find one. This was in the fall of 1953. Victimized by premature publicity! Haloid did not bring out its first copier, and change its name to Xerox, until a decade later. But

LITERARY 1/24 MACHINES

the experience presaged a pattern that was to repeat in my life: committing prematurely to writing systems which were not yet available.

In college I started accumulating file cards that fed toward my papers and writings; but they soon got out of hand. Every file card wanted to be many places at once, many needed to be pasted in the middle of several different documents and separately reworked, but needed to stay connected between documents as well. All methods of paper were wholly inadequate and imposed connective restrictions that masked the true structure of the ideas.

But then, in graduate school, I took a computer course.

COMPUTERS

My second year in graduate school, Fall 1960, I took a course in computer programming. The instructor, Arthur S. Couch, was an easy-going and reasonably well-informed guy. One of the things he told us right off the bat was that integrated circuits would make computers small and cheap very soon, even though the only computer at Harvard was the 7090 up at the Smithsonian Observatory-- a big machine indeed.

I will always be grateful that the course did not cover Fortran, and that instead we got into machine language and assembler-- the Real Stuff that let you see what really happened in the machine.

THE FIRST DESIGN, 1960

I announced as my term project a writing system for the 7090: the idea was to store your manuscripts in the computer, change them with various editorial operations, and print them out. (When this became commercialized years later, it was called "word processing." I called it, at the time, "text handling," which still seems to me the more appropriate term: you do not *process* words, you simply put them away and get them back out.)

My design for the term project went much farther, however; the notion of merely being able to revise text seemed to me obvious and inconsequential; the really *important* features would have to do with helping the user make organizing decisions. It seemed to me that a crucial aspect was being able to *compare alternative possibilities easily*: showing two versions of anything side by side, so the user writing at the screen could make detailed intercomparisons.

INTERCOMPARISON OF ALTERNATIVES
(two versions of "anything" side by side)

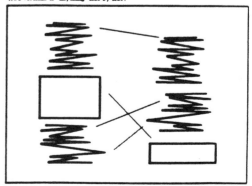

LITERARY 1/25 MACHINES

Thus the intercomparison of alternative versions was a central aspect of the first design. I also included, as features, both historical backtrack and revision by outline. (I'm not sure presently whether "links" were in the first specs or not.)

It seemed so simple and clear to me then. It still does. But like many beginning computerists, I mistook a clear view for a short distance.

While it was obvious that *interactive* computers-- "one person, one computer"-- would be along in a year or so (or so I assumed), the system that I designed at that time for the 7090 had to be configured around input commands punched on IBM cards. I wrote thousands of lines of 7090 assembler code, and had a dumb little input language worked out.

It was not finished on time; I got an incomplete for the course, and thus only a Master's degree. And the project has taken over twenty-five years to complete.

You might say that I chose the wrong problem to work on. But I have never felt that way. It was the *right* problem. It just took longer, and led further, than I expected.

THE SECOND DESIGN

There was a lot of talk around Cambridge in the early sixties about Computer-Assisted Instruction, for which there was a lot of money.

I was originally all for it. After talking with CAI people, though, and rather soon after getting into the subject, my original editing ideas were expanded, and became what I first called the "thousand theories program"-- an explorable CAI complex that would let you study many different theories on many different subjects, *at your choice*-- going in whatever directions seemed to you most appropriate.

This was a sharp departure from what others were doing. Computer-Assisted Instruction at that time was thought of as a form of tactical engineering to replace specific teaching chores in the conventional curriculum. Whereas I was proposing, and still believe, that new computer media would make it possible to *break away from curriculum*, allowing students to pursue their own chosen paths of intellectual development.

This idea rather quickly became what I would eventually call "hypertext"-- non-sequential forms of writing connected by links. This was essentially my second design.

This second design had become what I now call *chunk style hypertext*. The basic idea was of many separate paragraphs, each with many branching choices. (See Chapter 1.4.)

My other studies meant nothing to me now. I wanted to be in Computers-- but at that time there prevailed the silly notion that computers were "mathematical," and being a mathematical incompetent I was unable to get a job in the field.

I spent a year in the dolphin research laboratory of Dr. John C. Lilly. The dolphins were great, but I got no access to his LINC computer. I moved on to Vassar College, teaching sociology, and at last got a chance to publish my designs.

THE THIRD DESIGN, 1965

Now I was thinking about a third system, combining the two ideas: the original plan for screen editing and idea management, where you could compare alternative versions side by side on the screen, and the second idea of non-sequential writing. So a third system gradually became clear at Vassar. I concentrated on data structure. My notion was that of having sequences which could be linked together sideways; zippered lists, I called them then. These would permit certain intercomparisons and certain forms of non-sequential writing.*

ZIPPERED LISTS

LISTS WHICH INDEX EACH OTHER IN DIFFERENT SEQUENCES

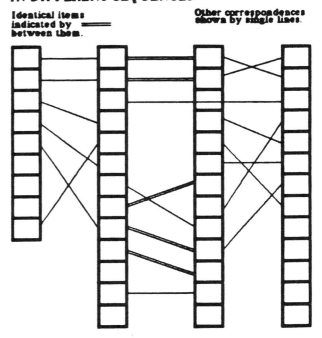

Identical items indicated by ===== between them.

Other correspondences shown by single lines.

---

*Note that this maps perfectly to the procedure used to restore Frank Capra's 1937 film "Lost Horizon" to the almost identical version re-released in 1986. Many scenes (especially those expressing pacifist and liberal sentiments) had been expunged from the film after its opening year; but those survived in various copies, some of the in 16mm, around the world.

For the reconstruction, *all copies were intercompared*; an accurate original sound track was restored from various sources, and fragments from various of the existing copies were fitted to the soundtrack where they were missing from the 35mm version. About six minutes of footage could not be found anywhere, and were filled in with stills.

LITERARY 1/27 MACHINES

It is interesting to note that this version (and possibly the first) contained a form of "outline processing," though I was as yet unaware that "outline processing," like "word processing," had originally been invented by Douglas Engelbart. (Note, of course, that these terms did not exist at the time.)

However, just as I rejected the concept we now call "word processing" from the beginning as too shallow, I also rejected "outline processing" as being too shallow as well; since this implies hierarchy, of which I have always been deeply suspicious.

Specifically, the "outline processing" in this system was to allow for intercomparisons between versions, in which an item could be an important heading in one version and a trivial point in another.

Zippered List
where
one item is important heading in one zip.
trivial in another

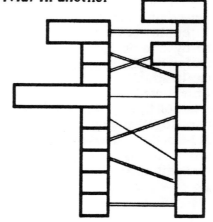

LITERARY 1/28 MACHINES

PUBLISHING ARTICLES

My first paper, on zippered lists, was accepted by the ACM national conference, 1965. It was in Cleveland, but even so, I was thrilled. The audience was some 800 strong, and they really liked my presentation. I was briefly lionized in the field. I got invited to a VIP-researcher wingding at Lincoln Labs.

Then people lost interest in what I said. I was talking about *the structure of ideas*, and thus how to set computers up to hold them. Nobody got it. Everybody was listening for something else. Some people didn't want to see what I was saying, calling it "blue-sky" and "arm-waving"-- in other words, they basically lacked the capacity to visualize. If I had understood years ago how hard it would be to explain and describe these things, and get these ideas across: how difficult it would be for most people to imagine these things-- conceptually, viscerally, and how they feel to the hand and look to the eye-- and how difficult it would be to persuade people of such a whole new paradigm, I would have gone about things differently. But I'm not sure how.*

I've also learned that most people are afraid of (and/or angered by) new words and ideas. Unless a thing comes on just the right silver platter, people don't want to think about it. This is why careful academics pretend to be so cautious and respectful when they introduce new ideas. (John Ahern, of Vassar College, has recently pointed out to me that most people *don't like to be told the big picture,* that it makes them angry; and that is why so much time is spent in articles and discussions, speeches and written articles on non-central matters and insufferable details, talking around the real issues.)

Since that time, always thinking it would help, I have spent an unconscionable amount of time writing articles and giving speeches. I have come to learn that communicating whole new big ideas, rather than small modifications of familiar ones, is a very great psychological challenge on both conceptual and emotional levels. (While for years it seemed these writings had been seen by nobody, now their cumulative impact is turning out to have been considerable; see bibliography.)

---

*I first published the term "hypertext," which I had chosen quite carefully, in 1965, along with "hyperfilm" and "hyperfile." I do not know whether I published the term "hypermedia" at that time or not, although I used it in my notes. This is the obvious generic for non-sequential and branching media; the problem is that since the word *media* is plural, you can't reasonably speak of a work in this mix as "*a* hypermedia," the way you can resasonable speak of a hypertext. On the other hand, just as we say "a multi-media prodution," I suppose that such noun forms as *hypermedia production* and *hypermedia unit* are reasonable. In any case, the term *"hypermedia"* has resurfaced, in approximately this usage.

LITERARY 1/29 MACHINES

SPOOKS

A government intelligence agency got in touch with me. I was impressed at their discernment, and eagerly responded to their offers of great money after "just one more proposal." But it gradually became clear that they were chowderheads, did not understand what I was saying, and were not going to come through with any backing. Much more time wasted.

A WORLDLY PUBLISHER

My next job was at a large book firm. I wrote to its head; he was somewhat taken with my ideas and hired me; I reported directly to him. I have found then and since that the people at the top listen and understand better. This man was the brightest I have ever met; he listened very well. Had I been a better politician we might have built the system.

At the publishing house I at last chose a very literary name for the evolving full design. I chose the name "Xanadu" for its connotations in literary circles. As the mysterious palace in Coleridge's poem "Kubla Khan"-- a great poem which he claimed to have mostly forgotten before he could write it down-- Xanadu seemed the perfect name for a *magic place of literary memory*.

My kingly boss almost backed the Xanadu project-- it would have been at an opening budget of a quarter of a million-- but

then they decided to go into computer-assisted instruction instead. I demurred, expressing my views of CAI as practiced at that time, and we parted company.

THE 1967 DESIGN

The design of that time was especially concerned with presenting and reworking *alternative versions of hypertext*. Thus it combined my original idea of editing alternative versions on screens with the powerful notion of non-sequential writing. This was to be not just for hypertext, but for intercomparing *alternative hypertext structures*. It used the zippered-list method to manage the intercomparison facilities that had obsessed me since 1960. The contents would be hypertexts, the intercomparison facilities would be managed by zippered lists.

ALTERNATIVE CHUNK-STYLE HYPERTEXTS
INTERCOMPARED THROUGH ZIPPERED LISTS

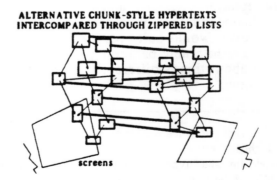

screens

LITERARY   1/30   MACHINES

I visualized this as a sort of super Executive's Console, self-contained. But the idea of communicating between such consoles was beginning to get through to me, and the nagging issue of shared access began to grow on me. (This was not finally solved until the work of the Implementation Squad twelve years later, in the summer of 1979.)

STAR WARS, 1968

I spent about a year working on military text systems for a big lab. Their system was already designed and I could do nothing to help, nor did I get any ideas from it.

THE BROWN UNIVERSITY HYPER-TEXT SYSTEM

I got involved with a text project at Brown University, whose objective (as it was explained to me at first) was to try out some of my hypertext ideas. For several years I went up there at my own expense, consulting in the development of the Hypertext Editing System (now called HES). However, the young programmers apparently were not briefed to see me as either instigator or co-designer, and seemed rather to consider me an intruder who was constantly "raving" and "flaming."

I argued continually for the elaboration of HES's hypertext features, whereas the programmers and their boss, Andries van Dam, emphasized *paper output*. It seemed to me that if we were going to be seriously concerned with hypertext, this emphasis on paper printout and formatting was a retrograde preoccupation.

Their view, of course, prevailed. (The Brown University Hypertext Editing System is still available from IBM's program library; see Carmody, et al. in bibliography.)

Ironically, the Brown Hypertext Editing System turned out to be very influential, since it was effectively the first visual computer text facility that beginners could use. But it had little to do with hypertext. I believe that if the project had emphasized on-line reading and writing, and their revolutionary implications, it would have had an impact at that time in moving us toward the real on-line future. When the system was to be demonstrated at the Joint Computer Conference, I believe in 1969, I arranged permission from the publishers of Nabokov's *Pale Fire*-- a brilliant poetic hypertext-- to use it in the demo. But the IBM people rejected this as "too far out." Thus progress must wait for the halt and the lame to catch up.

I think this pandering to the familiar, this emphasis on paper output, may have set progress back considerably. It represented a turning away from the real screen future to placate the lowest conceptual denominator of those who would see the system. This tendency persists today. There is an inane preoccupation with paper: the current stampede for "desktop publishing," and the paper orientation of the Macintosh computer, where everything has a "normal size"-- the size of printout. The great masses of computer users are still wedded to the Virtual Piece of Paper-- the VPOP Paperdigm-- because they have seen nothing better. I think we could have set a better precedent in 1969.

THE 1970 DESIGN: RING BUFFERS

In the 1968-70 era my concern was the organization of streams of data babbling through core memory, especially for use with the calligraphic displays of that time, which drew lines on screens (rather than today's carpet of dots). Based on this expected form of screen, I did clever stuff with respect to parallel ring buffers for display refreshment, but this later turned out not to be the heart of the problem.

THE 1972 DESIGN: A NEW BREAK-THROUGH

The years 1971 and 1972 were essentially devoted in my mind to the problem of disk management and editing-- which turned out to mean Data Structure-- especially, finding fast editing methods that would always be up to date.

THE XANADOERS

By this time an individual named Jonathan Fagin invested some money in what I was doing. This brought a sense of movement; I recruited two others who moved the work on considerably. These were John Ridgway, then a sophomore at Swarthmore, and Cal Daniels, who then worked at Minicomputer Systems, Inc., and who had written that company's cassette tape operating system.

JOHN RIDGWAY

A clever second-generation Swarthmore student with hair down to his shoulderblades-- incidentally, the first second-generation programmer I ever met (they were rare in those days)-- John Ridgway was an 1130 Fortran and folk-dancing whiz. And a very enjoyable guy. Naturally we implemented in 1130 Fortran.

CAL DANIELS

Soft-spoken, warmhearted, quietly clever, Cal lived in a section of Queens that looked like Old English houses, but the bachelor's interior of his own house was startling in orange and tiger upholstery. But neighborhood kids teemed in and out of his livingroom to play *chess*.

Good meals, long evenings of discussion. I would explain something and Cal would stroke his chin and bob his head and say "Mmm..." And it turned out he saw problems far past where I was looking.

Cal's death in 1978 was a sorrow to all of us.

LITERARY 1/32 MACHINES

Gas was cheap then. I zoomed a lot between my Manhattan apartment and scattered places, driving back and forth and back among Ridgway at Swarthmore, Daniels on Long Island and the R.E.S.I.S.T.O.R.S. kids' computer club in Princeton, talking the system, hashing details.

THE DISCOVERY OF THE ENFILADE

Anyhow, somehow we discovered the system we now call the first enfilade-- the Model T: a data structure that manages huge agglomerates of text and their arrangement in and out of core. With its attendant routines, the Model T enfilade handles the revision of serial data very quickly and very cleanly. Still secret, unfortunately, it is the granddaddy of the other enfilades which constitute our system.

Records of the discovery are spotty. However, it is clear that the Model T enfilade was fully formed by 6 March 1972, according to my design notes of that date.

Anyway, appropriate credit will be apportioned later when we can all sit down and figure out what really happened. Certainly it is the case that the help and advice from the R.E.S.I.S.T.O.R.S. computer club of Princeton (especially Nat Kuhn and Glen Babecki), and the detailed analyses of John and Cal, meant a great deal. I also vaguely recall jumping up and down and whooping with John Ridgway (in Parrish 22 at Swarthmore College) when we had discovered something incredible and codified it on the blackboard, but on combing hundreds of pages of notes that moment does not jump out at me.

TWO 1972 VERSIONS

In July 1972 the "Calgol" version was completed-- Cal Daniels' version of enfilade editing written in Algol-- but we had given back our rented Nova and had no chance to try to run it. (Too bad, because we could've had a fine, cheap "word processor" easily.)

Meanwhile John Ridgway continued with an interpretive version in 1130 Fortran. It eventually ran-- and actually drew a picture using its interpretive screen-language (which we called DINGO)-- on a Calcomp, in September 1973.

CIRCLE CAMPUS AND COMPUTER LIB

In '73 I was hired by the University of Illinois in Chicago, a strange concrete moonscape called Circle Campus (though the original traffic circle is long gone). A few weeks there made it clear I wouldn't fit in with their computer establishment, so I contrived to write *Computer Lib*. I published the book myself in, I believe, August of 1974. It was an instantaneous success. Hundreds of orders came in. (At this writing some 50,000 have been sold.) It didn't make a lot of money-- clumsy business arrangements-- but its hidden invitations brought in the guys who would finally finish

LITERARY 1/33 MACHINES

the Xanadu work. The book effectively said, if you want to join in a great endeavor to make the world's writings (and pictures and movies and music) instantly accessible and annotatable, come see me. And so they did.*

BILL BARUS

One was William F. Barus, whom I had known long ago when he was a kid. (When I was graduating from college he had helped me carry my cartons in his Boy Scout outfit.)

Now Bill Barus was a graduate student in philosophy, brilliant, famously incomprehensible, with the unworldly kindness and deep moralism of a Li'l Abner.

This was 1974 and 1975. It took Bill perhaps six months to work through with me the design of the system up to that date, since he was not satisfied merely to understand it; he needed to understand the theory behind each decision, the frame of mind, and the possible alternatives that might have been overlooked.

Then he thought about it for another six months, and tried out many conceptual alternatives. (We were sure, though, that we were going to create the system in PDP-11 machine language, using 16-bit binary codes for everything in the data structure.)

My precious system up to that point-- the 1972 design as implemented separately by John Ridgway and Cal Daniels-- was good on text storage but bad on links. Bill announced a solution that would fix that. His new method would allow linkages to keep up with all changes. It was instantaneous and permanent and could grow indefinitely. All changes, once made, left the file remaining in canonical order, which was an internal mandate of the system.

I did not understand Bill's solution for a long time. Like many others who have encountered his remarkable mind, I sometimes had great difficulty in following his ideas; so coming to understand the Barus method took *another* six months.

Until Barus's remarkable discovery, what we could do was essentially what anybody could do-- fast lookup that did not degrade too badly for large files. But Barus's work, which we refer to jocundly as "the eye in the pyramid," made possible an efficiently ever-linkable enfilade, a whole universe of poly-enfiladic structures. While his particular designs have been superseded, his stunning insights opened the way to the world of unlimited linkages we believe we have found.

---

*I have arbitrarily limited this enumeration to those who actually participated in some way in making or improving the code. The well-wishers, social participants, cheerer-uppers, POSSLQs, and members of the project who stayed only briefly would be too many to enumerate, so I've arbitrarily cut the list to the actual Xanadoers. Others are thanked in Section 5, "Acknowledgments."

LITERARY 1/34 MACHINES

By now the personal computer field had opened up, and Barus and I tried several business ventures "to support the Xanadu work." But as in most cases of doing B to support A, A quickly got swept aside as we got swamped.

On an off chance I got a brief teaching appointment at Swarthmore, a chance to teach my own stuff. It didn't work out well. It proved more difficult to teach my own stuff than other people's, not easier. But trying to say certain things clearly for the first time did help my thinking quite a bit.

THE FINAL IMPLEMENTATION SQUAD

During 1978 a group of accomplices finally coalesced for the final assault; pledging lives, fortunes and sacred honor, and mostly a whole lot of time.

We were devoted capitalists all-- I from hatred of committees, blunted creativity and the dilution of thought; they from desire for their own space shuttle. Virtually all of us had had awful school experiences; the fire that has driven our work was the shared hope for real change and liberation of the mind. Not your everyday people. Spacers, two of us, anxious to get off the planet immediately. And propelled by knowing we were onto something.

MARK MILLER

Mark Miller, at that time a Yale undergraduate and fan of *Computer Lib*, lived in Philadelphia. We talked virtuality (to be discussed later) for a while, then the Xanadu system. A superb programmer and remarkable theoretician with an infectious smile and ingratiating waddle, he makes everybody happy; this despite his constant complaints about there being too much gravity, and continual demand for the immediate abolition of all governments.

STUART GREENE

Stuart Greene had taken both my courses at Swarthmore, but went on to get a film degree at NYU. Devastatingly clever and probingly elfin, Stuart was teaching holography while he was in high school and frequently goes on Buddhist retreats. In all things requiring manual coordination he is astounding, supposedly due to Zen meditation.

ROGER GREGORY

Roger Gregory defies description. Roger Gregory defies everything. Once a mathematician, knowledgeable and rancorously opinionated on all subjects, he defies you to argue by expressing himself as fiercely as possible. Miraculously, most people like him a lot, perhaps because he wastes no energy in hypocrisy. Some, however, would find him unkempt. It is probably not the case that he inspired the character of Oscar the Grouch on *Sesame Street*-- aggressively messy with a heart of gold-- but this leads to puzzling questions of how *else* they might have come up with such a character.

LITERARY 1/35 MACHINES

I first met Roger at some science-fiction convention in Chicago. He thought I was onto something but had to think about enfilades a lot before he realized it could be done. In 1979 he gradually took over day-to-day supervision of the Xanadu project, cajoling, snarling, and demanding hotter spices; and now runs XOC, Inc., the development company.

ERIC HILL

While it was alleged that at fifteen he was involved in misdeeds involving a government computer over the phone, Eric was chortled out of juvenile court by an amused judge. In high school he was active in DECMUG (Digital Equipment Corporation MisUsers Group). He knows Systems. He was more suave and worldly than the rest of us even in high school, as he was in the summer of 1979.

ROLAND KING

Incredibly gaunt and thin, gentle and soft-spoken, Roland was a graduate student in formal linguistics when he joined us. The Vandyke beard suggests a Robin Hood, but underneath burns perhaps a fiercer Libertarian than all the rest of us. With his soft Southern accent, ever-present cigarette, faraway look and incredible graciousness, he is that member of the group on whom the term *gentleman* would sit most comfortably.

THE AUTHOR

And then there was Ted Nelson, glib, eager, impatient, always behind.

A LONG SUMMER'S DESIGN

In the summer of 1979 this group rented an idyllic tree-shaded house and we *designed*, restructuring the system from top to bottom. This was clearly necessary. Bill Barus's ingenious design had to be reworked for several reasons. He had opened the door and shown us the way; but a number of new and penetrating questions had to be answered, as we reached toward a generality not previously dreamed of.

The entire summer was spent exploring and reworking the algorithms and data structures and making sure it could all be done. No premature coders *we*. We had expected to get to coding much sooner, but that's not how it worked out. Everything had to be rethought from top to bottom. Ever probing and reformulating, the group redesigned Barus's linking enfilade system, designed the historical trace enfilade, and formulated the general theory of enfilades (that the work of Miller and Greene and Gregory). By various enfilade structures we were able to come up with a design that could grow forever without any of its performance parameters deteriorating unacceptably. Our enfilade data structures and methods

LITERARY 1/36 MACHINES

effectively refute Donald Knuth's list of desirable features that he says you can't have all at once (in his book *Fundamental Algorithms: Sorting and Searching*).*

It was a very special time: *dolce far niente* design sessions on the porch with blackboards, long evenings talking design while Stuart, with his back to us, conquered Apple Breakout with one ball over and over. A special experience was a number of afternoons we spent with the very wonderful John Mauchly (one of the inventors of the computer), listening to his reminiscences.

The group has fiercely and relentlessly pushed for generality. Several of my pet ideas went out the window, though they hung onto the sill for a time. One of those was the "literary link" formulation, expounded in various of my articles since about 1975, which is too tricky to go into at the present time.

By the end of the summer we got into actual programming. The language, of course, is Bell Labs' C.* Despite a constant lack of funds, we muddled through.

KING OF PRUSSIA

Part of the group continued on in the fall, renting a house in King of Prussia, Pennsylvania, a strange suburban area where tract homes and new-tech factories are crammed into a junction of expressways. King of Prussia is not easy to find your way around; Xanadu House, as it was dubbed, was lost in these suburbs. To find it you went down a certain road until you passed a six-foot painted statue of a chicken, then turned left.

During ths period, Mark was the principal coder, with Roger kibitzing and managing the household, and a number of friends and well-wishers dropping by from the nearby computer community. The details of the evolving design filled the living room on tall Formica whiteboards.

---

*Knuth, world authority on algorithms, is aware of our assertions and has been kind enough to mention them in public speeches, though as yet he has no direct knowledge of our methods.

*Lifeboat Associates' BDS C under CP/M-- the only C compiler available at that time for our computers-- pulled us through at a crucial early stage, thanks to its diligent young creator, Leor Zolman. So did an equipment loan from Harry Garland of Cromemco.

LITERARY 1/37 MACHINES

It was at this time that the last great inspiration of the project took place. Mark Miller had been puzzling over a number of key questions. One was how to handle multiple versions. Another was how to extend to a networked system with many storage computers and many users, and how to handle network growth on a decentralized basis.

Then all at once it came to Mark on a single night of immense realization: the unified addressing scheme we now call "tumblers." This is a unique numbering system and arithmetic which handles all these problems cleanly by a unified method. (See "Tumbling through the Docuverse," Chapter 4.) Roger, the mathematician, worked out the details with Mark and thus shares the credit. (Both Mark and Roger had by an odd coincidence studied transfinite numbers, a very esoteric topic, in college, and tumblers turned out to be closely related.)

K. ERIC DREXLER

It was at about this time that K. Eric Drexler, then of MIT, joined the group as a friend and analyst. He spent a great deal of time analyzing our algorithms, and came up with a number of new wrinkles and structures which we consider part of the enfilade family, though they taper off in new directions. His new book, *Engines of Creation*, is inspiring to us all.

THE EIGHTIES

Since that time, the group has dispersed and changed lifestyles. There have been various Xanadu weddings. Mark Miller is currently (November 1986) at Xerox PARC, Stuart Greene is at Apple. Until the system is ready I continue as writer and lecturer, propagating the faith and cleaning up other projects begun long ago.

Software development has continued under Roger Gregory: first in Ann Arbor, then in California-- Menlo Park and San Jose. At this writing we are on the verge of over-the-phone demonstration. The code begun in King of Prussia has grown up.

Many people are very eager to see the Xanadu system work. Perhaps none is so eager as the author of this book, who has been waiting for it for twenty-six years. (Talk about sharpening a very big pencil.)

Why a single design should have such importance to anybody is discussed in the next chapter.

LITERARY 1/38 MACHINES

AS WE MAY THINK

by Vannevar Bush

(This article first appeared in the July, 1945 issue of *The Atlantic Monthly*. Reprinted by permission.)

Of what lasting benefit has been man's use of science and of the new instruments which his research brought into existence? First, they have increased his control of his material environment. They have improved his food, his clothing, his shelter; they have increased his security and released him partly from the bondage of bare existence. They have given him increased knowledge of his own biological processes so that he has had a progressive freedom from disease and an increased span of life. They are illuminating the interactions of his physiological and psychological functions, giving promise of an improved mental health.

Science has provided the swiftest communication between individuals; it has provided a record of ideas and has enabled man to manipulate and to make extracts from that record so that knowledge evolves and endures throughout the life of a race rather than that of an individual.

There is a growing mountain of research. But there is increased evidence that we are being bogged down today as specialization extends. The investigator is staggered by the findings and conclusions of thousands of other workers--conclusions which he cannot find time to grasp, much less to remember, as they appear. Yet specialization becomes increasingly necessary for progress, and the effort to bridge between disciplines is correspondingly superficial.

Professionally, our methods of transmitting and reviewing the results of research are generations old and by now are totally inadequate for their purposes. If the aggregate time spent in writing scholarly works and in reading them could be evaluated, the ratio between these amounts of time might well be startling. Those who conscientiously attempt to keep abreast of current thought, even in restricted fields, by close and continuous reading might well shy away from an examination calculated to show how much of the previous month's efforts could be produced on call. Mendel's concept of the laws of genetics was lost to the world for a generation because his publication did not reach the few who were capable of grasping and extending it; and this sort of catastrophe is undoubtedly being repeated all about us, as truly significant attainments become lost in the mass of the

LITERARY 1/39 MACHINES

inconsequential.

The difficulty seems to be not so much that we publish unduly in view of the extent and variety of present-day interests, but rather that publication has been extended far beyond our present ability to make real use of the record. The summation of human experience is being expanded at a prodigious rate, and the means we use for threading through the consequent maze to the momentarily important item is the same as was used in the days of square-rigged ships.

But there are signs of a change as new and powerful instrumentalities come into use. Photocells capable of seeing things in a physical sense, advanced photography which can record what is seen or even what is not, thermionic tubes capable of controlling potent forces under the guidance of less power than a mosquito uses to vibrate his wings, cathode ray tubes rendering visible an occurance so brief that by comparison a microsecond is a long time, relay combinations which will carry out involved sequences of movements more reliably than any human operator and thousands of times as fast--there are plenty of mechanical aids with which to effect a transformation in scientific records.

Two centuries ago Leibnitz invented a calculating machine which embodied most of the essential features of recent keyboard devices, but it could not then come into use. The economics of the situation were against it: the labor involved in constructing it, before the days of mass production, exceeded the labor to be saved by its use, since all it could accomplish could be duplicated by sufficient use of pencil and paper. Moreover, it would have been subject to frequent breakdown, so that it could not have been depended upon; for at that time and long after, complexity and unreliability were synonymous.

Babbage, even with remarkably generous support for his time, could not produce his great arithmetical machine. His idea was sound enough, but construction and maintenance costs were then too heavy. Had a Pharoah been given detailed and explicit designs of an automobile, and had he understood them completely, it would have taxed the resources of his kingdom to have fashioned the thousands of parts for a single car, and that car would have broken down on the first trip to Giza.

Machines with interchangeable parts can now be constructed with great economy of effort. In spite of much complexity, they perform reliably. Witness the humble typewriter, or the movie camera, or the automobile. Electrical contacts have ceased to stick--note the automatic telephone exchange, which has hundreds of thousands of such contacts, and yet is reliable. A spider web of metal, sealed in a thin glass container, a wire heated to a brilliant glow, in short, the thermionic tube of radio sets, is made by the hundred million, tossed about in packages, plugged into sockets--and it works! Its gossamer parts, the precise location and alignment involved in its construction, would have occupied a master craftsman of the guild

LITERARY 1/40 MACHINES

for months; now it is built for thirty cents. The world has arrived at an age of cheap complex devices of great reliability; and something is bound to come of it.

THE SILVER IMAGE

A record, if it is to be useful to science, must be continuously extended, it must be stored, and above all it must be consulted. Today we make the record conventionally by writing and photography, followed by printing; but we also record on film, on wax disks, and on magnetic wires. Even if utterly new recording procedures do not appear, these present ones are certainly in the process of modification and extension.

Certainly progress in photography is not going to stop. Faster material and lenses, more automatic cameras, finer-grained sensitive compounds to allow an extension of the minicamera idea, are all imminent. Let us project this trend ahead to a logical, if not inevitable, outcome. The camera hound of the future wears on his forehead a lump a little larger that a walnut. It takes pictures 3 millimeters square, later to be projected or enlarged, which after all involves only a factor of 10 beyond present practice. The lens is of universal focus, down to any distance accommodated by the unaided eye, simply because it is of short focal length. There is a built-in photocell on the walnut such as we now have on at least one camera, which automatically adjusts exposure for a wide range of illumination. There is film in the walnut for a hundred exposures, and the

spring for operating its shutter and shifting its film is wound once and for all when the film clip is inserted. It produces its result in full color. It may well be stereoscopic, and record with two spaced glass eyes, for striking improvements in stereoscopic techniques are just around the corner.

The cord which trips its shutter may extend down a man's sleeve within easy reach of his fingers. A quick squeeze, and the picture is taken. On a pair of ordinary glasses is a square of fine lines near the top of one lens, where it is out of the way of ordinary vision. When an object appears in that square, it is lined up for its picture. As the scientist of the future moves about the laboratory or the field, every time he looks at something worthy of the record, he trips the shutter and in it goes, without even an audible click. It this all fantastic? The only fantastic thing about it is the idea of making as many pictures as would result from its use.

Will there be dry photography? It is already here in two forms. When Brady made his Civil War pictures, the plate had to be wet at the time of exposure. Now it has to be wet during development instead. In the future, perhaps it need not be wetted at all. There have long been films impregnated with diazo dyes which form a picture without development, so that it is already there as soon as the camera has been operated. An exposure to ammonia gas destroys the unexposed dye, and the picture can then be taken out into the light and examined. The process is now slow, but someone may

LITERARY 1/41 MACHINES

speed it up, and it has no grain difficulties such as now keep photographic researchers busy. Often it would be advantageous to be able to snap the camera and to look at the picture immediately.

Another process now in use is also slow, and more or less clumsy. For fifty years impregnated papers have been used which turn dark at every point where an electrical contact touches them, by reason of the chemical change thus produced in a iodine compound included in the paper. They have been used to make records, for a pointer moving across them can leave a trail behind. If the electrical potential on the pointer is varied as it moves, the line becomes light or dark in accordance with the potential.

This scheme is now used in facsimile transmission. The pointer draws a set of closely spaced lines across the paper one after another. As it moves, its potential is varied in accordance with a varying current received over wires from a distant station, where these variations are produced by a photocell which is similarly scanning a picture. At every instant the darkness of the line being drawn is made equal to the darkness of the point on the picture being observed by the photocell. Thus, when the whole picture has been covered, a replica appears at the receiving end.

A scene itself can be just as well looked over line-by-line by the photocell in this way as can a photograph of the scene.

This whole apparatus constitutes a camera, with the added feature, which can be dispensed with if desired, of making its picture at a distance. It is slow, and the picture is poor in detail. Still, it does give another process of dry photography, in which the picture is finished as soon as it is taken.

It would be a brave man who would predict that such a process will always remain clumsy, slow, and faulty in detail. Television equipment today transmits sixteen reasonably good pictures a second, and it involves only two essential differences from the process described above. For one, the record is made by a moving beam of electrons rather than a moving pointer, for the reason that an electron beam can sweep across the picture very rapidly indeed. The other dfference involves merely the use of a screen which glows momentarily when the electrons hit, rather than a chemically treated paper or film which is permanently altered. This speed is necessary in television, for motion pictures rather that stills are the object.

Use chemically treated film in place of the glowing screen, allow the apparatus to transmit one picture only rather than a succession, and use a rapid camera for dry photography. The treated film needs to be far faster in action than present examples, but it probably could be. More serious is the objection that this scheme would involve putting the film inside a vacuum chamber, for electron beams behave normally only in such a rarefied environment. This difficulty could

LITERARY 1/42 MACHINES

be avoided by allowing the electron beam to play on one side of a partition, and by pressing the film against the other side, if this partition were such as to allow the electrons to go through perpendicular to its surface, and to prevent them from spreading out sideways. Such partitions, in crude form, could certainly be constructed, and they will hardly hold up the general development.

Like dry photography, microphotography still has a long way to go. The basic scheme of reducing the size of the record, and examining it by projection rather than directly, has possibilities too great to be ignored. The combination of optical projection and photographic reduction is already producing some results in microfilm for scholarly purposes, and the potentialities are highly suggestive. Today, with microfilm, reductions by a linear factor of 20 can be employed and still produce full clarity when the material is re-enlarged for examination. The limits are set by the graininess of the film, the excellence of the optical system, and the efficiency of the light sources employed. All of these are rapidly improving.

Assume a linear ratio of 100 for future use. Consider film of the same thickness as paper, although thinner film will certainly be usable. Even under these conditions there would be a total factor of 10,000 between the bulk of the ordinary record in books and its microfilm replica. The *Encyclopaedia Britannica* could be reduced to the volume of a matchbox. The library of a million volumes could be compressed into one end of a desk. If the human race has produced since the invention of movable type a total record, in the form of magazines, newspapers, books, tracts, advertising blurbs, correspondence, having a volume corresponding to a billion books, the whole affair, assembled and compressed, could be lugged off in a moving van. Mere compression, of course, is not enough; one needs not only to make and store a record but also to be able to consult it, and this aspect of the matter comes later. Even the modern great library is not generally consulted; it is nibbled at by a few.

Compression is important, however, when it somes to costs. The material fo the microfilm *Britannica* would cost a nickel, and it could be mailed anywhere for a cent. What would it cost to print a million copies? To print a sheet of newpaper, in a large edition, costs a small fraction of a cent. The entire material of the *Britannica* in reduced microfilm form would go on a sheet eight and one-half by eleven inches. Once it is available, with the photographic reproduction methods of the future, duplicates in large quantities could probably be turned out for a cent apiece beyond the cost of materials. The preparation of the original copy? That introduces the next aspect of the subject.

VOCODER

To make the record, we now push a pencil or tap a typewriter. Then comes the process of digestion and correction, followed

LITERARY 1/43 MACHINES

by an intricate process of typesetting, printing, and distribution. To consider the first stage of the procedure, will the author of the future cease writing by hand or typewriter and talk directly to the record? He does so indirectly, by talking to a stenographer or a wax cylinder; but the elements are all present if he wishes to have his talk directly produce a typed record. All he needs to do is to take advantage of existing mechanisms and to alter his language.

At a recent World Fair a machine called Voder was shown. A girl stroked its keys and it emitted recognizable speech. No human vocal cords entered into the procedure at any point; the keys simply combined some electrically produced vibrations and passed these on to a loudspeaker. In the Bell Laboratories there is the converse of this machine, called a Vocoder. The loudspeaker is replaced by a microphone, which picks up sound. Speak to it, and the corresponding keys move. This may be one element of the postulated system.

The other element is found in the stenotype, that somewhat disconcerting device encountered usually at public meetings A girl strokes its keys languidly and looks about the room and sometimes at the speaker with a disquieting gaze. From it emerges a typed strip which records in a phonetically simplified language a record of what the speaker is supposed to have said. Later this strip is retyped into ordinary language, for in its nascent form it is intelligible only to the initiated. Combine these two elements, let the Vocoder run the stenotype, and the result is a machine which types when talked to.

Our present languages are not especially adapted to this sort of mechanization, it is true. It is strange that the inventors of universal languages have not seized upon the idea of producing one which better fitted the technique for transmitting and recording speech. Mechanization may yet force the issue, especially in the scientific field; whereupon scientific jargon would become still less ietligible to the layman.

One can now picture a future investigator in his laboratory. His hands are free, and he is not anchored. As he moves about and observes, he photographs and comments. Time is automatically recorded to tie the two records together. If he goes into the field, he may be connected by radio to his recorder. As he ponders over his notes in the evening, he again talks his comments into the record. His typed record, as well as his photographs, may both be in miniature, so that he projects them for examination.

Much needs to occur, however, between the collection of data and observations, the extraction of parallel material from the existing record, and the final insertion of new material into the general body of the common record. For mature thought there is no mechanical substitute. But creative thought and essentially repetitive thought are very different things. For the latter there are, and may be, powerful mechanical aids.

LITERARY 1/44 MACHINES

NAPIER'S BONES REVISITED

Adding a column of figures is a repetitive thought process, and it was long ago properly relagated to the machine. True, the machine is sometimes controlled by a keyboard, and thought of a sort enters in reading the figures and poking the corresponding keys, but even this is avoidable. Machines have been made which will read typed figures by photocells and then depress the corresponding keys; these are combinations of photocells for scanning the type, electric circuits for sorting the consequent variations, and relay circuits for interpreting the result into the action of solenoids to pull the keys down.

All this complication is needed because of the clumsy way in which we have learned to write figures. If we recorded them positionally, simply by the configuration of a set of dots on a card, the automatic reading mechanism would become comparatively simple. In fact, if the dots are holes, we have the punched-card machine long ago produced by Hollorith for the purposes of the census, and now used throughout business. Some types of complex businesses could hardly operate without these machines.

Adding is only one operation. To perform arithmetical computation involves also subtraction, multiplication, and division, and in addition some method for temporary storage of results, removal from storage for further manipulation, and recording of final results by printing. Machines for these purposes are now of two types: keyboard machines for accounting and the like, manually controlled for the insertion of data, and usually automatically controlled as far as the sequence of operations is concerned; and punched-card machines in which separate operations are usually delegated to a series of machines, and the cards then transferred bodily from one to another. Both forms are very useful; but as far as complex computations are concerned, both are still in embryo.

Rapid electrical counting appeared soon after the physicists found it desirable to count cosmic rays. For their own purposes the physicists promptly constructed thermionic-tube equipment capable of counting electrical impulses at the rate of 100,000 a second. The advanced arithmetical machines of the future will be electrical in nature, and they will perform at 100 times present speeds, or more.

Moreover, they will be far more versatile than present commercial machines, so that they may readily be adapted for a wide variety of operations. They will be controlled by a control card or film, they will select their own data and manipulate it in accordance with the instructions thus inserted, they will perform complex arithmetical computations at exceedingly high speed, and they will record results in such form as to be readily available for distribution or for later further manipulation. Such machines will have enormous appetites. One of them will take instructions and data from a whole roomful of people armed with simple keyboard punches, and will deliver sheets of

LITERARY   1/45   MACHINES

computed results every few minutes. There will always be plenty of things to compute in the detailed affairs of millions of people doing complicated things.

The repetitive processes of thought are not confined, however, to matters of arithmetic and statistics. In fact, every time one combines and records facts in accordance with established logical processes, the creative aspect of thinking is concerned only with the selection of the data and the process to be employed, and the manipulation thereafter is repetitive in nature and hence a fit matter to be relegated to the machines. Not so much has been done along these lines, beyond the bounds of arithmetic, as might be done, primarily because of the economics of the situation. The needs of business, and the extensive market obviously waiting, assured the advent of mass-produced arithmetical machines just as soon as production methods were sufficiently advanced.

With machines for advanced analysis, no such situation existed; for there was and is no extensive market; the users of advanced methods of manipulating data are a very small part of the population. There are, however, machines for solving differential equations--and functional and integral equations, for that matter. There are many special machines, such as the harmonic synthesizer which predicts the tides. There will be many more, appearing certainly first in the hands of the scientist and in small numbers.

If scientific reasoning were limited to the logical processes of arithmetic, we should not get far in our understanding of the physical world. One might as well attempt to grasp the game of poker entirely by the use of the mathematics of probability. The abacus, with its beads strung on parallel wires, led the Arabs to positional numeration and the concept of zero many centuries before the rest of the world; and it was a useful tool--so useful that it still exists.

It is a far cry from the abacus to the modern keyboard accounting machine. It will be an equal step to the arithmetical machine of the future. But even this new machine will not take the scientist where he needs to go. Relief must be secured from laborious detailed manipulation of higher mathematics as well, if the users of it are to free their brains for something more than repetitive detailed transformations in acccordance with established rules. A mathematician is not a man who can readily manipulate figures; often he cannot. He is not even a man who can readily perform the transformations of equations by the use of calculus. He is primarily an individual who is skilled in the use of symbolic logic on a high plane, and especially he is a man of intuitive judgement in the choice of the manipulative processes he employs.

All else he should be able to turn over to his mechanic, just as confidently as he turns over the propelling of his car to the intricate mechanism under the hood. Only then will mathematics be practically effective

LITERARY 1/46 MACHINES

in bringing the growing knowledge of atomistics to the useful solution of the advanced problems of chemistry, metallurgy, and biology. For this reason there will come more machines to handle advanced mathematics for the scientist. Some of them will be sufficiently bizarre to suit the most fastidious connoisseur of the present artifacts of civilization.

THE PERPETUAL AUDITOR

The scientist, however, is not the only person who manipulates data and examines the world about him by the use of logical processes, although he sometimes preserves this appearance by adopting into the fold anyone who becomes logical, much in the manner in which a British labor leader is elevated to knighthood. Whenever logical processes of thought are employed--that is, whenever thought for a time runs along an accepted groove--there is an opportunity for the machine. Formal logic used to be a keen instrument in the hands of the teacher in his trying of students' souls. It is readily possible to construct a machine which will manipulate premises in accordance with formal logic, simply by the clever use of relay circuits. Put a set of premises into such a device and turn the crank, and it will readily pass out conclusion after conclusion, all in accordance with logical law, and with no more slips than would be expected by a keyboard adding machine.

Logic can become enormously difficult, and it would undoubtedly be well to produce more assurance in its use. The machines for higher analysis have usually been equation solvers. Ideas are beginning to appear for equation transformers, which will rearrange the relationship expressed by an equation in accordance with strict and rather advanced logic. Progress is inhibited by the exceedingly crude way in which mathematicians express their relationships. They employ a symbolism which grew like Topsy and has little consistency; a strange fact in that most logical field.

A new sybolism, probably positional, must apparently precede the reduction of mathematical transformations to machine processes. Then, on beyond the strict logic of the mathematician, lies the application of logic in everyday affairs. We may some day click off arguments on a machine with the same assurance that we now enter sales on a cash register. But the machine of logic will not look like a cash register, even of the streamlined model.

So much for the manipulation of ideas and their insertion into the record. Thus far we seem to be worse off than before--for we can enormously extend the record; yet even in its present bulk we can hardly consult it. This is a much larger matter than merely the extraction of data for the purposes of scientific research; it involves the entire process by which man profits by his inheritance of acquired knowledge. The prime action of use is selection, and here we

LITERARY 1/47 MACHINES

are halting indeed. There may be millions of fine thoughts, and the account of the experience on which they are based, all encased within stone walls of acceptable architectural form; but if the scholar can get at only one a week by diligent search, his syntheses are not likely to keep up with the current scene.

Selection, in this broad sense, is a stone adze in the hands of a cabinet-maker. Yet, in a narrow sense and in other areas, something has already been done mechanically on selection. The personnel officer of a factory drops a stack of a few thousand employee cards into a selecting machine, sets a code in accordance with an established convention, and produces in a short time a list of all employees who live in Trenton and know Spanish. Even such devices are much too slow when it comes, for example, to matching a set of fingerprints with one of five million on file. Selection devices of this sort will soon be speeded up from their present rate of reviewing data at a few hundred a minute. By the use of photocells and microfilm they will survey items at the rate of a thousand a second, and will print out duplicates of those selected.

This process, however, is simple selection: it proceeds by examining in turn every one of a large set of items, and by picking out those which have certain specified characteristics. There is another form of selection best illustrated by the automatic telephone exchange. You dial a number and the machine selects and connects just one of a million possible stations. It does not run over them all. It pays attention only to a class given by a first digit, then only to a subclass of this given by the second digit, and so on; and thus proceeds rapidly and almost unerringly to the selected station. It requires a few seconds to make the selection, although the process could be speeded up if increased speed were economically warranted. If necessary, it could be made extremely fast by substituting thermionic-tube switching for mechanical switching, so that the full selection could be made in one one-hundredth of a second. No one would wish to spend the money necessary to make this change in the telephone system, but the general idea is applicable elsewhere.

Take the prosaic problem of the great department store. Every time a charge sale is made, there are a number of things to be done. The inventory needs to be revised, the salesman needs to be given credit for the sale, the general accounts need an entry, and, most important, the customer needs to be charged. A central records device has been developed in which much of this work is done conveniently. The salesman places on a stand the customer's identification card, his own card, and the card taked from the article sold--all punched cards. When he pulls a lever, contacts are made through the holes, machinery at a central point makes the necessary computations and entries, and the proper receipt is printed for the salesman to pass to the customer.

LITERARY 1/48 MACHINES

But there may be 10,000 charge customers doing business with the store, and before the full operation can be completed someone has to select the right card and insert it at the central office. Now rapid selection can slide just the proper card into position in an instant or two, and return it afterward. Another difficulty occurs, however. Someone must read a total on the card, so that the machine can add its computed item to it. Conceivably the cards might be of the dry photography type I have described. Existing totals could then be read by photocell, and the new total entered by an electron beam.

The cards may be in miniature, so that they occupy little space. They must move quickly. They need not be transfered far, but merely into position so that the photocell and recorder can operate on them. Positional dots can enter the data. At the end of the month a machine can readily be made to read these and to print an ordinary bill. With tube selection, in which no mechanical parts are involved in the switches, little time need be occupied in bringing the correct card into use--a second should suffice fo the entire operation. The whole record on the card may be made by magentic dots on a steel sheet if desired, instead of dots to be observed optically, following the scheme by which Poulsen long ago put speech on a magnetic wire. This method has the advantage of simplicity and ease of erasure. By using photography, however, one can arrange to project the record in enlarged form, and at a distance by using the process common in television equipment.

One can consider rapid selection of this form and distance projection for other purposes. To be able to key one sheet of a million before an operator in a second or two, with the possibility of then adding notes thereto, is suggestive in many ways. It might even be of use in libraries, but that is another story. At any rate, there are now some interesting combinations possible. One might, for example, speak to a microphone, in the manner described in connection with the speech-controlled typewriter, and thus make his selections. It would certainly beat the usual file clerk.

MEMEX

The real heart of the matter of selection, however, goes deeper than a lag in the adoption of mechanisms by libraries, or lack of development of devices for their use. Our ineptitude in getting at the record is largely caused by the artificiality of systems of indexing. When data of any sort are placed in storage, they are filed alphabetically or numerically, and information is found (when it is) by tracing it down from subclass to subclass. It can be in only one place, unless duplicates are used; one has to have rules as to which path will locate it, and the rules are cumbersome. Having found one item, moreover, one has to emerge from the system and re-enter on a new path.

The human mind does not work that way. It operates by association. With one item in its grasp, it snaps instantly to the next that is suggested by the association of

LITERARY 1/49 MACHINES

thoughts, in accordance with some intricate web of trails carried by the cells of the brain. It has other characteristics, of course; trails that are not frequently followed are prone to fade, items are not fully permanent, memory is transitory. Yet the speed of action, the intricacy of trails, the detail of mental pictures, is awe-inspiring beyond all else in nature.

Man can not hope fully to duplicate this mental process artificially, but he certainly ought to be able to learn from it. In minor ways he may even improve, for his records have relative permanency. The first idea, however, to be drawn from the anology concerns selection. Selection by association, rather than by indexing, may yet be mechanized. One cannot hope thus to equal the speed and flexibility with which the mind follows an associative trail, but it should be possible to beat the mind decisively in regard to the permanence and clarity of the items resurrected from storage.

Consider a future device for individual use, which is a sort of mechanized private file and library. It needs a name, and, to coin one at random, "memex" will do. A memex is a device in which an individual stores his books, records, and communications, and which is mechanized so that it may be consulted with exceeding speed and flexibility. It is an enlarged intimate supplement to his memory.

It consists of a desk, and while it can presumably be operated from a distance, it is primarily the piece of furniture at which he works. On the top are slanting transluscent screens, on which material can be projected for convenient reading. There is a keyboard, and sets of buttons and levers. Otherwise it looks like an ordinary desk.

In one end is the stored material. The matter of bulk is well taken care of by improved microfilm. Only a small part of the interior of the memex is devoted to storage, the rest to mechanism. Yet if the user inserted 5000 pages of material a day it would take him hundreds of years to fill the repository, so he can be profligate and enter material freely.

Most of the memex contents are purchased on microfilm ready for insertion. Books of all sorts, pictures, current periodicals, newspapers, are thus obtained and dropped into place. Business correspondence takes the same path. And there is provision for direct entry. On the top of the memex is a transparent platen. On this are placed longhand notes, photographs, memoranda, all sorts of things. When one is in place, the depression of a lever causes it to be photographed onto the next blank space in a section of the memex film, dry photography being employed.

There is, of course, provision for consultation of the record by the usual scheme of indexing. If the user wishes to consult a certain book, he taps its code on the keyboard, and the title page of the book promptly appears before him, projected onto

LITERARY 1/50 MACHINES

one of his viewing positions. Frequently used codes are mnemonic, so that he seldom consults his code book; but when he does, a single tap of a key projects it for his use. Moreover, he has supplemental levers. On deflecting one of these levers to the right he runs through the book before him, each paper in turn being projected at a speed which just allows a recognizing glance at each. If he deflects it further to the right, he steps through the book 10 pages at a time; still further at 100 pages at a time. Deflection to the left gives him tha same control backwards.

A special button transfers him immediately to the first page of the index. Any given book of his library can thus be called up and consulted with far greater facility than if it were taken from a shelf. As he has several projection positions, he can leave one item in position while he calls up another. He can add marginal notes and comments, taking advantage of one possible type of dry photography, and it could even be arranged so that he can do this by a stylus scheme, such as in now employed in the telautograph seen in railroad waiting rooms, just as though he had the physical page before him.

All this is conventional, except for the projection forward of present-day mechanisms and gadgetry. It affords an immediate step, however, to associative indexing, the basic idea of which is a provision whereby any item may be caused at will to select immediatly and automatically another. This is the essential feature of the memex. The process of tying two items together is the important thing.

When the user is building a trail, he names it, inserts the name in his code book, and taps it out on his keyboard. Before him are the two items to be joined, projected onto adjacent viewing positions. At the bottom of each there are a number of blank code spaces, and a pointer is set to indicate one of these on each item. The user taps a single key, and the items are permanently joined. In each code space appears the code word. Out of view, but also in the code space, is inserted a set of dots for photocell viewing; and on each item these dots by their positions designate the index number of the other item.

Thereafter, at any time, when one of these items is in view, the other can be instantly recalled merely by tapping a button below the corresponding code space. Moreover, when numerous items have been thus joined together to form a trail, they can be reviewed in turn, rapidly or slowly, by deflecting a lever like that used for turning the pages of a book. It is exactly as though the physical items had been gathered together from widely separated sources and bound together to form a new book. It is more than this, for any item can be joined into numerous trails.

The owner of the memex, let us say, is interested in the origin and properties of the bow and arrow. Specifically he is studying why the short Turkish bow was apparently

LITERARY 1/51 MACHINES

superior to the English long bow in the skirmishes of the Crusades. He has dozens of possible pertinent books and articles in his memex. First he runs through an encyclopedia, finds an interesting but sketchy article, leaves it projected. Next, in a history, he finds another pertinent item, and ties the two together. Thus he goes, building a trail of many items. Occasionally he inserts a comment of his own, either linking it into the main trail or joining it by a side trail to a particular item. When it becomes evident that the elastic properties of available materials had a great deal to do with the bow, he branches off on a side trail which takes him through textbooks of elasticity and tables of physical constants. He inserts a page of longhand analysis of his own. Thus he builds a trail of his interest through the maze of materials available to him.

And his trails do not fade. Several years later, his talk with a friend turns to the queer ways in which a people resist innovations, even of vital interest. He has an example, in the fact the the outranged Europeans still failed to adopt the Turkish bow. In fact, he has a trail on it. A touch brings up the codebook. Tapping a few keys projects the head of the trail. A lever runs through it at will, stopping at interesting items, going off on side excursions. It is an interesting trail, pertinent to the discussion. So he sets a reproducer in action, photographs the whole trail out, and passes it to his friend for insertion in his own memex, there to be linked into the more general trail.

PUSHING THE LIMITS

Wholly new forms of encyclopedias will appear, ready-make with a mesh of associative trails running through them, ready to be dropped into the memex and there amplified. The lawyer has at his touch the associated opinions and decisions of his whole experience and of the experience of friends and authorities. The patent attorney has on call the millions of issued patents, with familiar trails to every point of his client's intrerest. The physician, puzzled by a patient's reactions, strikes the trail established in studying an earlier similar case, and runs rapidly through analogous case histories, with side references to the classics for the pertinent anatomy and histology. The chemist, struggling with the sythesis of an organic compound, has all the chemical literature before him in his laboratory, with trails following the analogies of compounds, the side trails to their physical and chemical behavior .

The historian, with a vast chronological account of a people, parallels it with a skip trail which stops on the salient items, and can follow at any time comtemporary trails which lead him all over civilization at a particular epoch. There is a new profession of trail blazers, those who find delight in the task of establishing useful trails through the enormous mass of the common record. The inheritance from the master becomes not only his additions to the world's record, but for his disciples the

LITERARY 1/52 MACHINES

entire scaffolding by which they were erected.

Thus science may implement the ways in which man produces, stores, and consults the record of the race. It might be striking to outline the instrumentalities of the future more spectaculary, rather than to stick closely to methods and elements now known and undergoing rapid development, as has been done here. Technical difficulties of all sorts have been ignored, cetainly, but also ignored are means as yet unknown which may come any day to accelerate technical progress as violently as did the advent of the thermionic tube. In order that the picture may not be too commonplace, by reason of sticking to present-day patterns, it may be well to mention one such possibility, not to prophecy but merely to suggest, for prophecy based on extension of the known has substance, while prophecy founded on the unknown is only a doubly involved guess.

All our steps in creating or absorbing material of the record proceed through one of the senses--the tactile when we touch keys, the oral when we speak or listen, the visual when we read. Is it not possible that some day the path may be established more directly?

We know that when the eye sees, all the consequent information is transmitted to the brain by means of electrical vibrations in the channel of the optic nerve. This is an exact analogy with the electrical vibrations which occur in the cable of the television set: they convey the picture from the photcells which see it to the radio transmitter from which it is broadcast. We know further that if we can approach that cable with the proper instruments, we do not need to touch it; we can pick up those vibrations by electical induction and thus discover and reproduce the scene which is being transmitted, just as a telephone wire may be tapped for its message.

The impulses which flow in the arm nerves of a typist convey to her fingers the translated information which reaches her eye or ear, in order that the fingers may be caused to strike the proper keys. Might not these currents be intercepted, either in the original form in which information is conveyed to the brain, or in the marvelously metamorphosed form in which they then proceed to the hand?

By bone conduction we already introduce sounds into the nerve channels of the deaf in order that they may hear. Is it not possible that we may learn to introduce them without the present cumbersomeness of first transforming electrical vibrations to mechanical ones, which the human mechanism promptly transforms back to the electrical form? With a couple of electrodes on the skull the encephalograph now produces pen-and-ink traces which bear some relation to the electrical phenomena going on in the brain itself. True, the record in unintelligble, except as it points out certain

LITERARY 1/53 MACHINES

gross misfunctioning of the cerebral mechanism; but who would now place bounds on where such a thing may lead?

In the outside world, all forms of intelligence, whether of sound or sight, have been reduced to the form of varying currents in an electric circuit on order that they may be transmitted. Inside the human frame exactly the same sort of process occurs. Must we always transform to mechanical movements in order to proceed from one electrical phenomenon to another? It is a suggestive thought, but it hardly warrants prediction without losing touch with reality and immediateness.

Presumably man's spirit should be elevated if he can better review his shady past and analyze more completely and objectively his present problems. He has built a civilization so complex that he needs to mechanize his records more fully if he is to push his experiment to its logical conclusion and not merely become bogged down part way there by overtaxing his limited memory. His excursions may be more enjoyable if he can reaquire the priviledge of forgetting the manifold things he does not need to have immediately at hand, with some assurance that he can find them again if they prove important.

The applications of science have built man a well-supplied house, and are teaching him to live healthily herein. They have enabled him to throw masses of people against one another with cruel weapons.

They may yet allow him truly to encompass the great record and to grow in the wisdom of race experience. He may perish in conflict before he learns to wield that record for his true good. Yet, in the application of science to the needs and desires of man, it would seem to be a singularly unfortunate stage at which to terminate the process, or to lose hope as to the outcome.

ABOUT THE AUTHOR: Vannevar Bush was a pioneer in computer design who also distinguished himself as an engineer, an administrator, and a government offical. He became president of the Carnegie Institute in Washington, D.C., in 1939, and was chairman of the National Advisory Committee for Aeronautics from 1939 to 1941. In 1941, President Roosevelt appointed Bush the first director of the Office of Scientific Research and Development, an agency to coordinate federally funded defense research. In this capacity, he directed the activities of some 6000 leading American scientists in the application of science to warfare.

LITERARY 1/54 MACHINES

CHAPTER TWO

PROPOSAL FOR
A UNIVERSAL ELECTRONIC
PUBLISHING SYSTEM
AND ARCHIVE

Civilization ... has to do not with things
but with the invisible ties
that join one thing to another.

Antoine de Saint-Exupéry

We are all agreed that your theory is crazy.
The question which divides us is whether it is
crazy enough to have a chance of being correct.
My own feeling is that it is not crazy enough.

Niels Bohr
quoted in Kenneth Brower,
The Starship and the Canoe p. 46

'Tis a gift to be simple, 'Tis a gift to be free.

Shaker hymn

LITERARY 2/1 MACHINES

LITERARY 2/2 MACHINES

CHAPTER 2

PROPOSAL FOR
A UNIVERSAL ELECTRONIC
PUBLISHING SYSTEM AND ARCHIVE

PLAN OF THIS CHAPTER

This chapter is in nine sections, which introduce and elaborate on a very particular and precise design and plan. This chapter, design and plan are the heart of this book, a crossroad through which you are asked to pass repeatedly.

Some readers, especially those who may not have given these matters any thought, may find this material tough sledding the first time through. Therefore a *summary* level has been provided. (The bigger type.) Read that level on your first time through, or if you're in a hurry to get to another Chapter Three.

If this chapter is long and tedious to read, that is only because it strives for completeness. I am sure that in a few years from now everything in it will be quickly divined by small children sitting at screens which enact these principles. This is the painful irony of having to describe it rather than show it.

LITERARY 2/3 MACHINES

2.1 AN ELECTRONIC LITERARY SYSTEM

Here is the right way to do something by computer: first figure out what you *really* want to do and think about, instead of staying bogged down in what you usually do and think about when you don't use a computer.

This chapter is about one big idea: how materials stored electronically should be organized, and how the *right* system can be expanded to a universal instantaneous publishing system and archive for the world.

This first section is about the way we think information should be handled. In this chapter we will discuss this central idea, without technicalities. (The few "computer technicalities" are in footnotes.) In the later sections of this chapter we will consider how this idea had to be carried out, and what its details have to be.

This is the design of the system we propose for tomorrow's literature, tomorrow's office, and for the archives of our thought, controversy, art and architecture. But this is not merely an abstract design. It is now a functioning computer program, soon to be available on an experimental basis and later as a universal utility which we believe will be the manifest successor of the printed word as humanity now knows it. (This belief will be proven or disproven in the fullness of time; to understand why we believe it is to understand what this system will do, and its potentially revolutionary ramifications.)

So this will be a description of what we think we have created. We built this software to fulfill the virtuality we wanted rather than by selecting technical methods because they were convenient, as is more usually the custom.

The footnotes contain a few kibitzing remarks to those interested in how we have done it.*

---

*The Project Xanadu group has for some time been developing software to do what is described here with no complications for the user. Our way of seeing the world, as described here, is reflected in many ways in our unusual data structure.

To do efficiently what will be described here, we have had to overthrow all conventions and conventional assumptions about data handling and indexing, building from the bottom up a system that we think can grow indefinitely without choking on retrieval and transmission bottlenecks. We believe we have achieved this in our unique proprietary software.

We could only carry out this design with the help of certain technical developments which are for the present proprietary and secret. A number of radical discoveries in the field of computer indexing and retrieval render it possible to offer these services within seconds on configurations of present-day equipment, even, we believe, as the number of documents and service requests expands to astronomical figures. See "The Only Way It Could Work," Chapter 4.

LITERARY 2/4 MACHINES

For instance, we are going to look at ways of dealing with text based on its "true" structure, if we can figure out what that is.

THE DESIGN

We think this design is simple and basic, like running water or the telephone. Such a statement may be hard for some readers to believe, considering how many words and pictures it takes to describe it. Yet we think this design, once understood, is spare, parsimonious, clear and mandatory. (And that a few years from now, small children will understand it immediately when they get a chance to play with it.)

Unfortunately it is difficult to describe an interactive computer system so people can visualize it. Most people have not had practice in visualizing jumping and responding screen objects and presentations just from a writeup. Nonetheless, here we go.

The structure of documents and links to be described here is, for a computer system, unusually simple. This is all there is; we will describe it completely. We regard the simplicity of this design as its greatest virtue. *The user has no direct contact with technicalities.* The technicalities underneath are simply the means whereby certain exact and simple services are rapidly performed.

This is by no means the only possible design, but we believe it is the most comprehensive and powerful that can be. Whether ours is the right and best design is the central question for the reader to judge; but we believe there is such a thing as right and best. What we describe can be done: if not by us, then by somebody sometime. But if ours is not the right and best design, then it is on the reader's shoulders to come up with a better one.

Suggestions are welcome-- *if* you are sure you understand this design first.

THE INTRINSIC STRUCTURE IS WHAT YOU SHOULD SEE

The structure a user sees should be the *intrinsic* structure of his or her material, and not (as in many "word processing" systems) some combination of the material itself with some set of obtrusive conventions under which it is stored.

LITERARY 2/5 MACHINES

And we are going to create a service that simply stores and sends back different excerpts from this "true" structure of text.

WORLD AND VIEWPANE: BACK AND FRONT ENDS

Computer workscreens are to be the center of our coming worlds of work, of writing, of graphics. These aspects of our human world will be face-to-face with the screen. But what world will be on the computer screen? This is the central question.

The design of the storage for this new world is fundamental. What you store should be the *true and basic structure of the information you are dealing with*-- not some tricky arrangement that is carefully matched to some set of programs or hardware.

When you work on something at a computer screen, you should see that thing by itself, with no intrusion or distraction by the system. What the thing *is*-- its natural structure to the user-- is what you should see and work on: nothing less, nothing more, nothing else. It is therefore the representation of this structure-- of whatever structure the user may be concerned with-- that should concern us. But the things you work on can be staggeringly complex. So we must create a general system of representation that will automatically hold and present any possible structures you want to work on. (And keep track of their developing changes in a new and faithful accounting method.)

The necessary complexities for any given problem you may want to work on can be immensely intricate. That's why we must have a totally general system to represent, store and deliver any structures whatever-- but with new additional facilities that we believe are universally necessary, made applicable to every field of endeavor.

TRUE STRUCTURE

The world on the screen should deal with the true structure of the material seen and the work to be done on it.

The question in computerizing anything should be *what is the true structure*? Having answered that, you design a system that stores and shows that true structure.

What we will discuss here is representing the true structure of a certain kind of information, not how to show it. We believe that an orderly overall system can be developed for most types of written and graphical information and their instantaneous delivery. That is the storage system we will be discussing here. Think of this storage and delivery as a commodity service, as basic as telephone service, supplying your screen.

LITERARY 2/6 MACHINES

2.2 WHAT IS LITERATURE?

Literature is an ongoing system of interconnecting documents.

THE LITERARY PARADIGM

Our design is suggested by the one working precedent that we know of: literature.

A piece of writing-- say, a sheet of typed paper on the table-- looks alone and independent. This is quite misleading. Solitary it may be, but it may be also part of a literature.

By the term "a literature" we are not necssarily talking about *belles lettres* or leather-bound books. We mean it in the same broad sense of "the scientific literature," or that graduate-school question, "Have you looked at the literature?"

A literature is *a system of interconnected writings*. We do not offer this as our definition, but as a discovered fact. And almost all writing is part of some literature.

These interconnections do not exist on paper except in rudimentary form, and we have tended not to be aware of them. We see individual documents but not the literature, just as people see other individuals but tend not to see the society or culture that surround them.

The way people read and write is based in large part on these interconnections.

A person reads an article. He or she says to himself or herself, "Where have I seen something like that before? Oh, yes--" and the previous connection is brought mentally into play.

What is a document?

(You don't see the links.)

THE WEB OF CONNECTIONS IN SCIENCE

Consider how it works in science, and the day-to-day activities of an individual

LITERARY 2/9 MACHINES

In any ongoing literature, there is perpetual interpretation and reinterpretation, and links between documents help us follow the connections.

---

scientist, let's say a genetic theorist. She* reads current articles in the journals. These articles refer back, explicitly, to other writings; if our genetic theorist chooses to question the sources, or review their meaning, she is *following links* as she gets the books and journals and refers to them. Our genetic theorist may correspond with colleagues, mentioning what she has read, and receiving replies suggesting other things to read. (This correspondence, too, is thus connected to these other writings by implicit links.)

Say that our scientist, seeking to refresh her ideas, goes back to reading Darwin. She also derives inspiration from other things she reads-- the Bible, science fiction. These too link up to work going on in her mind.

Now writing, our scientist quotes and cites the things she has read in her own articles. (These links are explicit.) Other readers, taking interest in her sources, read the source documents for these quotes and citations (following the links).

And so it goes on. Our Western cultural tradition is a great procession of writings, all with links implicit and explicit between them.

Writings in principle remain continuously available-- both as recently quoted, and in their original inviolable incarnations-- in a great procession.

CONTROVERSY AND SHIFTING VIEW-POINT

Everyone argues over the interpretation of former writings, even the geneticist of our example. One author will cite a passage in Darwin to prove Darwin thought one thing, another will find another passage to try to prove he thought another.

And views of a field, and the way a field's own past is viewed within it, change. A formerly forgotten researcher may come to light (like Mendel), or a highly respected researcher may be discredited (like Cyril Burt). And so it goes, on and on. The past is continually changing-- or at least seems to be, as we view it.

---

*The literary tradition of English also uses the masculine pronoun for arbitrary examples like this-- "man as embracing woman"-- but I have become persuaded of the need for affirmative action in gender reference.

LITERARY 2/10 MACHINES

Exactly the same linked structure is implicit in the relation between business documents.

There is no predicting the use future people will make of what is written. Any summary we write today embodies a particular view: the perspective of a particular individual (or school of thought) at a particular time. We cannot know how things will be seen in the future. We must assume there will never be a final and definitive view of anything.

And yet this system functions.

LITERATURE IS DEBUGGED.

By that I mean that the system of writing and publication is a well-worked-out method and structure with deep and subtle workings.

In the evolution of the printed word, the mechanisms of quotation, citation and bibliography have been carefully adjusted in an evolving process. Scientific publication has one set of conventions, supermarket tabloids are much vaguer about sources, and most publications are somewhere in between.

Even though in every field there is an ever-changing flux of emphasis and perspective and distortion, and an ever-changing fashion in content and approach, the ongoing mechanism of written and published text furnishes a flexible vehicle for this change, continually adapting. Linkage structure between documents forms a flux of invisible threads and rubber bands that hold the thoughts together between documents.

LINKS IN BUSINESS TEXT

Linkage structure and its ramifications are surprisingly similar in the world of business.

A business letter will say, "In reply to your letter of the 13th..." Or a business form, another key communication, may say in effect, "In response to your order of the 24th of last month, we can supply only half of what you have asked for, but can fill the rest of the order with such-and-such item from our catalog." An internal company report will refer to previous reports. All of these citations may be thought of as cross-linkages among documents.

The point is clear, whether in science or business or *belles lettres*. Within bodies of writing, everywhere, there are linkages we tend not to see. The individual document, at hand, is what we deal with; we do not see the total linked collection of them all at once. But they are there, the documents not present as well as those that are, and **the grand** cat's-cradle among them all.

From this fundamental insight, we have endeavored to create a system for text editing and retrieval that will receive, and handle, and present, documents with links between them. We believe there is something very right about the existing system of literature; indeed we suspect that there are things right about it that we don't even know, as is true of Nature. And so we have tried to mirror, and replicate, and extend, existing literary structure as we have here described it.

LITERARY 2/12 MACHINES

2.3 A TRUE STORAGE SYSTEM FOR TEXT AND OTHER EVOLVING STRUCTURES

We are going to propose a way of keeping information that may seem odd and inefficient at first, but turns out to have remarkable power later on.

PROLOGUE:
MAKING EXTRA COPIES
ALL THE TIME

In most computer applications (such as that new game in town, "word processing"), it is often necessary to keep repeated copies. This frequent and disagreeable practice has several purposes.

The obvious purpose of making copies, often thwarted, is to assure the safety of recent work against various kinds of accident. But in the long run that is not important, since tomorrow's systems (like many of today's) will make reliable "safety copies" automatically.

However, there is another unrelated reason for an individual's making copies. This is to keep track of former states of the work, in case mistakes or wrong decisions need to be undone, to reconsider old choices, or otherwise look at former states. This need, *backtrack*, is serious and important. (We do not need to go back through previous material often, but if we need to do it at all we ought to be able to do it right.)

These two separate purposes-- safety and backtrack-- have been accidentally fused into a single conventional solution, the storage of repeated full copies; but if we assume that safety can be handled inside the system, away from the user, then historical backtrack becomes a separate issue, for which the conventional means of computer storage-- making a complete copy of everything you've done so far-- is rather silly. If what you're doing is making repeated small changes and additions, then you are repeatedly storing the unchanged material, redundantly. Department of Redundancy Department.

CONVENTIONAL BLOCK STORAGE

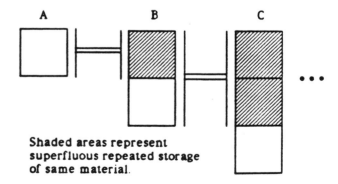

Shaded areas represent
superfluous repeated storage
of same material.

LITERARY 2/13 MACHINES

Under many circumstances the writer, or "text user," needs to reach back to a former condition. This is in the nature of creative work.

Virtually all of computerdom is built around this curious convention of storing whole copies of each current version.* Most computer people will tell you that is the way God intended computers to be used.

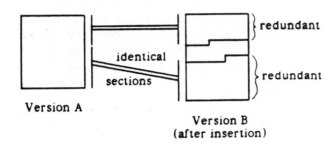

Version A

Version B
(after insertion)

Not so: computers can be programmed any way you like. What we are talking about is creating *new* ways of doing things that will make life easier. (This does mean throwing out a lot of the software that now exists, but that is the price of getting what we really need.)

THE ALTERNATIVE

Making extra copies to keep track of changing work is simple, but cluttering and dumb. Instead, suppose we create an automatic storage system that takes care of all changes and backtrack automatically. As a user makes changes, the changes go directly into the storage system; filed, as it were, chronologically.** Now with the proper sort of indexing scheme, the storage facility we've mentioned ought also to be able to deal with the problem of historical backtrack.

Think of it this way. An evolving document is really not just a block of text characters, Scrabble tiles all in a row; it is an ongoing changing flux. Think of its progress through time as a sort of braid or vortex.

A document is really

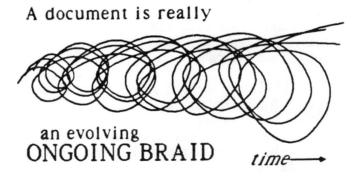

an evolving
ONGOING BRAID   *time*⟶

---

*Including block-transfer circuitry, most display buffering, and the disk routines supplied with conventional operating systems.

**(Of course, since the storage system assimilates all changes, it becomes nearly the whole "word processor," except for the user's front-end controls and display.)

LITERARY 2/14 MACHINES

The true storage of text should be in a system that stores each change and fragment individually, assimilating each change as it arrives, but keeping the former changes; integrating them all by means of an indexing method that allows any previous instant to be reconstructed.

Think of the process of making editorial changes as re-twisting this braid when its parts are rearranged, added or subtracted,

EDITING

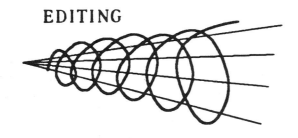

and think then of successive versions of the document, at successive instants of time, as *slices* in this space-time vortex.

INSTANTANEOUS VERSIONS ARE

CURRENT VERSION

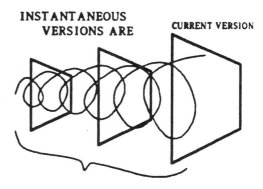

INSTANTANEOUS SLICES

Very well: the file management system we are talking about automatically keeps track of the changes and the pieces, so that when you ask for a given part of a given version at a given time, it comes to your screen.

The user may then refer not merely to the *present* version of the document; he or she may go back in time to any previous version. The user must also be able to follow a specific section back through time, and study its previous states.

LITERARY 2/15 MACHINES

This can be done efficiently if the user is reading from a computer screen; since you can set up the system to reconstruct hastily any piece that is wanted at the instant it is wanted. THE PART YOU WANT COMES WHEN YOU ASK FOR IT.

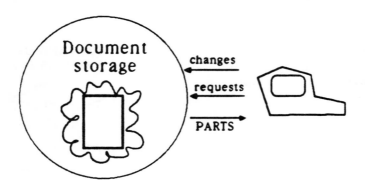

PART-POUNCE

This system is built around the assumption that you are reading from a screen, not from paper. When you "go to a certain part" of a document, the whole document is not ready to show; yet the system gives you that *part* instantly, *assembling it on the run* from the many fragments of its actual storage.*

We call this *pounce*. You pounce like a cat on a given thing, and it seems to be there, having been constructed while you are, as it were, in midair. Unlike things which *de*materialize when you pounce on them, like cotton candy, this *materializes* when you pounce on it.

---

*Obviously such a system departs from conventional "block" storage, and instead stores material in fragments under control of a master directory that indexes by time, position, and other things.

This method stores the document canonically as a system of evolving and alternative versions, instantly constructed as needed from the stored fragments, pointers and lists of our unusual data structure. Thus there is no "main" version of a

LITERARY 2/16 MACHINES

This is the *true* structure of text, because text is best viewed as an evolving, Protean structure.

You get *the part you want next*; the mistake of the conventional computer field has been to assume that the whole document had to be formed and ready in storage.

You ask for

A CERTAIN PART

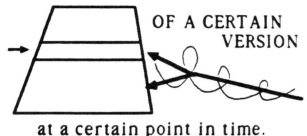

OF A CERTAIN VERSION

at a certain point in time.

ANOTHER VISUALIZATION

The canonical documents in this system can store the same material in numerous different versions-- as, for example, in the successive drafts of a novel.

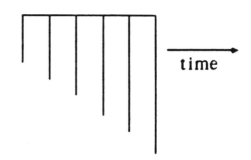

time

INDEXING VORTEX

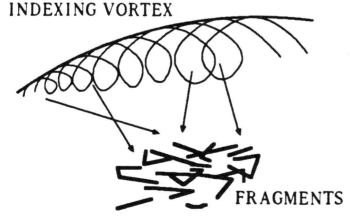

FRAGMENTS

thing, just the ongoing accumulation of pieces and changes, some of whose permutations have names and special linkages. In other words, our system treats all versions of a document as views extracted from the same aggregated object. It will be readily apparent that this changes the whole style of disk access, and mates uneasily with conventional operating systems, from CP/M to IBM's OS, which

LITERARY 2/17 MACHINES

Such storage permits easy reconstruction of previous states for mental clarification, fresh starts, and transfusions of previous ideas. It also permits multiple uses of the same materials for alternative versions and "boilerplate."

While the user of a customary editing or word processing system may scroll through an individual document, the user of this system may scroll in

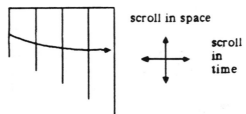

scroll in space

scroll
in
time

time as well as space, watching the changes in a given passage as the system enacts its successive modifications.

---

are designed to deliver whole files or continuations of files. The illustration depicts the operating system as Frankenstein's monster with a silver tray. (This presents inconveniences which may usually be *defeated*, but that just adds another level of indirection.)

And storage space is saved by not having to keep redundant parts. This in itself is not very important until the amount of redundantly stored material becomes very large-- but it can become very large very quickly as full versions are repeatedly saved-- which today's software methods require.

FILEWISE OP SYSTEMS WON'T DO

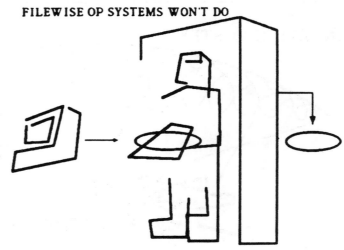

LITERARY 2/18 MACHINES

This same approach-- storage as an evolving structure with backtrack-- may be extended to all forms of data that are created by individuals.

Versions of a document set apart for other reasons-- "alternative" versions-- may likewise be flipped through or efficiently compared side by side.

We call this system of storage Prismatic because we may think of a given part, or section, as being prismatically refracted when we pass from one version to another. We believe our Prismatic storage can support virtually instantaneous retrieval of any portion of any version (historical or alternative).

of alternative versions (or *Alts*)-- more than one arrangement of the same materials, a facility that writers and programmers will certainly use when it becomes readily available. Alts are also important in many boilerplate applications, such as law and public relations, where the same materials are churned out repeatedly in different arrangements and variations. A master indexing scheme will greatly reduce storage requirements in these applications, as well as make the relations among the Alts much clearer.*

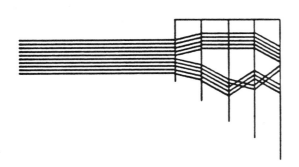

ALTERNATIVE VERSIONS

This same scheme can be expanded to allow the easy maintenance, creation and use

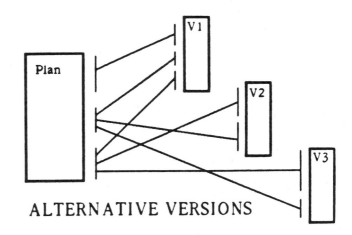

ALTERNATIVE VERSIONS

---

*Since alternative versions share common storage of the document's fragments, there is no waste of space.

LITERARY 2/19 MACHINES

Pictures, music, and graphical data structures created at a screen, three-dimensional structures for design and graphic arts, evolve in the same way and should be stored in the same way.

Actually, we may best visualize these alternative versions as a *tree* in the ongoing braid, a forking arrangement whereby one document becomes two, each of these daughter documents may in turn become others, etc.

TREE OF
ALTERNATIVE VERSIONS

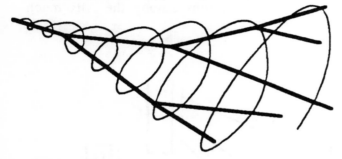

SHOWING COMMONALITIES: What Is the Same, What Is Different

Of course, a facility that holds multiple versions of the same material, and allows historical backtrack, is not terribly useful unless it can help you intercompare them in detail-- unless it can show you, word for word, what parts of two versions are the same.*

Lawyers need this to compare wordings. Congressmen need this to compare different draft versions of bills. Authors need it to see what has happened to specific passages in their writings between drafts. Biologists and anatomists need it to compare corresponding parts of animals graphically.

ANY FORMS OF DATA

This principle of storage and indexing by pieces and changes works not merely for text; it can be used for any forms of data structure.

HISTORICAL TRACE
OF ANYTHING

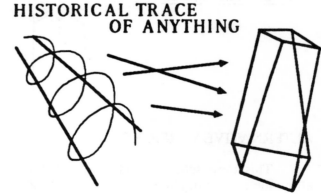

---

*(Such intercomparisons are sometimes possible in conventional computer systems, but they require the use of complex search commands among various related files.)

LITERARY 2/20 MACHINES

We propose an evolutionary structure, the *docuplex*, as the basic storage structure for electronic literature.

Thus if you are designing a building on a computer screen, as architects now do, you may browse through the changing design in the sequence you modified it over time, and create alternative versions as you like which share the common material.

Example.

Many kinds of equipment exist in multiple versions and designs. One example is an excellent airplane, the Boeing 747, which comes in over a dozen versions that you may order from the factory. Designers, engineers and customers should be able to call up any view of any model and see the corresponding parts on any other models. This is important for a variety of purposes; such manipulation should be possible *wherever there are corresponding structures.*

In *Computer Lib* I proposed the term "thinkertoy" for a computer screen facility which will permit the detailed intercomparison of complex alternatives. I still believe this will be one of the most fundamental structures of our working lives, once there exist systems such as these (and clean interactive front ends for these purposes).

Using the data structure and programs we have described, it is possible to store alternative designs and texts (such as the variant 747s) as *one unified data pool*, with the forking-version facility reading the variant designs directly out of this single structure.

FIRST SIMPLIFICATION

By creating such a capable storage system, we have greatly simplified the life of the text user. The nuisance of backup (and the spurious nonsense-task of finding *names* for backup files) are eliminated. But more important, we have unified all versions (previous and alternative) in a unified structure, what we may call a *docuplex*, permitting part-pounce on present, past and variant structures. The user may scroll through any two versions to see corresponding parts; and much more.

STAGE ONE ALL TOGETHER

I have so far presented several new capabilities that I think are important: *alternative versions* and *historical backtrack*, both with *commonality display*; and another vital capability, *links*, which I will explain shortly.

So let us call this Stage One: a system of computer storage that holds pieces of a thing, not big blocks, and assembles them instantly into whatever part of whatever version you ask for; and shows you which parts are the same between related versions.

Thus there are four kinds of movement inside a document: within the document's own topology (forward and back for simple text, links between parts in hypertext, between layers in windowing text), plus historical forward and back, and corresponding parts in alternative versions.

Let us call such a storage system a hyperfile.

You don't *have* to use these facilities. You can store text in long blocks if you wish. But if the facility is there, then the people who need it can use it.

Perhaps most important, these facilities provide a building-block for what is to be described in what follows.

2.4 A LINKING SYSTEM FOR TEXT AND OTHER DATA

Such an evolutionary storage structure makes the creation and maintenance of links between documents much cleaner and easier.

LINKS ARE PART OF THE WRITING

Links are intrinsic to documents, and have been for millennia.

A link is simply a connection between parts of text or other material. It is put in by a human. Links are made by individuals as pathways for the reader's exploration; thus they are parts of the actual document, part of the writing.

So the system we are describing must allow you to create links of any kind you want between any things you want.

LINK TYPES

As perhaps the simplest type of link, a user may create *book-marks*-- places he or she may want to re-enter text when returning to it.

JUMP-LINK

A link may be thought of as a jump opportunity, like a conventional footnote. If the author wants, such opportunities become part of the text structure. An asterisk, say, signals that "there's something to jump to from here." If you point at it with your lightpen (or mouse or whatever), Bingo!-- you're now at the footnote, or whatever else the author took you to. If you don't like it there, hit some sort of a Return Button and your screen goes back to where you were before and no harm has been done.

JUMPING ON A LINK

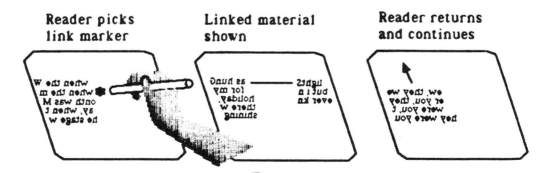

Reader picks link marker   Linked material shown   Reader returns and continues

LITERARY 2/23 MACHINES

You may want links for commentaries, bookmarks and placemarkers, footnotes, marginal notes, hypertext jumps and innumerable other uses; but they are very hard to keep in place with conventional computer storage structure.*

MARGINAL NOTES, SIDE-BY-SIDE WRITING

Marginal notes are another simple and important type of link. (Where the "margin" of the screen is-- that is, how to show them-- is a matter particular to your own screen setup.)

A user may also make side-by-side connections of other types. On contemplating any two pieces of text, he or she may make a link between them. Thereafter, when he or she displays either piece of text, and *asks to see the links*, a link-symbol is displayed, and the other attached text-- if he or she wishes to see it.

PARALLEL LINKED TEXT

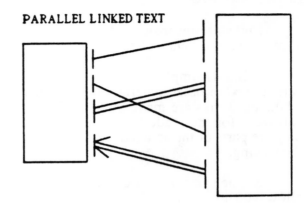

Naturally, making a marginal note consists of writing the note and hooking the link.

---

*LINKS + PRISMATICS -> USABILITY

Most computer schemes for linkage face the terrible problem of "updating" the links as text is modified and successive versions come into being. The present scheme dodges this problem smartly: a link is attached, not to a positional address in a given version, but to specific characters, and simply stays with these characters wherever they go. Thus Prismatic storage solves the considerable problem of link maintenance.

VIRTUAL YELLOW STICKERS

So-called "yellow stickers," marketed since the 1970s under such names as Post-It Notes (3M trademark), have been used in business and scholarship for temporary notes on printed material and other papers. The link method described here may be used for the same purposes. I stress this to indicate that the ease and low cost of such linked materials means that they may be used freely.

HYPERTEXT

The link facility gives us much more than the attachment of mere odds and ends. It permits fully non-sequential writing, or hypertext.

Links work together with the features described earlier; they have to. The links allow the creation of non-sequential writings, bookmarks and jump-structured graphics of many kinds. But *if you are going to have links you really need historical backtrack and alternative versions.*

Why? Because if you make some links to another author's document on Monday and its author goes on making changes, perhaps on Wednesday you'd like to follow those links into the present version. They'd better still be attached to the right parts, even though the parts may have moved. And being able to intercompare versions for shared material allows the links on compound alternatives to be studied and intercompared in depth.

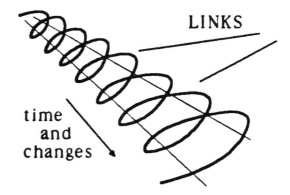

Thus the link stays where you put it through historical backtrack and in alternative versions-- if you choose to see it.

LITERARY 2/25 MACHINES

However, the evolutionary storage we have already described allows any links to be associated firmly with the pieces of data in any evolving structure, wherever those pieces may migrate to as changes occur.

This simple facility-- the jump-link capability-- leads immediately to all sorts of new text forms: for scholarship, for teaching, for fiction, for hyper-poetry. This makes possible a certain free-form serendipitous browsing.

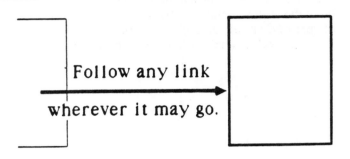

Follow any link wherever it may go.

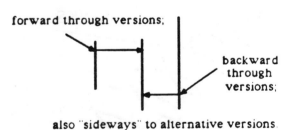

forward through versions;

backward through versions;

also "sideways" to alternative versions.

Essentially, the link seizes a point or span (or any other structure) in the Prismatic Document and holds to it. Links may be refractively followed from a point or span in one version to corresponding places in any other version. Thus a link to one version of a Prismatic Document is a link to all versions.

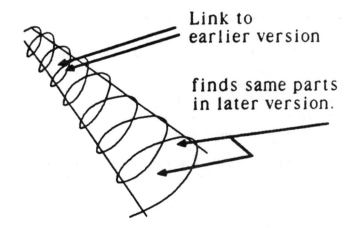

Link to earlier version

finds same parts in later version.

The effects, then, of links, alts and backtrack are in some sense multiplicative: together they give you a united facility of great power.

LITERARY 2/26 MACHINES

And any types of link may be created.

ANY TYPES OF LINK

A proper system should allow any types of link whatever, and there is a myriad of possible types.

In principle we allow any types of link to be defined by the sophisticated user.*

LINKS AND FRONT ENDS

How to *show* links is a Front-End Function, meaning that your screen machine can show them any way you like. Your front-end machine must also manage your other special needs: keeping track of where you go as you browse, taking note of your favorite places, and otherwise supporting your habits of work.

AS YOU RAMBLE,

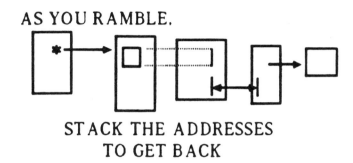

STACK THE ADDRESSES
TO GET BACK

---

*As presently defined, links are between spans of bytes. However, many extensions to this scheme are possible. These include point-to-point links, point-to-span, and span-to-span, having any separate names and functions desired. It will also be possible to have links with multiple endpoints, attaching to different kinds of object.

ANY KIND OF LINK

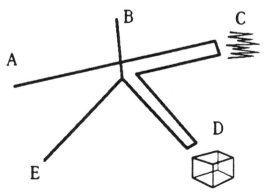

LITERARY 2/27 MACHINES

LINKING AMONGST ALL DATA TYPES

ALL DATA STRUCTURES
MAY BE MARRIED

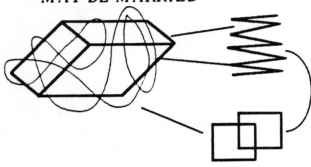

There must be no restrictions as to data types. For instance, why should you just have links on *text?* We believe you should be able to put footnotes and marginal notes and branching jumps on pictures, on music-- on any forms of data. (And it must be possible for such attached materials themselves to be pictures, music or whatever.)

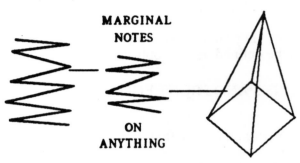

MARGINAL NOTES

ON ANYTHING

Consider, for example, an arbitrary type of link which we may call a "wuffle." A wuffle, let us say, connects a span of text, a picture, and a footnote. These are the *endparts*; together they constitute a wuffle's *end-set.*.

link-type specifier

wuffle

with the end-parts

C   B   A

→ span of text

→ picture

→ footnote-link

Directionality, if any, is given in the link-type definition. Note that end-parts may not hang together as they evolve (e.g. text sections):

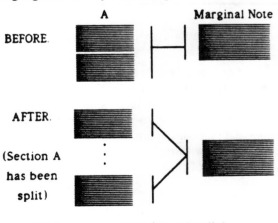

Links may even attach to other links.

LITERARY 2/28 MACHINES

2.5 THE DOCUMENT CONVENTION

From these beginnings, it will be possible to create many levels of organization and overlay-- but first let us identify the most fundamental unit. This unit comes from ancient reality, but in the new system is a combination of both a technical structure and an ownership convention.

So far we allow the storage of any sort of text (or other data) and any sort of links between arbitrary sections of the text or data.

But if it were possible for just anybody freely to put in and change just anything, we would stand to get simply a chaotic blur, a single muddy pool.

The solution is straightforward and traditional, and derives from literature as we have known it. We make sure that everything stored is divided precisely into *separate documents*.

A document consists of anything that someone wishes to store. It is designated by somebody to *be* a document; it may contain text, graphics, links, or window-links-- or any combination of these-- that the owner has created.

By this convention, then, *everything in the system is a document and has an owner.* No free-floating materials exist. Thus the Gettysburg Address is a document; "Jabberwocky" is a document; and a set of links between them, were someone to create it, would be yet a separate document.

What this convention really does is stress the singularity of each document, its external and internal borders. Thus, we focus on the integrity of the "document" as we've known it. Evolutionary continuity is unambiguous.

OWNERSHIP

Every document has an *owner*, the person who created and stored it (or someone who arranged it to be created and stored, such as a publishing company). The rightful copyright holder, or someone who has permission from the copyright holder and pays for storage, is the owner as far as the system is concerned.

Only the owner has a right to withdraw a document or change it.

(Although there are ways that others may conveniently create changed *versions* to suit their needs, as we will see in a later section.)

Ancient documents, no longer having a current owner, are considered to be owned

LITERARY 2/29 MACHINES

We will call this unit a *document*. It has an owner and (ordinarily) a name. We propose this unit (and its available connections) to replace the conventional concept of the *file* (which is intrinsically sequential).

A document normally consists of *contents*-- text, graphics, music, etc.-- and *links* to other documents.

---

by the system-- or preferably by some high-minded literary body that oversees their royalties. (See "Tuning the System," a Chapter 4.)

LOCATION AND OWNERSHIP OF LINKS

Links may be created within or between documents. But each link *resides in one place, the document that contains it.*

Links, just like text, are owned. Every link is part of a particular document and has an owner.

However, links in one document may attach to another document or collection of documents.

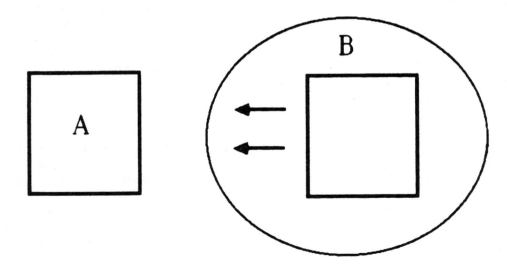

LITERARY 2/30 MACHINES

Every link, then, is part of a document.

Putting it another way, a document consists of its contents and its out-links.

And that's all.

Ordinarily a document consists of its *contents* (including history and alternatives) and its *out-links*, the links it contains that point to other documents. By contrast, a document's *in-links* are those stored elsewhere which point to *it*. These out-links are under control of its owner, whereas its in-links are not.*

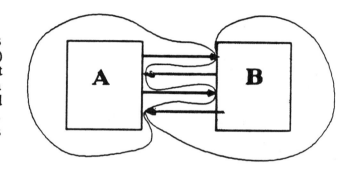

---

*More elaborate cases are possible, however. For instance, links between documents may reside in yet others.

Links between documents may reside in yet others.

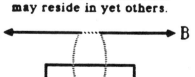

LITERARY 2/31 MACHINES

2.6 COMPOUND WINDOWING DOCUMENTS

These ground rules about documents, links and ownership provide a clean basis for the creation of complex multi-level document structures-- criss-crossing superdocuments of many parts-- collected in new structural wholes.

Given the exact document boundaries and ownership already mentioned, we can now create an orderly arrangement permitting far more complex documents to be stored. We also provide an arrangement allowing other individuals freely to make their own modifications on the stored documents. This we do by allowing what we call "compound documents."

The logic of these compound documents is simple and derives from the concept of document ownership. Every document has an owner. The integrity of this document is maintained; no one may change it but the owner.

But someone else may create a document which quotes it as much as desired. This mechanism we call the *quote-window* or *quote-link*. Through a "window" in the new document we see a portion of the old. We may also call this an *inclusion*.

The windows of a windowing document are themselves actually particular links between documents. No copy is made of the quoted material; rather, a quote-link symbol (or its essential equivalent) is placed in the quoting document. This quotation does not affect the integrity or uniqueness or ownership of the original document, since nothing has been copied from it.

WINDOWS

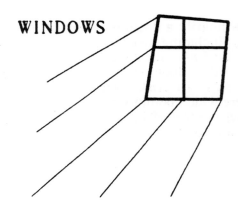

The quote-window is in fact the previous mechanism of *commonality display*-- showing what bytes are the same between two versions. But we extend the mechanisms so that one document can point to another and share some of its bytes in common.

And so a compound document consists of parts of old documents together with new material. Or we may say it really consists of *quote-links and new material*.

LITERARY 2/32 MACHINES

Each compound document is like the other documents: it has an owner and receives royalties.

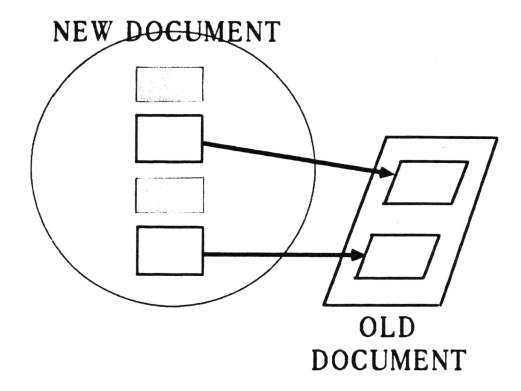

NEW DOCUMENT

OLD DOCUMENT

Through the same document conventions, the compound structures maintain the same conventions of integrity and ownership.

The compound document, too, has its own integrity, though the windowed materials are still part of their original documents.

Anything stored by one user on the system may be quoted-- adopted into a document-- by another person writing on the system (provided that the document being quoted is publicly available). This freedom of windowing applies, of course, to all forms of data, including pictures, musical notation, etc.

LITERARY 2/33 MACHINES

MANY LEVELS

Think of the present document as a sheet of glass. It may have writing painted on it by the present author; it may have clear glass, windowing to something else; the next pane may be in turn made of more layers of painted glass, with more windows, and so on indefinitely.

Only when you *step through* the window-- turning one glass page and going on in the next-- do you reach the original that you wanted. But stepping through the window means you are now in another work.

A document may have a window to another document, and that one to yet another, indefinitely. Thus A contains part of B, and so on. One document can be built upon another, and yet another document can be built upon that one, indefinitely: each having links to what was already in place.

A reader may either explore the immediate document, including the materials that show through; or "step through the window" to explore unseen parts of the next document, or the one beyond, and so on. After exploring a further document, the reader may return to the first gateway document, through which he or she came, or proceed further on tangents that have become available.

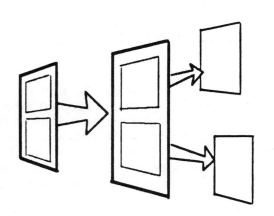

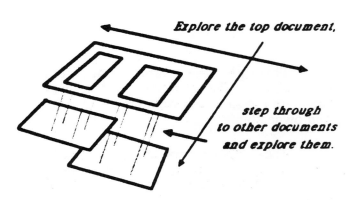

Explore the top document,

step through to other documents and explore them.

LITERARY 2/34 MACHINES

Document A can *include* Document B, even though Document B is *owned by* someone else.

By this simple, sweeping mechanism, all manner of different requirements and specialized uses are reduced to a single structure.

Example. The annual report of a corporation has a brief paragraph about each division of the company, with summary operating figures for the year. These paragraphs and figures are quoted from other documents which explain the matters more fully; the reader may easily step through to study them further.

Example. A children's story is ilustrated with pictures. If the child wants to "reach through the window," each picture is found to be part of a larger picture, with another story attached.

Example. A scholar writes a new interpretation of ancient Greek society, with numerous quotations from the writings of those times. Each quotation is a window, allowing the reader to step through and read the original.

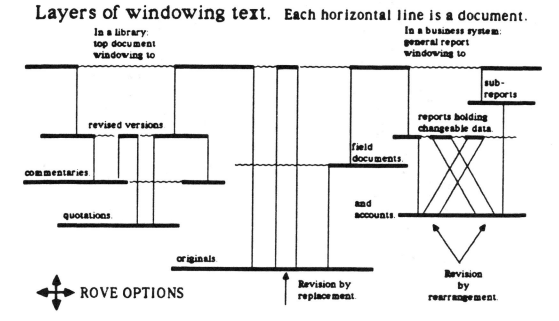

WINDOW SANDWICH

Layers of windowing text. Each horizontal line is a document.

LITERARY 2/35 MACHINES

THE PAYOFF BEGINS

These new methods of storage, based on the document and new kinds of links, have enormous advantages, and dramatically simplify a host of problems.

1. SPACE

First, of course, they save a great deal of space, if the same material is used in numerous documents.

2. UPDATE

No copying operations are required among the documents throughout the system, and thus we solve the problems of update-- especially the problem of updating documents which depend on other documents. We solve this problem simply by windowing to a changing document. Thus the problem of *distributed update*, so familiar throughout the technical world, disappears.

DISTRIBUTED UPDATE
Many documents updated automatically by windowing

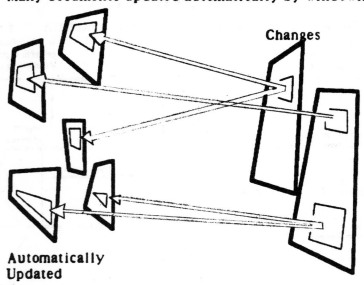

Changes

Automatically
Updated

LITERARY 2/36 MACHINES

Since quoted material only has to reside in its place of origin, and not in the other documents that quote it, other documents that quote it may be automatically "updated" when the owner of the quoted material changes it.

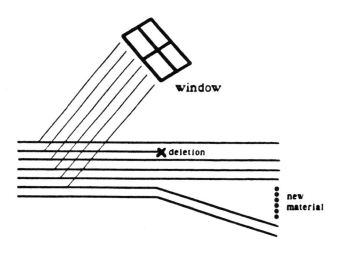

Note also, however, that a quotation-- an inclusion window-- may be fixed to another document in two ways: at a certain point in *time*, in which case revisions are seen by the user only when he or she asks, "What has this passage become?" Or second, at a relatively fixed location in the document *space*, in which case updates are seen automatically.*

TWO-WAY READING

As already stated, it is possible for the reader to ask to see the materials which are windowed to *by* a given document. However, it must also be possible for the reader to ask to see whatever documents *window to* the current document. Both are available at any time.

DERIVATIVE DOCUMENTS

A particular form of compound document is one which consists expicitly of an original and changes to it-- which may be made by anyone. (We may call this a *derivative* document).

The integrity of each document is maintained by keeping the two aspects separate: derivative documents are permanently defined (and stored) in terms of the originals and the changes.

Indeed, a document may consist merely of changes to another document. A nice example is the wonderful revision of Lincoln's Gettysburg Address by Doodles Weaver, showing how it might have been corrected by a stuffy highschool teacher. (This appeared in MAD some years ago.) Weaver's publication, put on this system, would consists of the changes on Lincoln's original (with the pointers to that original), along with Weaver's title and prefatory note.

*There are therefore two types of inclusion links: *floating in time* and *fixed in time*. But distinguishing among them-- for instance, suggesting

the most recent version to the reader-- is a front-end function.

ALTERNATIVE VERSIONS BY OWNERS AND NON-OWNERS

Alternative versions of anything may be created and published by anyone, whether or not he or she owns the document to which the alternative is being published. Because of the rules of ownership, however, the method differs slightly.

1. BY OWNERS -- AS PART OF THE SAME DOCUMENT

A document owner may create alternative arrangements of the same material, all *within* the same document.* In that case these alternatives are stored as separate, simultaneously available versions under the same document name, sharing material and forking on its historical tree. We may call this *versioning by descent.*

Owner's alternative versions

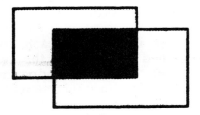

Shared bytes under same document name and account

Non-owner's alternative version

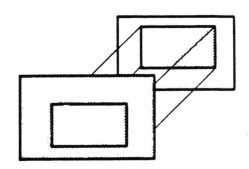

Shared bytes windowing from one account to another

---

*Documents and their versions are two separate aspects of the name-and-address mechanism of the system. See "Tumbling through the Docuverse," a Chapter 4.

LITERARY 2/38 MACHINES

2. BY NON-OWNERS -- AS OTHER DOCUMENTS

Another user, however, is free to create his or her own alternative version of the document he or she does not own. This, then, becomes a *windowing* document using the shared materials by including them. We may call this *versioning by inclusion.*

INTERCOMPARISON DOCUMENT

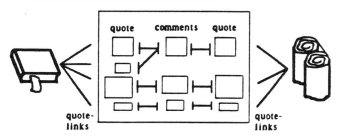

INTERCOMPARISON DOCUMENTS

A document that points out relations among other documents we may call an *intercomparison document.* Such documents may be easily created, say, to point out relations betwen the Bible and the Dead Sea Scrolls.

COMPOUNDING OF OTHER LINK TYPES

These structures may of course nest. Note especially that *links*, like text and pictures, *may be quoted.* All link types may interweave with quote-links and be themselves quoted. This makes possible compound documents to any remove, where one document links to another, and so on. One document, embracing another, takes it into itself by inclusion.

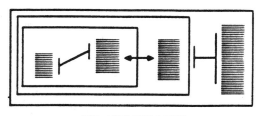

... TO ANY REMOVE

And this creates a basis for all kinds of hypertext-- linked, parallel, windowing.

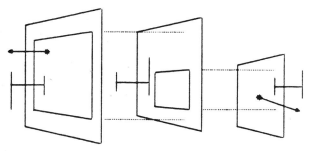

COMPOUND NESTED LINKS

AN INTERESTING WORLD

It will be noted that we have here defined an interesting and rich sort of world-- a world in which we are relieved of complications from conventional computer

LITERARY 2/39 MACHINES

filing; yet in which we have greatly enhanced our abilities to specify and express compound relations of every sort.

A WORLD OF INTER~~ACTIVE~~ *TWINGLED*

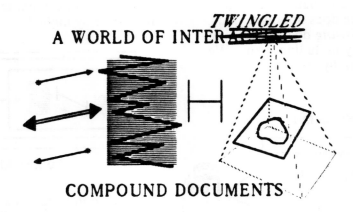

COMPOUND DOCUMENTS

...BUT A SIMPLE ONE

This world nevertheless remains simple in design. The virtuality is simple in structure and repeats in layers. You always know where you are, and can at once ascertain the home document of any specific word or character.

DOCUMENT COMPLEXITY
does not mean

IMPLEMENTATION COMPLEXITY

LITERARY 2/40 MACHINES

2.7 ELECTRONIC PUBLISHING:
MAKING THE LITERARY SYSTEM UNIVERSAL

Our system is not intended just as a private facility, but also as a method of publication. Thus a carefully designed system of publication, including conventions for copyright and royalty-- surprisingly like that of paper publishing-- has been worked out.

We have talked so far about storing and delivering compound documents and hypertexts. I claim that this represents an extension of the true structure of text.

The orderliness and power of this approach are very suggestive. Given the hyperfile with links that we just expounded: Why can't we extend it into a full publishing system?

Suppose that the hyper-documents already stored could be reached and used by anyone. All that we need additionally is the ability for any user whatever to create links *among* them-- to make bookmarks and marginal notes, to quote from them by direct excision. And why not, indeed, allow users to *publish* assemblies and collections of compound documents building on the others?

Very well. Let us try to put together a publishing system-- that is, an overall arrangement whereby the documents stored in this "true" structure may be made available publicly.

What does this mean exactly? Well, a publishing system, as we see it, should include provisions for privacy, copyright, royalty and accounting.

PUBLIC AND PRIVATE

The idea of "publication" in this system, as it is clarified below, will show what we mean by both private and public documents.

A PUBLICATION SYSTEM

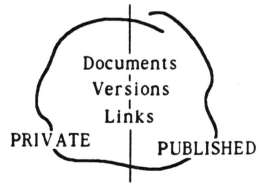

LITERARY 2/41 MACHINES

We can therefore have a system of electronic publishing that feeds to your computer screen exactly what you ask for, as soon as you ask for it; with royalties divided between the document owners in exact proportion to how much of their materials are transmitted or used.

A document may be *private or published*. A published document may include text, links, alternative versions and historical backtrack. But it need not.

Any user may store anything on the system. Unless specified otherwise it is a private document. A private document may be read and linked-to only by the owner and his or her associates. A published document is available to anyone, and may be read and linked-to by anyone.

INTERNAL COPYRIGHT CONVENTION

To bypass some legal problems, we foresee establishing copyright convention *internal to the network* and contractually agreed upon by all participants. To wit, if you publish a thing through the network, you have to agree to the same rules as everybody else-- which are intended to create a fair balance of incentives. More on this later, when the choices described here will be further discussed. (See "Tuning the System" a Chapter 4.)

LINKING TO WHAT-HAVE-YOU

Any user may read, or otherwise employ, any published document on the system, or any private document to which he or she has legitimate access. The user can make any kind of links to any document from his or her own documents, private or not.

NO CONTROL OVER IN-LINKS

Accessibility and free linking make a two-sided coin. On the one hand, each user is free to link to anything privately or publicly. By the same token, *each author of a published work is relinquishing the right to control links into that work*. This relinquishment must also be part of the publishing contract.

THE ACT OF PUBLICATION

If the user chooses to publish a document, he or she may do so with relative ease, making it available to anyone throughout the network. It is then a published document. It is added to the master list of published documents, and readout from its address space is opened to all users.

Because publication is an important act, both for authors and readers, we make publication a solemn event, to be undertaken cautiously. It could be effected merely by a

LITERARY 2/42 MACHINES

"Private" materials are available only to their owners or designees; "published" materials are available to anyone, yielding a royalty to the owners.

"publish" button on the user's console-- but the dangers of rash publication to an individual's reputation, legal liabilities and career could be great. Some formalized techniques are therefore required for "committing to publish"-- probably a ceremony and signature; presumably signing a contract on something very like a credit-card triplicate slip. The author signs an "I hereby publish" form, after which not only is the document universally available, but the author can't easily withdraw it from publication. (See "The Contracts," Chapter 3.)

NO WITHDRAWAL; SUPERSESSION; OTHERS' LINKS

It is in the common interest that a thing once published *stay* published, as in the world of paper. Other readers and users will come to depend on its accessibility. Consequently its author may not withdraw it except by lengthy due process.

However, for corrections and amendments, the author may readily publish a *superseding* document, but the former version must remain on the network. This is vital because of the links other users may have made to it-- which can now reach through from the previous version (to which they were originally attached) into the newer version.

FOLLOWING OLD LINKS TO THE CURRENT VERSION

When a document is updated, a reader will ordinarily want to see the new version-- but the reader may be following a link made to an older version.

However, the user's front-end machine may easily be set up to follow the link to the same passage in the most recent version-- if it's still there.

SUPERSESSION WITH NOTICE

Fresh readers turning to an old version of a document will ordinarily be directed to the new, unless they have reason to consult the old-- which is of course contained in the same docuplex.

But an author's wishes with regard to new versions may be posted in the presentation instructions for a document. These are interpreted by the reader's front-end screen machine.

ROYALTY FOR USE

In our planned service, there is a royalty on every byte transmitted. This is paid automatically by the user to the owner every time a fragment is summoned, as part of the proportional use of byte delivery.

LITERARY 2/43 MACHINES

Private documents can link and window to public ones.

Each publishing owner must consent to the standard royalty-- say, a thousandth of a cent per byte-- and each reader contributes those few cents automatically as he or she reads along, as part of the cost of using the system. This is a proportion (probably between ten and twenty percent) of the byte-delivery charges. If the byte delivery charge for servicing a user is, say, $2 per screen-hour, then the royalty will be 10c to 20c for that hour. This is deducted automatically from the back-end fees.

COST OF USAGE

EXTERNALITIES

    Cost of screen machine
       (ownership or rental)

    Transmission
       (to commercial transmission companies)

....

BACK-END FEES (to storage vendors, etc.)

    Byte delivery (per byte delivered)
      Included: royalty reserve
    Search Resource Units (SRUs)

    Cost of Private Storage
      Maintenance fees on private storage

    Publishing fees

    Cost of Publishing Storage
      Maintenance fees on public storage

The royalty goes to the *owner*. We say "owner" here to avoid having to distinguish between authors and publishers; but this distinction, and dividing up the proceeds among author and publisher, is a matter of private arrangements that are of no concern at the system level. (Royalties for non-owned documents go to a non-profit Author's Fund.)

PRIVASHING AND WITHDRAWAL

An author who wishes to render his work universally available, but wishes also to retain the right to withdraw it at any time, has a simple means for so doing. The author simply designates his or her document as a private document with unrestricted distribution. Anyone may have access to it or use it, but the owner is free to withdraw it irrecallably or change it unrecognizably at any time. Those who linked to it may complain to the owner, but this is a matter for private recourse.

No royalty is received for the use of privashed documents. This increases an author's incentive to publish, which is for the general benefit of all.

PRIVATE SALE OF INFORMATION

Those information purveyors not satisfied with the system's standardized royalty are free to store what they like as private encoded documents and then sell access to these documents, or sell the secret code to make them readable, or whatever. These are private transactions and do not

LITERARY 2/44 MACHINES

This is a radical and daring idea: a new form of reading and writing, in a way just like the old (but faster), with quotations and marginalia and citations. Yet it will also be socially self-constructing into a vast new traversable framework, a new literature.

---

involve the system either technically or legally.

THE REAL POWER: PUBLISHING COMPOUND DOCUMENTS

The windowing approaches already mentioned automatically furnish a general solution to the "copyright problem" with regard to quotation and citation, simply by this means: authors who are windowed in a document automatically get royalties as well. When a quotation is sent out, the owner of the *quoted* document gets that increment of royalty. The royalties are paid to the owner of each document seen in proportion to its use.

Since the copyright holder gets an automatic royalty, *anything may be quoted without further permission.* That is, permission has already been granted: for part of the publication contract is the provision, "I agree that anyone may link and window to my document." Publication through such a net requires your permission for your work to be quoted *ad lib.* If you publish something, anyone can use it, and you always get a royalty automatically, either when it is read directly or whenever a quotation from it is read. Fair.

PUBLISHING MODIFIED VERSIONS

Thus users may create *new published documents out of old ones indefinitely,* making whatever changes seem appropriate-- without damaging the originals. This is done by inclusion links.

This means a whole new pluralistic publishing form. If anything which is *already* published can be included in anything *newly* published, any new viewpoint can be fairly presented by an easily-made annotated collage. (The old viewpoint is still present and available as well, since the reader can always say, "Show me what this was originally," a request which is also built in.)

If a modified document is read, the original owner and the modifier split the royalty in proportion to who wrote what, as determined automatically. (For royalties on links, see "Tuning the System," a Chapter 4.)

For example, my great-grandfather, Edmund Gale Jewett, believed that one word in *Hamlet* was incorrect. (He claimed that it should have been *siege* of troubles, not "sea" of troubles, in the "to be or not to be" soliloquy.)

LITERARY 2/45 MACHINES

Given that anything on such a network may be available instantly, such an arrangement promises an extraordinary new level of capability. For not only may simple documents be accessed at once, but compounded and windowing documents may be overlaid on anything-- promising a new degree of understandability through what is added later.

Very well: if *Hamlet* is already on the system, then E.G. Jewett could publish his own *Hamlet* very easily: a quote-link to the first part of the original, just up to "sea" in the soliloquy; then the word "siege;" then a quote-link to the rest of the play.

Note the modest cost should Jewett publish this: the storage cost for a few hundred bytes (ID, pointers and the one change, a single word).

Now, the obvious rules of the road should be as follows:

1. Shakespeare's *Hamlet* is of course unchanged and available instantly.

2. Jewett's modified version of *Hamlet*, composed of two quote-links to the original and one new word, is also available instantly. (Jewett may give it any title he wants.)

3. Shakespeare-- or rather the Authors' Fund-- gets the royalties for whatever of Shakespeare's *Hamlet* is summoned by readers.

4. When people read Jewett's *Hamlet*, the Author's Fund still gets the royalty on Shakespeare's behalf almost all the time. But Jewett gets a tiny proportional royalty for the change he has made, whenever that part is sent out to a reader.

5. Anyone reading Jewett's *Hamlet* can say, "Show me the original of this next to it," or just "Take me to the original."

6. Anyone reading Shakespeare's *Hamlet* can say: "What documents have links to this?" or "Are there any alternative versions?" and get a list that includes Jewett's version.

SECURITY RAMIFICATIONS OF WINDOWING

These ideas simplify the creation of rationally-ordered document dissemination systems with clear-cut security. A document can only window documents with the same, or lesser, security level. For instance, a private document may window a published document, but not vice versa. But this principle may also be used for windowing among documents with different permission lists, or different levels of encryption. Thus the more secure document would window

LITERARY 2/46 MACHINES

It is our unusual hope and vision that this system, with its simplicity of approach and efficiency of implementation, will become the standard publishing and archival medium of the future.

---

into the less secure documents, but not vice versa.

SHOWING AND SIEVING IN-LINKS

The reader should be able to ask, for a given document or place in the document, "What connects here from other documents?"-- and be shown all these outside conections without appreciable delay.*

ALL LINKS IN

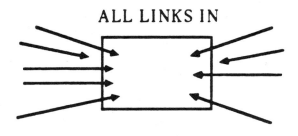

But there may be too many. Indeed, for *Alice in Wonderland* or the U.S. Constitution, the number could be in the squillions.

Thus it becomes necessary to apply some kind of filter, saying, "What links come in from Spain? From last week? From last year in Marienbad?"-- and see the number of such links at once, followed by the linked documents themselves if desired.

This must all be fast enough to please the impatient on-line user. And we believe it can be done. This filtering by different attributes we call "sieving"; and it can only be set up for a comparatively small number of traits-- say, location and author and time.**

ALL END-USE IS LEGITIMATE

The user may employ any screen machine to view and manipulate these documents, in any style. Viewing-methods and manipulations are up to the designers of the equipment and viewing program. *No restraint is contemplated as to what use may be made of the materials found on the system, since no restraint is possible.*

There is no way whatever to ascertain or control what happens at the users' terminals. Therefore *perforce* all use

---

*Technically knowledgeable readers may note that *this* is the hardest feature. This is the stopper. But we believe it can be done.

**Of course, any amount of additional sieving can be put in at the front end.

LITERARY 2/47 MACHINES

whatever is legitimate, and anyone who plans to be vulnerable to "misuse," whatever he or she thinks that may be, had better keep his or her stuff off the system.

PRINTOUT AND COPIES AT USER END

Users are thus free to make printed copies, or keep disk copies for their own use. Note that if a user prints out a document, or saves the data on his or her own disk, he or she has *paid* a royalty on its supply and transmission. It is *paid up*, just as a paperback bought at the drugstore has had its royalty paid up. And if a copyright holder cannot be satisfied with this arrangement-- even knowing no other is possible-- he or she had better withhold his or her stuff from this system.

WHAT THE COPY LOSES

Note also that he or she who makes a paper copy or disk is losing all dynamic link connections, and is left with the inert, non-interactive copy. And that will be a considerable deprivation in the world we are talking about.

Remember the analogy between text and water. Water flows freely, ice does not. The free-flowing, *live* documents on the network are subject to constant new use and linkage, and those new links continually become interactively available. Any detached copy someone keeps is frozen and *dead*, lacking access to the new linkage (and, if there were any substantial body of in-links at the time the copy was made, probably most of those as well).

WHAT'S A PUBLISHER?

Publishing simply means the marketing and public sale of copies of documents. Traditionally, an *author* is someone who creates a work (whether or not on his or her own initiative). A *publisher* is a businessperson or firm that takes the business initiative, deciding to publish (that is, to manufacture and publicly sell the work), fronting the money to print, warehouse, and advertise. He, she, or it also assumes certain legal risks from which he, she or it usually guards the author (notably those risks regarding libel, plagiarism, or "national security" considerations). The publisher may also encourage and cajole the author, buck him or her up, *advance him or her money* for work unfinished, and finally erect a plaque to his or her memory on the Hotel Chelsea in New York. (Of course, the author may also be his or her own publisher-- like William Blake, Walt Whitman and the present author.)

Ownership and copyright are split between author and publisher according to their own negotiated private arrangement.

Even if (as we believe) compound hypertext is the writing of the future, and a system like ours is the printing press of the future, *the publisher of the future can do all these things in exactly the same way.* Except now there is no "printing and warehousing," but a certain required minimum disk rental. Thus a "publisher" is someone who pays for the rapid accessibility of materials and benefits from their use along with the author.

LITERARY 2/48 MACHINES

ON-LINE BOOKS AND MAGAZINES

Is it all just one big stew? Are such useful units as the "book" and the "journal" just lost in the goulash? Not at all.

Just the fact that things are on an electronic system does not threaten their integrity (as many suppose); indeed, every unit fully retains its integrity in the present system.

A *book* is still a comparatively large unit of writing or anthology, written and publshed by specific people on specific dates.

A *magazine or journal* is still a collection of shorter pieces which is regularly edited and published by the same person or people, and regularly published at a specific time. It may of course window material from elsewhere, including that which has been previously published.

Magazines and journals will have great importance in such a publishing system (as they do in the paper world) because they will furnish stabilized views of the world, offering a predictable kind of material, and bringing in, and evaluating, ideas from all over. That they are now become electronic, and window into other materials, is an enhancement of their previous functions, and not a change in principle.

DIRECTORIES AND CATEGORIES

Two system directories, maintained by the system itself, are anticipated: author and title, no more.

Other directories would essentially involve categorization, as do the Dewey Decimal and Library of Congress catalog systems, or the Yellow Pages of the phone book.

There is nothing wrong with categorization. It is, however, by its nature transient: category systems have a half-life, and categorizations begin to look fairly stupid after a few years. (Indeed, simple categorizations of computer articles in computer bibliographies of fifteen years ago have already begun to look stupid.) The army designation of "Pong Balls, Ping" has a certain universal character to it.

All category-systems make some sense, few stay good for long. (However, the Yellow Pages categories are an interesting exception, being dreadful to begin with. Indeed, though they are supposedly updated from time to time, the Yellow Pages improve only at glacial speed. It took them years to add "copying" as a category: over a decade after the first Xerox copier, you still had to look up places to make copies under "Photo Prints." It took similarly long for them to have a category called "Computers" (preferring instead "Data Processing Equipment and Supplies," which refers to only one corner of computerdom.) And sometimes it is simply impossible to find a simple thing, because the categorists of Yellow Pagination have it stuffed under some unthinkable heading (like black-and-white

TV cameras under "surveillance").)

How can we avoid categorical decay on our system? Keep the categories *out of the system level*. Categories are *user business*; let users publish categorical directories and collect royalties for their use.

Anyone may publish his or her own document lists, categorized in any way he or she imagines, and have users bounce through them in search of whatever they think they may find.

There are no special rules governing particular kinds of document (such as the "bulletin board," "teleconference"). While many other people's text systems require special rules which foster incompatibility, we have found that all special features of other systems can be mapped clearly into our document structure or moved into front-end functions.

PARTIAL PUBLICATION

A whole document need not be published. That is, someone may publish only *part* of a document, keeping the rest private. Very well: now the owner arranges for the *private* document to window into the published materials, so that the owner personally sees the whole, *real* document on the screen, windowing from the private to the published.

Historical backtrack, alts, etc., may also be held privately in a common pool, some of whose documents have entered the "published" world.

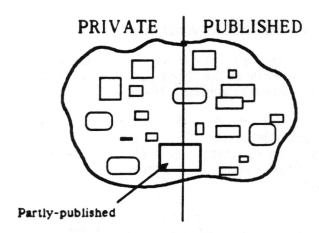

PRIVATE   PUBLISHED

Partly-published

USE WITH SEPARATE OR UNCOOPERATIVE DATA STORES

There are many purveyors of less comprehensive services who tell us, in effect, "Ha ha, we've got the copyrighted material, you can go hang."

Maybe yes, maybe no. Suppose that Company Y has some key legal document on line and copyrighted-- say, the Napoleonic Code-- and you need to make marginal notes, but the company that publishes it on line offers no such facility.

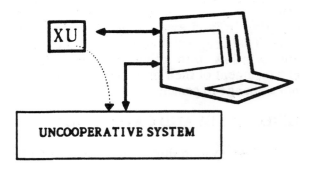

XU

UNCOOPERATIVE SYSTEM

LITERARY 2/50 MACHINES

Well then! Connect to ours and theirs at the same time. Write your marginal notes on our system, with the linking information; then your front end can call up their Controlled Document and show it along with the notes you've stored on our system, just as though the whole compound document were on our system.

In the general case, then, we can marry our data structures and linking facility even to the on-line material whose purveyors do not wish to cooperate.

Or suppose you have private material you do not wish to expose through communication lines, even in encrypted form. Nevertheless, the system we are discussing can help you with detailed linkages, backtracks, etc., even though it runs on a public system: for you may use its indexing facilities to control your privately-stored data, sight unseen. Your data stays home, while the indexing to it is stored blind on the net-- the contents it controls being wholly unknowable to any party but you.

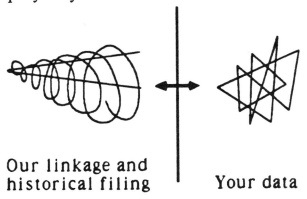

Our linkage and historical filing | Your data

VIDEODISC CONNECTIONS

There has been a great deal of whoop-te-do recently about videodiscs, the laser-tracking storage devices that hold one or more hours of TV or still images on a platter. The Philips and Pioneer versions offer freeze-frame and random frame addressability. Very well: they are a fast image playout that can be hooked up to our indexing for various purposes. (See Chapter 4. "Use with Videodisc and Motion Pictures.")

Another use of the term "videodisc," causing total confusion, refers to certain high-density laserdiscs used not for video but for digital storage. (Most recently these have been called by the odd term "CD ROMs.") We are often asked whether these "videodiscs" will be useful for our system, and the answer is yes, but they aren't being used for video, they're just big disks, and such hardware issues are not and have never been the central problem.

(The widely-touted notion that laserdiscs will be useful for text libraries seems a little silly, since they make it possible to access only what you actually have *right there on the disk in the room*, while a hypertext network will allow immediate access to everything on the whole network; a vast difference which will widen continually. Even as disk capacity expands, the size and interconnective complexity and diversity of tomorrow's hypertext repository will outstrip it. Regardless of what the hardware will do, there is *no way* that a disk at your facility can store "everything," because "everything" refers not to a well-bounded body but to an ongoing avalanche, greatly changing every day. Thus what is at the individual's site falls quickly behind. But even if such schemes for immense local text storage have serious impact, we believe we have the best software for indexing the individual's file server.)

Then there are the *write-once* videodiscs, and yes, they too will be useful, but this is just part of the continuing and predictable improvement of hardware.

LITERARY 2/52 MACHINES

2.8 DISTRIBUTION AND NETWORKING

It might conceivably be possible to do all this-- the grand publishing network-- out of one feeder machine, somewhere in the world, but there are a lot of disadvantages to that approach.

In the previous sections of this chapter we have concentrated on the conceptual structure of the proposed system. So far, it might be supposed that the service could be provided from a single computer, or "centralized data bank."

And it is easy to think that centralizing it in a single great unit will more easily treat all documents and their versions as an interconnected whole because they are stored in the same place.

This turns out not to be so. There are fairly definite limits on what one machine can hold and the number of users it can provide services to. For the services described here to be seriously expanded to large numbers, it will be necessary to "network" the service through multiple computers distributed throughout the nation and the world. For this system must be able to grow without size limit, containing in its body of available writings whatever anyone has stored from anyplace on the network.

So we turn to the idea of storing the materials on a network of computers. But we do not want the virtuality-- the conceptual structure, the style of response-- to change.

A user should get anything he or she asks for an instant or so after the request, even if it comes from far away-- even if some parts of it come from one faraway place, other parts from other faraway places; however widely scattered its parts may be in their storage and ownership.

ALL DOCUMENTS INSTANTANEOUS

no matter whence

All of storage near and far must therefore become a united whole-- what is now called a "distributed data base." Actual locations become essentially invisible to the user; or, in that traditional phrase, "You don't care where it's stored." The documents and their links unite into what is essentially a swirling complex of equi-accessible unity, a single great universal text and data grid, or, as we call it, the *docuverse*.

In principle it is possible to extend this system of storage and publication to a whole network of feeder computers.

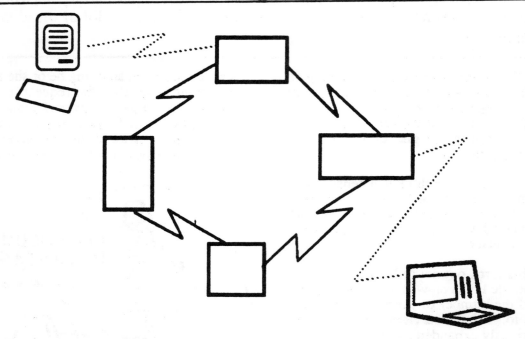

A user at any location may store what he or she wishes; links may be created by anyone, from anywhere, to a document anywhere else, any part of which can be summoned on command. Given today's network technologies, this is not really difficult; this part of the system-- the immediate delivery of anything from within a large arbitrary network of computers-- is not far-fetched. From a nuts-and-bolts point of view the material is more efficiently dispersed among holding stations united by a communication network. This is essentially state of the art.

But the software field is not quite so far along. From the software point of view-- needing to unite the documents into a single, instantly-available docuverse-- a number of challenges exist.

One is that multiple copies of each document must be distributed about the network for safety-- in a shifting distribution that keeps up with demand and other needs. Another is that these copies-- even with their historical-trace backpacks-- must be *updated in place*. And every change must somehow be known throughout the network the instant

LITERARY 2/54 MACHINES

Thus the stored literary contents of all the computers on the network must be continually united into a single, accessible whole.

---

it happens, with new things at once assimilated into the great corpus.

Multinode distribution with fast change

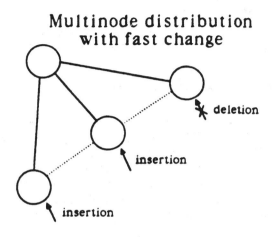

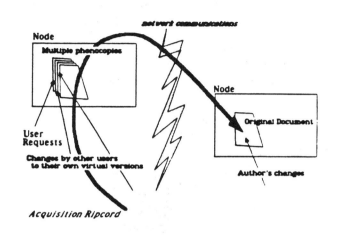

Moreover, while copies of all information cannot be stored in each location, enough of a trace or string must be in each place to pull in whatever is needed from wherever it is-- a "ripcord" to unleash any selected document.

NETWORK CONNECTIONS

Essentially the network will have two connection speeds; the fast lines that unite the stations, and the slow links to users.

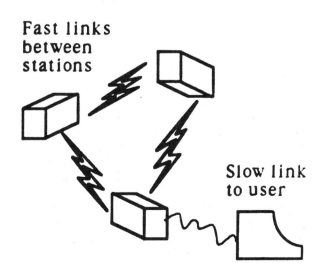

LITERARY 2/55 MACHINES

Users should be able to connect to the contemplated network by whatever channels are most convenient for them: directly (at Stations or Stands), and via communication links such as Telenet and telephone. The network will of course also tie to other digital networks, either in the amateur market (such as The Source and PCNet), or the professional world (such as ARPAnet).

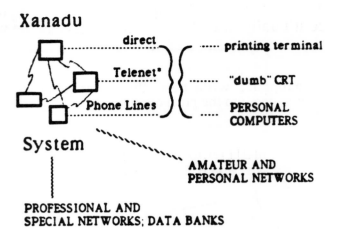

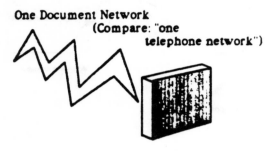

One Document Network
(Compare: "one telephone network")

Gateway Systems
(timesharing, videotext...)

We intend that the contemplated service will hook up to all ethical vendors who wish to offer gateway service to our docuverse.

For the connections between stations, the mechanics of computer networking are fairly straightforward, and we need not go into them here. The so-called "packet" approach (now being standardized under the name X.25) allows direct commercial hookup through various vendors. More high-budget and high-flying approaches can use direct satellite links between stations, which are available and feasible now.

"How big will the total storage be?" people ask. The answer is, *as big as people will pay for*. Everything stored has to have money behind it. The system will grow as long as paying demand increases-- which should be for a considerable period. No matter how big the network grows, you will be able to get anything in it very quickly-- as long as disks are added to the system to accommodate new paid-up storage.

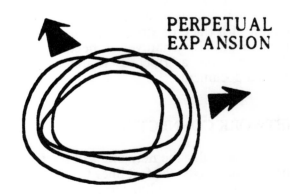

PERPETUAL EXPANSION

LITERARY 2/56 MACHINES

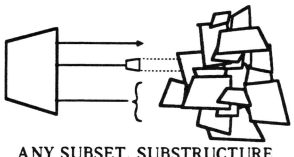

ANY SUBSET, SUBSTRUCTURE OR GROUPING

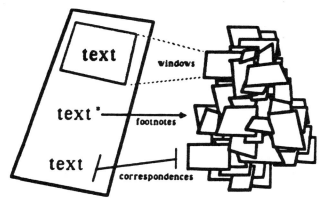

WINDOWING INTO THE PRIOR LITERATURE--
previous public contents of entire network

THE GREAT HOPE AND CONJECTURE OF INSTANT UNIFICATION

Perhaps the most important thing, and certainly the hardest part to believe, is that everything on such a network-- any subset, substructure or grouping-- can come to the user immediately, even as the aggregation grows to tremendous size.

First, let's be clear what we mean by "immediately."

We mean very quickly, even though there will be variations. If you telephone San Francisco from Chicago, you get through "immediately"-- that is, within perhaps three to fifteen seconds, with an off chance of having to wait thirty. We're talking about figures like that.*

---

*Now, as human habitation grows beyond the planet and speed-of-light considerations become significant, obviously performance will degrade. For off-planet users (or earthbound users calling an off-planet station), the usual performance figure must be *added to* the transmission time. Obviously, too, if interstellar travel is ever achieved, transmission delays will degrade response time to months and years. However, some thought has been given to this problem in the overall design: see "Tumbling Through the Docuverse," a Chapter 4.

LITERARY 2/57 MACHINES

In any case, for comparatively local service (on-planet or nearby), we may look forward to "instant" retrieval of whatever is asked for. This means essentially that *all documents become a single instantaneous whole.*

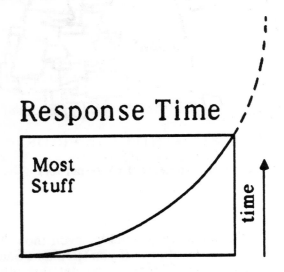

This in turn means that compound documents of any kind become effectively as accessible as simple ones. And we may read and write accordingly.

LITERARY 2/58 MACHINES

2.9 VITAL ISSUES

Thus we have the framework of a complete, radically different way of handling information.

THE PROGRESSIVE CLARIFICATION OF WORK

A problem in using computers is that our ideas of what we are doing constantly change, but the arrangements of storage become fixed and difficult to modify. Thus our files and divisions of work become ever more different from the way we now think of our work, requiring constant compromises.

With this type of storage, however, the current versions of everything will be available at all times in their most recent arrangement, with previous arrangements no longer any encumbrance or limitation.

Our evolving views and ideas may be continually reshaped *while keeping track of origins and interconnections*, which becomes vital in any complex area.

USER PRIVACY: A VITAL ISSUE

The network will not, may not monitor what is read or what is written in private documents. But these matters are not easy to guarantee. (See "Freedom in Our Time and Beyond," a Chapter 3.)

A PRINTING PRESS

We consider that this system may best be considered as the printing press of the future.

FREEDOM OF THE PRESS

If this system is a printing press, we can brook no greater restriction on its functions than on conventional printing. Freedom of the press has been challenged by tyrants and scoundrels since the time of Gutenberg. Such challenges will happen again, and worse, on this new playing-field. We must be ready.

LEGAL GOOD BEHAVIOR

Plainly, the system must live within the law. However, what the law *is* may often not be clear. Grey areas (for the USA) involve pornography, libel, and "national security" (often meaning matters embarrassing to a political administration). Indeed, the U.S. government has begun restricting computer text systems on the pretext that someone, somewhere, had used them for "child pornography." The political battle for freedom of electronic information has begun.

There is no thinking out all these eventualities. But the system we propose is a libertarian system: restrict it, and all will lose.

Numerous issues of personal freedom are conspicuously present.

JOHN DOE PUBLICATION

Normally publication will be by accountable individuals and companies with known residence or place of business. Still, there is no reason that anonymous publication by walk-in and transient users of this system should not be allowed. We may call this "John Doe publication."

PEREMPTORY CHALLENGE OF JOHN DOE PUBLICATION

However, John Doe publication is more sensitive to challenge, since the John Does do not hang around to defend their acts.

Hence peremptory challenges of John Doe publications must carry weight.

Consider libelous or uncomplimentary John Doe graffiti defaming specific individuals. If John Doe is not available, the affected individual must be able to effect removal of the materials by peremptory challenge.

CHALLENGE OF DEFENDED MATERIALS

However, where materials are published by accountable individuals or firms, peremptory challenge no longer holds water, and removal must be by negotiation or by court order.

COPYRIGHT VIOLATIONS

Since fair use of the system includes making and following any windows into any available document (and all who publish on the network necesarily submit to this arrangement), people are much freer to do whatever they like with whatever is available. But there are still possible forms of copyright violation.

Once materials are outside the system and the user's screen machine, normal copyright law applies. Thus going outside "fair use"-- for instance, making magnetic or paper copies of documents and giving them away or selling them without the user's permission-- is just as tortious and illegal as it would be without our system. Enforcement, of course, is the victim's problem. But our system introduces no changes to this situation.

One form of copyright violation is frequently mentioned. It is this: what if someone *makes a copy* of materials published by someone else on the system, then *re-enters them as his or her own in order to obtain royalties?*

As long as it went undetected, this scheme would work. However, the violator is exposing himself or herself, if detected, to a prima facie case of copyright violation. Identical materials found to be on the system

LITERARY 2/60 MACHINES

What we call "tuning" the system is the development of simple, fair and well-balanced arrangements and pricing that will balance users' incentives for the flexible and reasonable use of the system. (See "Tuning the System," a Chapter 4.)

---

with two different entry dates raise clear-cut questions. Whichever author proves ownership on the basis of outside evidence has the other nailed.

PLURALISM--
AND NEW UNDERSTANDING

What is in such a publishing network may be revised by anyone, reinterpreted, redesigned. Anyone can publish a *new* version of Thomas Aquinas, Ayn Rand, Einstein, or whoever else's writings are on the system, attempting to reach the true and *correct* formulations that always seem to elude the person ahead of you. And no harm is done, no credit lost, to the originals.

PLURALISM!

Anyone may revise anything-- harmlessly

The same applies to explanations. Most scientists and philosophers are not the ones to clarify their own work. The writings of a Niebuhr or a Talcott Parsons need to be considerably clarified by other commentators before most people can understand them.

Very well. With the capacity for any number of compound windowing documents, good explainers-- the Asimovs of tomorrow-- can take what is already there, and add the many clarifications that will bring understanding.

Is this chaos? *Not at all.* Because at any one time, you are within one specific document, the work of a specific author. If this work is windowing to other documents, nevertheless you are not "in" the others, but viewing them through the present author's filter.

ETERNAL REVISION

There is no Final Word. There can be no final version, no last thought. There is always a new view, a new idea, a reinterpretation. And literature, which we propose to electronify, is a system for preserving continuity in the face of this fact.

LITERARY 2/61 MACHINES

Computer scientists have frequently spoken of how we may store and make available "information" and "knowledge"-- terms which suggest that these are uniform and recognizable commmodities. For the purposes of education, scholarship and art they are not.

But writings and documents, created and owned by people, are clear to us now and can remain clear in the electronic future. Windowing hypertext offers the possibility that all writings may be forever revised and reinterpreted by new scholars, summarizers, popularizers, anthologizers; and that we may continue to know where we are and what we are doing as we read and write.

We are not the only ones who propose to electronify literature, making all its parts and corners swiftly available. But the naive approach, now heard from the "videodisc" enthusiasts, proposes only to bring individual documents when ordered separately, ignoring their interconnections. The newer videodisc idea, CDI (Compact Disk Interactive), *freezes the interactive structure*-- a considerable restriction.

We propose a broadening alternative: the ability always to add new connections.

The interconnections are as important as the words; and following the continuing variations and re-uses demands a simple but subtle system for instantaneous access to any *part* of any document and any possible *connection* between documents, and for the unending creation of new variants and connections, forever. In the light of these concerns we offer this system, and believe it to be the vital next step for humanity and civilization.

ETERNAL REVISION

LITERARY 2/62 MACHINES

CHAPTERS THREE

LITERARY 3/1 MACHINES

SUMMARY OF THE XANADU™ HYPERTEXT SYSTEM

People mistake generality for vagueness.

Roger Gregory

While the system is conceptually simple, it is amazing how many different ways there are to think about it and describe it. We take this as indicating its generality.

Some of these descriptions are listed below, both as one-liners and in an essay form. Readers may find them useful for communicating to others, or for reviewing their own understanding of the system.

SUMMARY OF THE XANADU™ HYPERTEXT SYSTEM:

ONE-LINERS

"A literary system of authorship, ownership, quotation and linkage."

"A pluralistic publishing and archiving medium with open hypertext and semi-closed framing."

"A distributed repository scheme for worldwide electronic publishing."

"A system to promote cumulative order and the equitable coexistence of many viewpoints."

"A vessel for the true shape of information--without having to cut it or jam it."

"A mapping system between storage and virtual documents."

"A distributed server network for documents made out of pooled boilerplate."

"A storage arrangement for linking between arbitrary collections of material."

"A seamless data architecture for linked electronic publishing."

"A linking system for keeping track of anything."

"An applicative virtual document system for applying sequential and non-sequential structure to material that arrived out of sequence and unstructured."

"A grand address space for everything, parts of which can be in different places at once."

"A way of tying it all together and not

LITERARY 3/2 MACHINES

losing anything."

"A way of including anything in anything else."

(See also the various generic descriptions under "The Trademarks," a Chapter Five.)

SUMMARY OF THE XANADU™ HYPERTEXT SYSTEM:

SHORTEST DESCRIPTION

The Xanadu™ Hypertext System is a form of storage: a new computer filing system which stores and delivers new kinds of documents. These documents may have any form and contents, but may also have links and inclusions from other documents. A user may request parts of documents or may follow links, both within and between documents. The user may easily see highlighted intercomparisons between documents.

This structure is the same regardless of size: a small Xanadu system will hold and clarify an individual's work, the full network is intended to supply millions of documents to millions of simultaneous users, all following links and windows throughout the growing body of hypertext.

Xanadu Document

Links

Historical Movement

Within-Document Roving

(however many dimensions)

Alternative Versions

A document has its conceptual dimensions plus three:
LINKS, ALTS, HIST

LITERARY 3/3 MACHINES

SUMMARY OF THE XANADU™ HYPERTEXT SYSTEM:

MEDIUM-LENGTH DESCRIPTION

The Xanadu™ Hypertext System is a new form of storage intended to simplify and clarify computer use, and make possible new forms of instantaneous electronic publication.

Running on a single computer, it is a file server for the storage and delivery of text, graphics and other digital information with previously impossible arrangements and services. These new arrangements include links and windows between documents, as well as non-sequential writing (hypertext).

It will also reveal and clarify commonalities between documents and among versions, simplifying both storage and comprehensibility. Thus even running on a single computer, it will simplify computer operations, clarify storage, and clarify and simplify office and document work for individuals and corporations.

In the full world-wide network, it will permit the publication and instantaneous world-wide delivery of interconnected works having immense new power to huge numbers of users.

SUMMARY OF THE XANADU™ HYPERTEXT SYSTEM:

EXTENDED DESCRIPTION

The Xanadu™ Hypertext System is software for the unique organization of computer storage and the rapid delivery of its contents to users. All forms of material--text, pictures, musical notations, even photographs and recordings--may be digitally stored on it. Most importantly, the new forms of interconnection this makes possible among these materials are profound and revealing.

It is a system for the rapid delivery of linked documents (which may share material) and the assimilation and storage of changes. System facilities permit promiscuous linkage and windowing among all materials; with special features for alternative versions, historical backtrack and arbitrary collaging. It is based on new technicalities which are of no concern to the user, and materials are stored in locations the user need not know about.

Any forms of data will eventually share these facilities of linking and inclusions, although each needs separate implementation. Bit-map graphics will be stored in such a way as to allow panning (graphical scrolling) and zoom (continuously increasing or decreasing magnification) as incremental data deliveries. (How your screen machine will show them is another matter.) Three-dimensional objects, when implemented, may be collaged by users into compund objects, scenes from history, enactments and artwork.

It's exactly one system that comes in small, medium and very large. In all cases it is a back-end storage feeder--or "file server,"

LITERARY 3/4 MACHINES

in the current vernacular--for holding and sending out documents which are connected in any possible way (arbitrary topology).

Single-user and multi-user versions for individual and coprorate uses will simplify and clarify the user's storage and the interrelations of data--helping your information evolve toward better organization by small increments.

The single-user system will run on personal computers (such as the extended-memory PC clone and the megabyte Macintosh). The multi-user version will provide document services to a network of computers among corporate users.

Custom front ends of any kind are possible. While any sort of terminal may be connected to the system, its best operation requires a full computer in the user's terminal, programmed to handle display functions, interchange protocol, and other work. A front-end program is any program, running on a user's screen machine or other computer, for any purpose and behaving in any manner, which delivers to and extracts from the Xanadu storage system.

A complete network of publishing with royalty has been carefully planned. All users will have access to all public documents instantaneously (not counting network delays). Every byte delivered to the user will return a minute royalty to the document of origin.

In this expected publishing network,

Xanadu storage will provide linked access to new and powerful forms of interconnected data and writing in compound documents, the storage of which may be distributed.

Its unique facilities of backtrack, linkage and windowing will allow the creation of new forms of multi-level, explorable collections and collages of material--without losing the well-defined authorship and ownership of all parts.

Anyone may publish collaged and windowing documents having finely-divided ownership. There are simple categories of publication (private and public) and low, comparatively flat costs of usage.

Any part of any available document will be accessible from any port on any computer in the net at any time, at prices comparable to storage on other computer systems.

Users may connect their home or office computers of any kind to this network, whether by dialup, GTE Telenet, leased line, twisted pair, or nearby wink-laser. (Each machine will need its own front-end program, however.)

Services will be differentiated mainly with respect to speed of terminal (1200 baud the minimum). No users will be restricted as to what public documents they may access, though private documents will be restricted as specified by their owners.

The system's contents will be supplied

LITERARY 3/5 MACHINES

by customers only. There will be no participation by the Xanadu enterprise in the publishing process itself; neither contents nor indexing will be provided by the system, these being rightful endeavors of the customers.

The system will exert no supervision or censorship on stored or published materials, and court orders will be required for the removal of any material held in a stable account. However, publishers and individuals will be thoroughly warned about legal exposure and pitfalls.

Publishing requires an up-front payment of one year's disk rental. A secondary publisher using windowed material need only pay the cost of pointer storage.

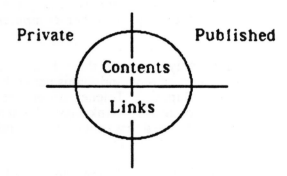

Private documents are available only to the owner and the owner's designees. Published documents are available to anyone, and yield a royalty to the owner; they may be updated at will, but the earlier contents remain available. They may not be withdrawn from publication except after six months' notice or court order. "Privashed" documents are available to anyone, and may be changed at will, but yield no royalty.

We believe this will make possible a whole new universe of knowledge and understanding.

It is presently on line as an experimental prototype. Later, we expect to offer it in object form to users for both personal and corporate computers, first in single-user, then multi-user configurations. After that comes the network with publishing royalty, which we believe can grow as fast as demand.

In one business scenario, the intended public operation of the publishing system will be out of a chain of suburban or roadside stations, called Silverstands™. New users will learn the operation of the system at such stands, and local users may dial into their nearest Silverstand. Silverstand personnel ("Conductors") will include both local people and an itinerant corps of circulating smarties.

The actual code of the system is a medium-sized program in the C language, currently running under the Unix operating system.

"HOW IS IT DIFFERENT FROM THE SOURCE?"

Many public-access computer systems now offer text services. One of the best

LITERARY 3/6 MACHINES

known is The Source, so we often get this question.

Unlike general-purpose time-sharing systems such as The Source, which can run many kinds of programs and furnishes text services simply as one class of available program, ours is a *specialized* storage form for what we believe is the *most generalized* form of storage. Our system does not permit the running of user programs.

The Source, and other currently available text services, do not support linkage, windows, alternative versions or historical backtrack as they supply their stored documents, let alone maintain these connective structures as documents change.

LITERARY 3/7 MACHINES

PROBLEMS OF HYPERTEXT

In this chapter I will discuss problems of hypertext; indeed, the problems faced by some current hypertext systems.

Everybody gets the idea of hypertext now: that you can write sections of text on screen, and attach them together in ways that affect the structure of the subject, your mental associations, and more.

Hypertext is also the most promising way of understanding complex structure. For instance, on-line aircraft maintenance documentation is already being put onto hypertext systems. In fact this is the only way to document large systems usefully, once they get to a certain level of complexity.

"ORDINARY" HYPERTEXT

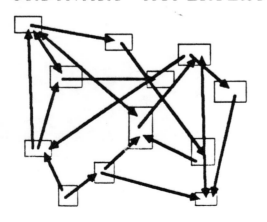

And everyone says at the beginning, Hypertext is easy! All we need is a way to read and write a lot of pieces, and connect them together.

That's all you need for a day or two. The problems go much deeper.

THE FRAMING PROBLEM

As collections of material grow, being able to isolate subcollections is very important.

This is a deep conceptual issue. As the number of interconnected parts of a hypertext grows, how can we restrict our concerns to any subsection? How can we cut down the size of the subject, when all those interconnections crisscross in so many ways? Even when you know what you want to consider, how can you *turn off* the rest? You would like to create your own *arbitrary closed context* from larger complexes of materals.

(Of course, somebody could decide *for* you what was relevant, but that wouldn't be hypertext.)

I call this the *framing* problem: being able to frame only a part of a large complex, to close a shell around a subset and make it seem like the whole world.

LITERARY 3/8 MACHINES

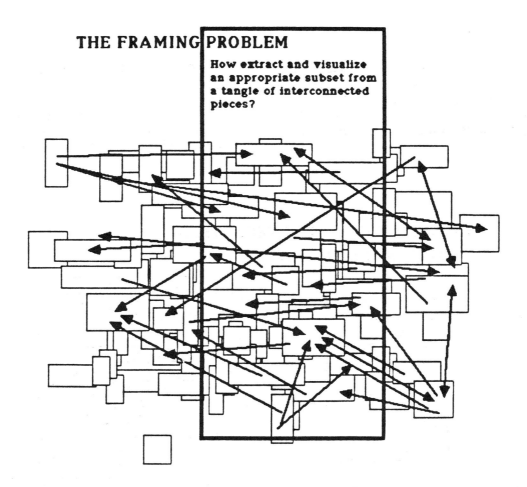

THE FRAMING PROBLEM

How extract and visualize an appropriate subset from a tangle of interconnected pieces?

COMPLEX ALTERNATIVES AND INTERCOMPARISON

One of the most important things that the computer workstation can do is help the user *understand complexity*. As designs and structures evolve, it is vital to see how they relate to complex alternatives.

A vital aspect of this is to show and highlight different versions, parallel structures, alternative designs--*the detailed resemblances and differences* between complex structures.

These alternatives may be different designs for future growth; they may be

LITERARY 3/9 MACHINES

alternative strategies; they may be different interpretations. In *Computer Lib* I called such intercomparison systems "Thinkertoys," expecting them to become common, but as yet no such systems have been built in the general case.

FRAMING AND INTERCOMPARISON COMBINED

Taking the two problems of framing and intercomparison in combination, we get a more complex issue: how can we

THE NEED FOR INTERCOMPARISON OF COMPLEX OBJECTS

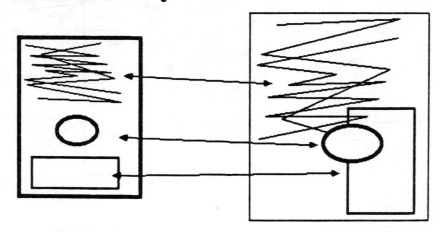

designs, plans, negotiations ...

LITERARY 3/10 MACHINES

intercompare the details of *framed, closed contexts?* This will be important wherever there is controversy and difficulty in handling large bodies of interconnected materials.

LINK TYPES

As complexes of connected materials grow, the number of links begins to drown

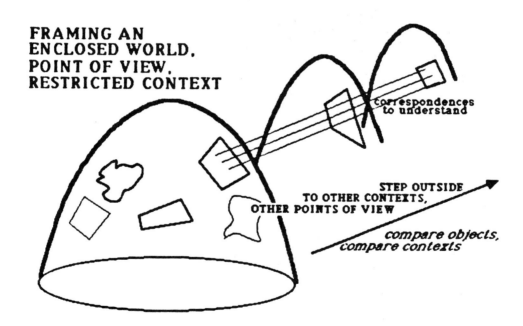

FRAMING AN ENCLOSED WORLD, POINT OF VIEW, RESTRICTED CONTEXT

Correspondences to understand

STEP OUTSIDE TO OTHER CONTEXTS, OTHER POINTS OF VIEW

compare objects, compare contexts

LITERARY 3/11 MACHINES

us rapidly. Allowing *link types* is one way to clarify the system: typed links allow the user to reduce the context of what is shown.

VERSIONING AND HISTORICAL BACKTRACK

We often have to keep similar files organized in several different ways: for instance, the same program set up for different computers. Or it is desirable to maintain several possible designs or plans at once. These are examples of the *versioning* problem.

As collections of interconnected materials grow, it also becomes increasingly important to understand them in terms of

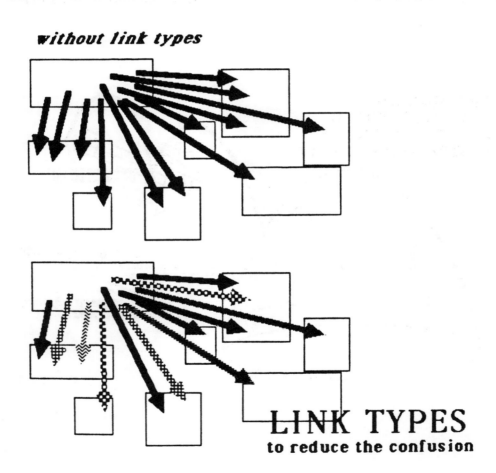

without link types

LINK TYPES
to reduce the confusion

LITERARY 3/12 MACHINES

what they were, and to keep track of changes in structure.

Being able to go back through changes, and perhaps restore an earlier state, is called the problem of *historical backtrack*. For simple, linear textual documents this can be done by storing lists of changes and undoing them; and indeed several commercial versioning and backtrack systems are now on the market. But it is rather more difficult to do this for hypertext.

Moreover, *highlighting the corresponding parts* is a vital aspect of intercomparison.

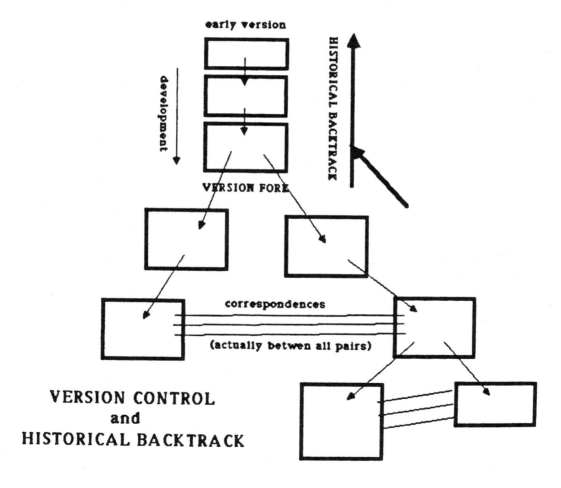

LITERARY 3/13 MACHINES

CLOSED CONTEXTS AND OPEN MEDIA

Just as it is important to be able to work only with a closed context of material, it is vital to be able to *open* a closed context. This is especially important with today's new media, where designers are able to imprison users as never before. You could always turn the page of a book, or slam it shut. Not so today: in computer-assisted instruction, in the proposed interactive disks (CDI), and in many other forms of interactive media, designers can make it impossible for you to move on, to follow a pathway of your own choosing. To say nothing of leaving a comment for the next guy.

This must change; and so we need a master indexing scheme that will *embrace other hypermedia*, and allow the leaving of comments, and the creation of alternative pathways amongst pre-canned materials, by others.

In open hypermedia, others can add to any production or re-use its parts as they see fit. Anyone can do new things with the same material, freely.

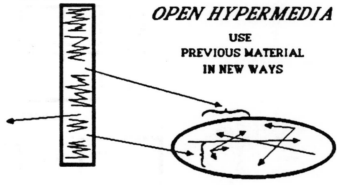

OPEN HYPERMEDIA

USE
PREVIOUS MATERIAL
IN NEW WAYS

CLOSED HYPERMEDIA

It is a balance of rights: the first author and publisher have a right to show you something *their* way; but users have a right to employ these things as *they* choose. Under freedom it can be no other way. As long as the original's context is preserved, ongoing new ones must be allowed.

Thus the Xanadu system is designed as a *universal open hypermedia environment*. The originating author or publisher may create a closed environment; then another

LITERARY 3/14 MACHINES

author may anthologize, or otherwise re-use, parts of the same document in a *new* closed environment; but the inquiring user must be able to step from closed environment to closed environment, intercomparing the parts, with complete freedom.

ADDING THESE ASPECTS LATER

In the "all we need" approach, with which most hypertext projects are begun, all these problems tend to be swept aside, with good reason. *They're hard to do*. But then, later in the life of a hypertext project, the developers start *adding* features of this type. Unfortunately, trying to add such things later is very different from designing them in at the start. And so it is hard to build much of this into the hypertext systems now existent.

You now hear people say things like, "We don't need anything as complicated as Xanadu." This is wrong on two levels. First, the Xanadu system can be arbitrarily simple at the user level; and second, that as soon as you start *adding* features like networking and link types and historical backtrack and framing, it becomes a complex morass, and what you really need is a system designed from the start to have all these features.

TOWARD A SUBCULTURE OF INTELLECT

Intellectualism is not a specific body of knowledge or a subculture, but a questioning, observing, hypothesizing outlook.

There are no intellectual subjects. For someone used to learning, to grabbing vocabulary and ideas, the elements of a new subject can come quickly. The more diagrams you have seen, the more words you know, the more theories you have heard, the more easily you can grasp the next one and assimilate it to the snowball of ideas already rolling around in your head.

In an era of school-induced stupor, punch-and-judy news and video narcosis, we hope the Xanadu System will encourage depth and a never-ending procession of new insights.

But it will be important to build a central constituency--a subculture to form a nucleus at the center of this new world.

The realm of intellect has had long connections to the establishment, and has been hoary and stuffy since the Middle Ages. A nice allegory of this is Hermann Hesse's heavy novel *Magister Ludi*, which is about a future subculture of generalists who look for resemblances and connections across all knowledge. But they have an elaborate competitive hierarchy like chess masters-- establishment nexocrats contributing to no one else.

In our time, a comparable organization is Mensa, a group of elitist establishment test-takers. (Founded, interestingly, by Cyril Burt, now discredited for his apparently fraudulent researches on intelligence.) But this is an exclusive club, not an open arrangement for the general benefit.

We propose to give momentum to our system by the creation of a new subculture which provides an alternative to the stuffiness of the rest of the intellectual world. This will be wide open to everyone, especially whoop-te-do enthusiasts who enjoy sharing their sophistications.

There are presently two different intellectual subcultures in America. I distinguish them because they are more or less out of touch with one another:

One is the academic and traditional intellectual culture--of the universities, of grand English, of *Harper's* and *The New Yorker*.

A second is the new generalist subculture--a populist movement that unites science-fiction and popular science. *Omni* magazine is its beginner's dream book, the popular science magazines are its outposts; and *Whole Earth Review* is its pinnacle.

I think these two subcultures can and should be brought together, and that the

LITERARY 3/16 MACHINES

Xanadu Hypertext System is the way to do this.

We think we can build a new subculture of intellect, intellect in a new and enthusiastic style--more like the science fiction subculture than Academia.

Here is a bunch of people who are paid to sit around and make things interesting for you. A national corps of peripatetic smarties plus the local bright kids are the Xanadu Conductors. The locals, kids of all ages, run the stand; the national Xanadu Hypercorps™ move around, share insights and explorations, do demos constantly for each other and for the local kids at a given stand, showing them what's new and what they've recently discovered in different subject realms on the system.

The Xanadu Hypercorps is expected to be an unusual and elite group. They will circulate among Xanadu stations transmitting skills and outlook. They will not be people who can program or repair a computer; rather, like the stewards and stewardesses of the airlines, they will know how to make users comfortable. Also how to help them be productive and enjoy themselves within their intended budget. Like good librarians the Hypercorps will have an understanding of what materials are available, but they will know how to deal with an avalanche, rather than a trickle, of ideas and information. Like good teachers they will have a sense of how to convey ideas. Like good woodsmen they will have a sense of the trails and byways of the territory to be explored. And like academics they will have a personal love for

one or more topics that they will watch and study in their free time on the system.

The customers who hang around the stands will become an active subculture-- including the bright, the verbal, and those interested in everything. Just as in music circles it is customary to know about symphonies and in sports circles it is customary to know about scores, in Xanadu circles it is customary to know about everything: to exchange interesting anecdotes, remarkable facts, extraordinary interconnections--and hold conversations with a Xanadu screen near at hand for reference. They'll be a subculture of generalists who act more like trivia freaks or D&D players.

There'll be festivals and events: Hypercons, Kublacons and Front-End Functions, Footnote Festivals and Intertwingularity Expos. There'll probably be an argot; perhaps Porlock and Rosebud codes, something like the ten-codes of CB radio. It's a fast lane for Zips, a picture-book for Bozos, and for night people as well as day.

A CULT?

Yes, call it a cult if that makes the idea clearer; but a secular cult of fascination with ideas and their uses, ready to wrap itself around the new or the old.

Cults do not just happen. They are constructed. If they become successful, it is through careful planning and insight about what works.

LITERARY 3/17 MACHINES

WHAT WORKS?

This cult offers a social system with its own status ladder (highest are the travelling generalists), a promise of "education" to reassure parents with--it's better than pinball, right? And cheaper per hour.

LITERARY 3/18 MACHINES

FREEDOM IN OUR TIME AND BEYOND

Freedom is indivisible.

Rumpole of the Bailey

Eternal vigilance is the price of freedom.

John Philpot Curran,
as popularly misquoted

Freedom is not a simple experience. And as technology becomes more sophisticated, living in freedom--which means living with constant, changing choice--will only become more complex.

Emily Prager

Tomorrow's hypertext networks have immense political ramifications, and there are many struggles to come. Many vested interests may turn out to be opposed to freedom.

It is important to see *why* the issues of freedom hinge so tightly on what many laymen would consider to be obscure technical issues.

On-line text systems may or may not become universal or replace much of paper publishing. Whichever view you take, the questions are *what these systems are to be like*; what things are to be available, and to whom, and under what circumstances; and who may put things in, and who is responsible for their contents, and who may censor them, and who may protest the contents, and what gets thrown away on whose decision; and what is to be their relation to the archiving of our heritage, and how accessible they are to be, and how reliably and accessibly the personal, national and human heritages are to be preserved. For rolled into such designs and prospects is the whole future of humanity, and, indeed, the future of the past and the future of the future--meaning the *kinds* of future that become forbidden, or possible.

These problems have been waiting.

LITERARY 3/19 MACHINES

The Xanadu group did not create them. The problems will be the same whether our system is adopted generally, or somebody else's, or no system at all--meaning a mess that is less for everybody.

Senator Robert Packwood (D-OR) has called for a "bill of information rights" that will serve us in the age of digital media and transmission. But this concern seems to have reached few others in the political arena.

NEW FORMS OF IMPRISONMENT

New forms of restriction and imprisonment involving computer screens are turning up, some with the best intentions.

The reader of a book can close it or skip to the ending. In some new environments, such as Computer-Assisted Instruction, it is possible to trap the user fully, giving him or her no options whatever except what the planner intended, with no overview and no way to step out of it. I submit that this can be highly oppressive, and is not our free tradition.

In a related development, some advocates of Artificial Intelligence would have computers decide what the reader shall see. As a filtering service this may be just what you want--but the danger is its evolving into a circumscription of your rights, where the choice is no longer yours.

A whole new set of rules is about to be generated. You may be supposing you have freedoms that aren't there anymore.

Consider wiretapping. Time was when a wiretapper sat in the basement with earphones under his fedora. No more. Your phone now can be tapped by a person thousands of miles away who simply gives the proper commands, as beeps, to your ESS switching station. Or so I am told by my telephone-knowledgeable friends, and I believe them.

So in principle, if we ever get the Wrong Sort of Government, they can study your life from your telephone use like an open book. So that particular form of freedom may have slipped away quietly.

What, then, about your computer transmissions? (Computer transmissions will be a basic form of communication for individuals soon.)

An ominous situation has already arisen. The U.S. government has given its approval to a system of encoding that you can buy on a chip. This system is called DES, Data Encryption Standard. Since you can prime it with a secret 56-bit "key," it is thought that running your transmissions through it acts like an electronic shredder, hopelessly garbling your transmissions except to the other party, who presumably knows the key you are transmitting with.

There is only one problem. The DES system stands impeached. Researchers on both coasts have accused this method of being easily breakable by the National Security Agency, the government's decoding

LITERARY 3/20 MACHINES

arm; many believe it a fraud perpetrated by the U.S. government to make all "encoded" transmissions readable by intelligence agencies.

Another system of codes has been proposed that supposedly can't be broken by *any* extant computer in less than millions of years. This is the RSA code, originally proposed by Hellmann and Diffie of Stanford, and developed by Rivest, Shamir and Adelman of MIT. It has several remarkable properties, among them being the ability to exchange unbreakable messages between strangers who have not had a chance to swap code keys; the ability to co-sign electronic documents that anyone can read and know you signed; and more. And the U.S. government tried to suppress it.

This may seem faroff to the average reader--perhaps as faroff as television seemed in the nineteen-thirties. Then consider the following:

If you are not careful, some government may be able to read your private computer documents in the future at any time.

THE MINISTRY OF TRUTH

In Orwell's *1984* the Ministry of Truth told lies and changed history. This was done by judicious snipping, disposal and replacement of paper.

As documents go electronic, however, no longer need paper be involved. A reference article, say, in an encyclopedia can be changed simply by storing another one in its place--and poof! history is changed.

There is no typography or watermark to check. Characters sent on the wire are all alike. But the right sort of *encoding*--what is called an *authentication* code--may help us know when documents have been fraudulently replaced. Authentication codes, too, the government is trying to suppress. When you're looking at the what purports to be the Mona Lisa on your screen fifty years from now, and she has a mustache, don't say I didn't warn you.

THE THOUGHT POLICE

Freedom of the press has been challenged by tyrants and scoundrels since Gutenberg. The problem now has new forms.

The Thought Police in *1984* couldn't really read your mind, but they knew enough psychology to have good suspicions.

Tomorrow's real-life Thought Police will have detailed access to a huge number of incidental records about your life, from banks and auto registration and so on--instantly investigable.

But will they also keep track of, and punish, *who says what* on text networks? For if we may be easily punished for the words we let slip, it will be as if freedom of speech and the press had been obliterated all at once.

LITERARY 3/21 MACHINES

And suppose you keep silent. Will they be able to find out what you *read*?

This is one of the most serious problems of the present moment. We thought it was further off, but in the fall of 1986 certain government figures announced that henceforth we the public would be limited as to what on-line information we could get, and we were further informed that they would be watching who reads what.

This particular threat was overcome, but plainly the forces of evil stand ready to take over any second.*

THE NEAR BATTLE

It may be easy to tell whether the battle for hope in our time is lost or won; simply ask whether there is instantaneous access to the many voices of science; of politics, the proposals and the arguments, wherever they may come from; the many facts and asserted facts which implicitly support or undercut various points of view--without their being censored, stifled, drowned out, smeared and scribbled over by those who want only their views heard, tainted by fraud and forgery, obliterated by bomb or threat or mysterious disappearance. These are the freedoms we have called "freedom of speech" and "freedom of the press." But digital storage will be the new microphone and printing press, and so access to it will be the battleground of freedom in the future. Knowing what kind of new printing press is possible should help you understand the freedoms that are truly yours--if you fight for them.

THINK FAST

These problems are real and present, and have been here waiting for us all along. Far on the horizon as they may now appear, soon they will be on us like a tornado. The way to approach these issues, I believe, is not to sit in a corner and tremble, like a rabbit in a tiger cage hoping it won't be eaten, but to run between the legs of the beast before it fully wakes up.

Electronic freedoms will be at the center of the whirlwind of the coming years. Either we will fight for them, or they will be taken from us like candy from a child.

The future will go on for a long time. And it will be a protracted war between those who wish to have access to information--the first need of a free people--and those who wish to suppress that access. This war will last as long as humanity endures.

---

*See T. Nelson, *Computer Lib*, second edition, "Great Issues," for further discussion of this topic.

LITERARY 3/22 MACHINES

THE INDEXING OF MOVIES AND VIDEODISCS

There as yet exists no sensible means by which motion pictures may be annotated by different commentators in a common bank of writings. Similarly, there exist no good film-editing systems that support the intercomparison of complex alternatives.

Tomorrow's nonsequential movie media--hypermovies and "interactive videodiscs"--require new depths of access by users. Though interactive videodiscs have begun to proliferate, it is only as closed systems to which others may not add or make variations. This is unacceptable in the long term.

Xanadu indexing is needed for films and video, from raw footage through editing to archive, and for on-line interactive presentations of every kind.

LITERARY 3/23 MACHINES

MUSIC: AN EXAMPLE

A key form of data is *music*. While conventional musical staff notation has been adapted to computer storage, and many computer-based *performance* systems are being constructed, the overall problems of musical archiving, cataloging, annotation and scholarship have not had a unified software base from which they may proceed rationally; let alone from which they may be correlated with performance.

What we propose goes far beyond the storage of notes (which will of course allow front-end performance); but will allow for the cataloguing, annotation and charting of interconnections amongst the whole corpus of musical scores and recordings.

From a given Mozart piece, say, it will be possible to get to every document which mentions or comments on that piece; every musical composition which quotes from that piece; and every recording of that piece or its derivatives.

Students, scholars and listeners should all deeply benefit.

LITERARY 3/24 MACHINES

CIVILIZATION AND ITS DISK-CONTENTS:
THE ARCHIVING PROBLEM

"The future isn't what it used to be," as they say. But then, neither is the past. Books disappear. Knowledge of the past is lost. Libraries *burn*, and each time, we are diminished.

The loss of the library at Alexandria in ancient times is still one of the greatest losses in human history. But such things continue. A major library with hundreds of thousands of manuscripts from American history burnt earlier in this century. The Jewish Museum library in New York burnt in 1970, with the loss of manuscripts centuries old. And in popular movies (such as "Chinatown" and "Defense of the Realm"), we see heroes ripping things out of library books with a polite cough.

This attrition of the heritage can in principle be stopped.

Only digital archives give us long-term hope for preserving our heritage--not just writings, but text, paintings (stored as detailed photographs), sculpture, architecture, whatever.

There are many bombs and fires to come. The system this book proposes is a generalized and self-networking structure that can eventually be put in deep rock and deep space--Iron Mountain or the asteroid belt. In the long run, only a digital system of the kind described in this book can provide security for the human heritage of literature, art and science.

But who is to control and safeguard these systems becomes the next question. And it is well to remember Ray Bradbury's book *Fahrenheit 451*--in which different individuals accepted the task of preserving individual books by memory. This allegory may take on new meanings in a world whose future rulers would like to alter the past--a common conceit in such occupations.

LITERARY 3/25 MACHINES

CHAPTERS FOUR

LITERARY 4/1 MACHINES

THE ONLY WAY IT COULD WORK

THE ONLY WAY IT CAN POSSIBLY BE DONE

An ever-growing network, instantaneously supplying text and graphics to millions of users, would be utterly impossible if it slowed down too fast as it grew. (It can't be linear. The system cannot slow down by half as its size doubles. Degradation must be much gentler than that.)

While there will be slowdowns in certain internal mechanisms, we believe they are under control. The point is that performance must slow down only a *little* as the network grows a *lot*. And we believe we can do this.

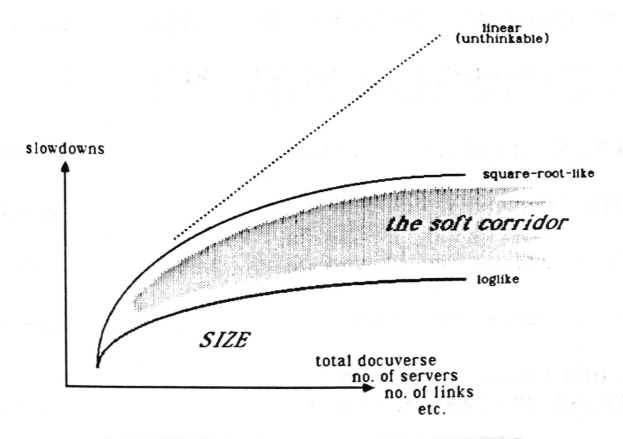

LITERARY 4/2 MACHINES

THE SOFT CORRIDOR: BETWEEN A LOG AND A SQUARE ROOT

Some conventional methods, such as B-trees, permit rapid insertion and deletion in large structures. The slowdown as structure grows is *logarithmic*.

Similarly, the ideas promoted in this book could not possibly be contemplated unless we found comparable performance curves for the methods we chose. We had to find methods of storage, editing and linking which *all*, singly and in combination, deteriorated in performance very little as the universe grew. We believe we have achieved this, with slowdown functions between log and square root--enough to be offset by hardware speedup.

As in other dynamic-function problems, analytic proof is not possible, so this is an empirical question to be proven or disproven in the fullness of time.

LITERARY 4/3 MACHINES

TUNING THE SYSTEM

The objective of this system is not any one aspect, but to *have* a system: a rational system of storage that can lead to a rationally-structured, universal hypertext network. *The whole system is the objective.*

This means having a system that everyone agrees is carefully reasoned and fair--a system that will catch on and take off.

Thus different aspects of the system's plan must be tuned against one another to get it all balanced.

The system's design is a unified whole, but we may think of it as a combination of structures: the basic conceptual structure, plus a technical structure which makes it possible, and a contractual structure which makes it possible for people to use it confidently. These aspects taken together make a unified design. Because the conceptual structure required very fast lookup within a tightly organized but large linked system, we had to develop a particular technical structure; and because the conceptual structure expects participants to behave in certain ways, these are embraced in the contract offered to users. These provisions are necessary for the orderly and confident use of published material by many people.

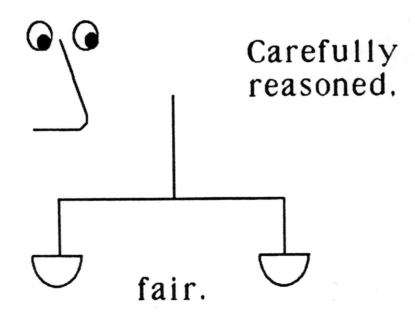

Carefully reasoned,

fair.

LITERARY 4/4 MACHINES

We are concerned with the balance of customer incentives to help foster our overall goals. In the coalescing final design of the system, contracts, categories of service and pricing are all subject to reconsideration.

There have been many discussions and arguments about incentives. Basically, they come down to a price list; and what those prices will be will simply have to be established by the market. We may need to study possible cost functions for reducing possible Babel; or for cutting less-recent accessibilities in order to be practical.

The system has two business commandments, viz.:

1. EVERYBODY MAKES MONEY: there exist many opportunities for profitable participation.

2. ALL SERVICES MUST BE SELF-SUPPORTING. Subsidy between one aspect of the system and another could only work temporarily. This means, for example, that archival storage must be economically self-sustaining.

ROYALTIES

A partial exception is the royalty issues. From an administrative and programming point of view it is cleaner and more verifiable for royalties to be fixed per byte shipped, especially since this is a relatively small part of the cost of using the system.

ADVERTISING

The system does not discriminate in any way among "types" of documents by content. Advertising is thus perforce allowed.

However, suggestions that advertising can somehow pay for generalized use of the system, as with TV and magazines, have pitfalls. Specifically, there is no foreseeable way to find out what is actually being *shown* on a screen; thus advertising could be automatically screened out in many ways, defeating the usefulness of it. So it is not clear that advertising subsidy is feasible.

Further discussion of business considerations is taken up in the Chapters Five.

LITERARY 4/5 MACHINES

THE XANADU DOCUMENT

Note that we are describing Xanadu 87.1; various extensions will be made to other forms of data, including pictures, movies, 3D data objects, sound tracks, DNA, and--by reference--external objects of various types: persons, places, things.

The Xanadu document is the unit of the system. There is almost nothing in the Xanadu system but Xanadu documents.

The Xanadu document may have any structure (sequential or not) and may hold any type of information.

In Chapter Zero we spoke of *xanalogical storage*, to wit:

all materials are in a shared pool, but divided into units;

each element has a unit of origin;

units may be made from new material and/or contents of previous units;

there may be arbitrary links between sections of units.

The Xanadu document is the design for our xanalogical unit. The particular structure of the unit we have designed is given here.

It consists of bytes in sequence, some of which are native to other documents; these are present "by inclusion," and have virtual addresses in the present document. The same is true for links.

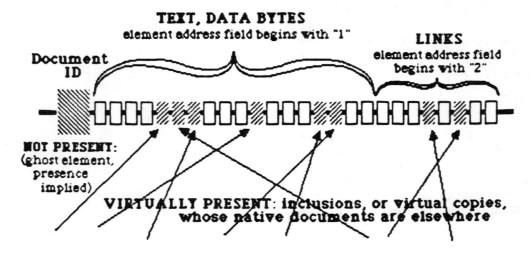

TEXT, DATA BYTES
element address field begins with "1"

LINKS
element address field begins with "2"

Document ID

NOT PRESENT:
(ghost element, presence implied)

VIRTUALLY PRESENT: inclusions, or virtual copies, whose native documents are elsewhere

LITERARY 4/6 MACHINES

The Xanadu document is a unit of virtual structure. It is not a *physical* unit; it may be assembled wholly or partly from other Xanadu documents; the contents of an individual document may be scattered throughout the docuverse; the document may have derivative copies throughout the network of servers; its only physical constraint is that a principal nucleus record must reside in its home Server.

The Xanadu document may be considered at two levels. We may call these the upper and lower virtuality.

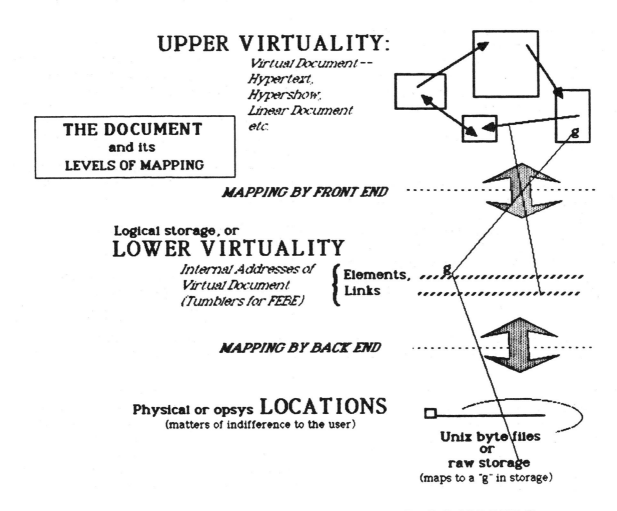

UPPER VIRTUALITY:

Virtual Document -- Hypertext, Hypershow, Linear Document etc.

THE DOCUMENT
and its
LEVELS OF MAPPING

MAPPING BY FRONT END

Logical storage, or
LOWER VIRTUALITY

Internal Addresses of Virtual Document (Tumblers for FEBE)

{ Elements, Links

MAPPING BY BACK END

Physical or opsys LOCATIONS
(matters of indifference to the user)

Unix byte files
or
raw storage
(maps to a "g" in storage)

LITERARY 4/7 MACHINES

UPPER VIRTUALITY

At the user level, a Xanadu document may have any shape or form. It may consist of linear text or hypertext, printable graphics, 3D graphics and CAD/CAM data, seismographic data numbers, branching movies, symphonic scores, and so on.

In some of these documents, such as hypertext and hypermovies, links may be a part of the user's virtuality; in other documents, links may not be perceived by the user at all. (However, this may depend somewhat on the front ends used.)

LOWER VIRTUALITY: XANADU LOGICAL STORAGE

Users are concerned with whatever upper-level structures they wish to see and think about. These structures must be mapped to our internal generalized mechanisms by the application designer, and by programs created by the designer in the front end. These programs communicate through the FEBE protocol to Xanadu logical storage.

Whatever the upper-level contents, all are mapped to a logical storage level representing final data and links. This we may call the lower virtuality.*

TWO VERY DIFFERENT ELEMENTS

At the lower virtuality, or inner logical level, the Xanadu document has only two types of element, different in several respects.

At this inner level, the Xanadu document is a *flat file with links*. This makes it uniquely appropriate as a universal archival standard, permitting all data to be mapped to it without invasive differences based on different software details and style. Certain aspects of the data remain separate and scannable. Other aspects of data are separated as links. The same data may be indexed by many different collections of links in mutually non-interfering ways.

OWNERSHIP AND CONTROL OF DOCUMENTS

Since a Xanadu document may logically contain any parts of any other Xanadu document, a key aspect of the document's internal structure has to do with *ownership and control*. Every element has an owner, who owns it in the sense of

---

*Why call it a virtuality if it's only a mechanism? Because this mechanism impinges on the whole Xanadu world. (Remember that "virtuality" means conceptual structure and/or feel.)

This conceptual structure is a public matter.

It is addressed by the FEBE protocol (see "Protocols," a Chapter 4) and is of close concern to designers of front-end applications. Moreover, this conceptual structure will become known to the user community to a certain degree, much as the Dewey Decimal System is somewhat known to many readers of text.

LITERARY 4/8 MACHINES

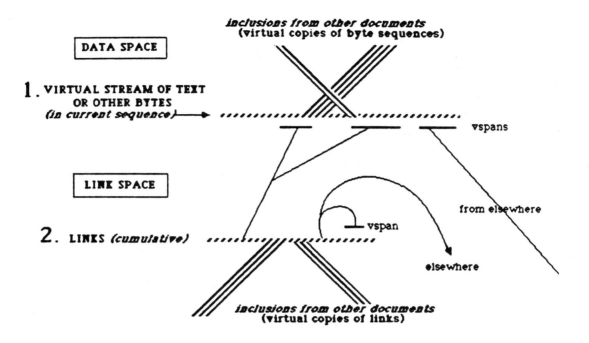

DATA SPACE

1. VIRTUAL STREAM OF TEXT OR OTHER BYTES
(in current sequence)

*inclusions from other documents
(virtual copies of byte sequences)*

vspans

LINK SPACE

2. LINKS *(cumulative)*

vspan

from elsewhere

elsewhere

*inclusions from other documents
(virtual copies of links)*

DELETED BYTES (///////////////////)
DELETED LINKS (///////////////////)
*(not currently addressable,
awaiting historical backtrack functions;
may remain included in other versions.)*

**A DOCUMENT'S
TECHNICAL
CONTENTS**

receiving royalties and who has the right to make certain changes in the original. This is reflected in the internal logic.

The rules governing the ownership, nativity and connection of document contents are based on the system of literature itself.

A document may use bytes or links from anywhere else. However, the logic governing this use is somewhat different for bytes and links.

All bytes and links have a *native document*--the document in which they were created, and by which they are logically owned. This is not the same as their *home* document; a link, in particular, may have several *home* documents but only one *native* document. (See "The Structure of Links," a Chapter 4.)

LITERARY 4/9 MACHINES

BYTES CAN BE ELSEWHERE: USES OF A LINKS-ONLY SYSTEM

Normally, tumbler-space contains bytes and links. However, since this system is concerned with the organization of storage, and not necessarily with holding the things stored, it is possible for a user's tumbler-space to store *no bytes*, only *links*. Nodes and accounts may keep their contents elsewhere for privacy, or for use on a when-and-if basis.

Properly understood, then, *this is a system for keeping track of interconnections.* The things which are interconnected can be somewhere else entirely; keeping them on our system is merely an additional convenience for the user.

THE VIRTUAL STREAM OF CONTENT BYTES

Content bytes have a logical sequence, an order in which they are stored. What this sequence means, and how it is used in a given case, depends on the document.

The sequence of content bytes may be used in any way by front-end applications. However, such sequence may not be relevant at all to what the user sees and the conceptual structure of what the front end is doing.

Still, the back end maintains this sequence through such functions as deletion, insertion and rearrangement. Thus any front-end applications using changing sequential material (such as the editing of linear text) are encouraged to use these mechanisms for updating and maintaining such data sequences.

CONTENTS, OR FINAL DATA

Content bytes (or *final data*) are the actual primary matter of the documents. In the case of text, these consist of alphabetical letters, spaces and punctuation marks--but no codes of any kind, as are common in the materials stored by word processors.

In the case of graphics (not implemented in XU.87.1), the content bytes are pixel information or other final data, and any organizing information is handled by links.

Where the system is being used to index externally-stored materials, there are no content bytes or final data. Instead, users may export the Xanadu logical addresses themselves for their needs in mapping external materials.

LINKS

Links are individual units which mark and connect final data. All indications of positions and relationships are handled by the link mechanism. (For the logic of this see a Chapter 4, "The Structure of Links.")

INCLUSION AND OWNERSHIP OF CONTENT BYTES

The virtual byte stream of a document may include bytes from any other document.

LITERARY 4/10 MACHINES

Bytes native elsewhere have an ordinal position in the byte stream just as if they were native to the document. Non-native byte-spans are called *inclusions* or *virtual copies*.

HOW ARE NATIVE BYTES DIFFERENT?

Native bytes of a document are those actually stored under its control and found directly in storage under its control; all other bytes are obtained by front-end or back-end requests to their home locations.

Non-native bytes are as much a logical part of a document as native bytes. Bytes which are logically native to other documents are treated in most ways identically: they are literally counted as part of the document (counted, that is, in the byte stream), and delivered to users in the same way--though delivered from different sources.

The only differences have to do with how directly available these bytes are, and with royalty and withdrawability. Byte-delivery royalties are paid to the accounts of the bytes' home documents.

Note that the owner of a document may delete bytes from the owner's current version, but those bytes remain in all other documents where they have been included.

THE VIRTUAL SPAN ADDRESS

Logical addressing of the byte stream is in the form of *virtual spans*, or *vspans*. These are sequences of bytes in the document's virtual byte stream, regardless of their native origin. *Thus a vspan within one document may contain bytes native to any number of documents.*

The numbers with which a vspan is described (and specified between front and back end) are explained in "Tumbling through the Docuverse," a Chapter 4.

The address of a byte in its native document is of no concern to the user or to the front end; indeed, it may be constantly changing; the front-end application is unaware of this.

LINKS

The structure of links is described in a Chapter 4 by that name.

A link is a logical unit put into a document by users, or by front ends, and maintained by the back end. The front end has no access to the link's internal mechanisms or raw data, but only to its behavior as defined by the FEBE protocol.

Unlike data bytes, a link is logically part of only one document, its home document.

The native links of a document are a second stream of addressable units. They are not presently editable or rearrangeable.

However, the link stream may be addressed as spans in the same way as a byte stream. This makes it possible for links to link to links, as described in the link chapter.

LITERARY 4/11 MACHINES

A link need not point anywhere in its home document. Its home document indicates who owns it, and not what it points to. Conversely, links connecting parts of a document need not reside in that document.

INCLUSION AND OWNERSHIP OF LINKS

A link is not "included" in other documents, as final bytes are. Rather, it has a *home* document, but it may *apply* to materials in any other documents.

The *endsets* of a link are the things it points to. A link may have any number of endsets pointing anywhere (see link chapter for their meaning).

THE STORAGE LEVEL

Final data bytes and links are stored in locations of no concern to the user. Where they are stored is chosen by the back end using proprietary Xanadu algorithms.

Front-end functions do not have access to the direct storage level.

WRITE-ONCE MEMORY

All algorithms have been chosen to be suitable for write-once memory (also called WORM, Write-Once Read-Many). Thus physical storage, like addressing in the system, may be done uniquely and permanently.

LITERARY 4/12 MACHINES

HUMBERS: A CUSTOM INTEGER SYSTEM
VARIABLE-LENGTH BINARY NUMBERS
FOR SMALL AND HUGE INTEGERS

Humber stands for "humungous number."[*] Humbers are numbers we have designed for this system, a notation for positive integers.[**] They are a data structure of the class usually called Bignums, that is, a way of representing numbers that may range up to very great size; but we have tailored them also to be very *small* in their representation when they represent small quantities. Thus the humber is an accordion-like notation, very short when a number is small, and as large as it needs to be when the number is big.

The humber is one or more bytes.

Consider its first byte.

The first (or Completeness) bit signals whether the number is *complete in this byte.* If this bit is unset, or zero, the remaining

SHORT HUMBER

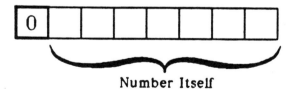

Number Itself

seven bits hold the number itself (0 to 127), and the entire number is stored in the one byte.

If the Completeness bit is set, or one, that means the remaining bits of this byte specify the length, in bytes, of the number, in binary. thus the humber may range up to $2^{(127 \times 8)}-1$, a number high above the trillions and larger than needed very soon..

Note some advantages of this scheme. Small incremental humbers are one byte long. But very large humbers adhere to the same format; thus only one set of "humber arithmetic" routines is necessary.

THE TRUE ZERO

The Completeness bit is zero if the actual number is within the byte, 1 if it is not; this choice makes an all-zero byte a true zero (a fact which will be seen to be a useful choice for the tumbler mechanism). See "Tumbling through the Docuverse," a Chapter 4.

OVERHEAD

Note also that these numbers occupy

---

[*]It originally stood for "Huffman-encoded number," which (strictly speaking) it is not, so we don't need to explain what that is.

[**]Humbers are the work of Roger Gregory, Mark Miller and Stuart Greene, done in the summer of 1979.

LITERARY 4/13 MACHINES

no more space than they need; they are short most of the time (when needed for small incrementation) and stretch out whenever needed without any change in the generalized manipulation routines. There is little overhead: the completeness bit, the first byte (if over 128), and no more than seven bits in the length of the mantissa, if over 128.

LONG HUMBER

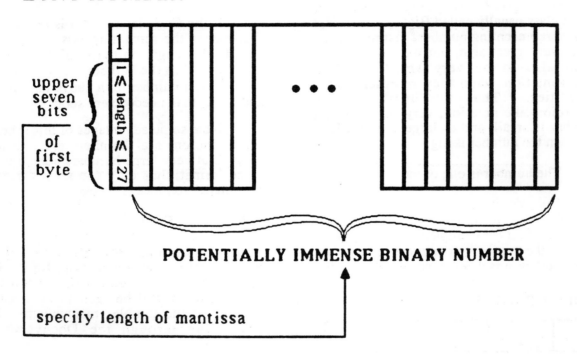

upper seven bits

of first byte

1

$1 \leqslant \text{length} \leqslant 127$

· · ·

specify length of mantissa

POTENTIALLY IMMENSE BINARY NUMBER

LITERARY 4/14 MACHINES

TUMBLING THROUGH THE DOCUVERSE:
DESIGNER ADDRESSES FOR EVERYTHING

A Write-Once Address System of Forking Multipart Integers
Specifying A Master Ever-Growing Tree-Address Space

Our kingdom is already twice the size of Spain,
and every day we drift makes it bigger.

The Kaiser
in Werner Herzog's film
"Aguirre, The Wrath of God"

THE NUMBERING PROBLEM

Besides the actual contents of our system--text, graphical data, and other notations representing things people want to look at and manipulate--the system must keep track of a lot of numbers. These are the internal numbers that are used for counts and pointers, and the overall scheme of where things are and how to get to them. They are integers. Some of these numbers have to be very very big. Others (in fact most of them) are small.

Our universe of documents (or docuverse) is potentially immense, and will grow unpredictably. Numerical addresses in our system can therefore grow very large. But they must also work with small increments and offsets. Designing the address space and notational representation has also therefore been crucial and difficult.

One assumption would treat the docuverse as a large integer domain, sparsely occupied by assigned document addresses. That way lies madness: it would mean unoccupied areas using up many, many precious bits.

It is not obvious--it was certainly not obvious to us at the outset--how to specify such a universe in any tractable form, with an indexing scheme that can possibly grow very large and still be cogent and parsimonious on the small-scale integer manipulations within individual documents.

The types of numbers we have chosen to use are an interesting exercise in notational engineering.

LITERARY 4/15 MACHINES

Our solution has two parts. One is to use a compound number which we call a *humber*. (Discussed elsewhere.) The other is the main addressing scheme of the system, which we call *tumblers*.

We chose the word "tumbler" partly because it sounded like "number," and partly because of our scheme's curious relation to the rotary mechanisms of locks--which also slide and increment independently with respect to one another, and are also called "tumblers."

Tumbler addressing is concerned with the management of storage--the spontaneous creation of places to put things, and remembrance of where they are.

Tumbler addressing is used throughout the system, as its common currency both external and internal.

Tumblers are an unusual form of numeration and arithmetic invented by Mark Miller in a rush of inspiration and developed by the group to index the Xanadu network and docuverse.

First we will discuss the idea of tumblers in general, where it came from and how it developed; then the specific form of tumblers we chose for mapping the Xanadu network and docuverse; then the public tumbler operations of the Xanadu system.

FACING IT DOWN

The planned docuverse as it faced us in 1980 looked like a sprawling and intractable-seeming collection of unpredictable materials. Two main problems stood out: the unpredictable growth of the network, and how to manage many different versions of a given document. It further had to address the problems of document storage on the network, and indeed the whole literary system of authorship, ownership, quotation and linkage.

In one big flash of insight, Mark Miller saw that everything could be named within a common structure, and that an arithmetic could be developed for this structure to be the common internal language throughout the search procedures of the system. It took some months to work this idea out in sufficient detail.

Many people suppose that there are only a few kinds of "numbers" and that they are all well understood by mathematicians. Actually, there are many kinds of numbers, and sometimes it is best to invent your own, so they will have just the properties you need. In which case they may not be well-known at all, or have been worked out by anybody yet.* This we did.

---

*This is a variant of an odd branch of mathematics called "transfinite arithmetic," which we need not get into. For those who are interested, however, tumbler arithmetic is the inverse of transfinite arithmetic, where transfinite numbers become the *denominators* of the tumblers. Hence Miller and Gregory call these "transfinitesimal" numbers.

LITERARY 4/16 MACHINES

Here are some of the problems addressed--that is, confronted, subdued, and at last numerically addressed--by the tumbler system:

Finding a manageable address-space for an ever-growing network of serving units--call them computers, nodes or file servers, as you will--a network with no center.

Finding a manageable address-space for an ever-expanding system of documents, growing unpredictably on this network.

Finding a manageable address-space for an ever-expanding number of authors and publishers, business users, scholars, and miscellaneous accounts.

Finding a manageable address-space for an ever-proliferating system of versions of documents, some controlled by their originators and others not.

For all these things it had to be assumed that no one would be in charge of the docuverse; that while it was growing continually, there would be no center. Further, we assumed that the number of compatible nodes will grow indefinitely but in hard-to-predict patterns.

We drew some inspiration from the Dewey Decimal system, which, despite its faults, does not waste a lot of space on empty characters. This leads to insights about forking numbers--numbers which may be continually separated to make more numbers--which we have developed in an unusual way.

A MANAGEMENT SCHEME

This is not just a numbering scheme, but an implicit structure whereby the docuverse and server network can continue to remain organized as they grow.

DECENTRALIZED

This is straightforward; no central administration or supervision is necessary.

OWNED NUMBERS AND BAPTISM

The basic principle is that of *owned numbers*. Numbers are owned by individuals or companies, and subnumbers under them are bestowed on other individuals and companies on whatever basis the owners choose. Whoever owns a specific node, account, document or version may in turn designate (respectively) new nodes, accounts, documents and versions, by forking their integers. We often call this the "baptism" of new numbers.

(The numbers are, of course, the tumblers whereof we speak.)

INDEPENDENT OF THE CONTENTS' STRUCTURE

Tumbler-space is tree-structured,

though its contents will usually not be. Tumblers do not affect the user-level structure of the documents; they only provide a mapping mechanism, and impose no categorization and no structure on the contents of a document.

INDEPENDENT OF SUBJECT AND CATEGORY

When we call tumblers an "indexing method," this has nothing to do with the kind of indexing people do by subject and category, but rather with the technical forms of indexing needed to manage storage--the computer equivalent of allocating shelf-space.

INDEPENDENT OF MECHANISM

Note that tumblers are an addressing scheme, not a mechanism of the system; it is essentially independent of the real internal mechanisms of the system. These mechanisms are for the present still proprietary and undisclosed.

INDEPENDENT OF TIME

Note that "time" is not included in the tumbler. Time is kept track of separately.

GENERAL TUMBLERS

The tumbler is a multi-part number with some rather remarkable features. It is intended to keep track of hereditary successions of various kinds, while reducing the overall indexing manipulations to tractable arithmetic form, while handling increments and offsets--whether local or very large--with creditable brevity. These increments and offsets, naturally, can cross the lines between nodes and accounts, documents and versions. So the docuverse is all really one big forking document.

Tumblers are the principal currency of the FEBE protocol (discussed in "The Protocols of Xanadu," another Chapter 4), and the common currency of the internal workings of the Xanadu system.

The tumbler is a type of elaborate (not "complex") number and its arithmetic. With its routines of addition and subtraction, it provides a master scheme for the full--always full, but always growing--address space.

It deals with positions and collections of documents and their contents--points and spans in an expandable tree-space.

The network of server nodes, too, is mapped to this tree-space. (It is important to stress that this is an addressing scheme which in no way assumes or imposes a tree structure on the material contained.)

Tumbler-space is an accordion-like master address space, potentially very very large, which includes notational provisions for the complex relations between documents, their forebears, their owners, their home locations on the network and the expansion of the network itself.

LITERARY 4/18 MACHINES

INSERTION

New items may be continually inserted in tumbler-space *while the other addresses remain valid.*

This means that any address of any document in an ever-growing network may be specified by a permanent tumbler address.

This works for servers, accounts, documents, versions, and text itself.

FORKING

A server node, or station, has ancestors and may have possible descendant nodes. An account, too, and a document, all have possible descendants.

The entire tumbler works like that: nodes can spin off nodes; accounts can spin off accounts; nodes can spin off accounts; and so on. Thus all numeration in the docuverse is compressed into a single mechanism.

ANATOMY OF THE TUMBLER

A tumbler consists of a series of integers. Each integer has no upper limit; since its number base is irrelevant, we call it a "digit." The digits of the tumbler are separated by minor dividers, or points.

Examples of tumbler digits:

.373.   .675923.   .40.

ALL ADDRESSES REMAIN VALID

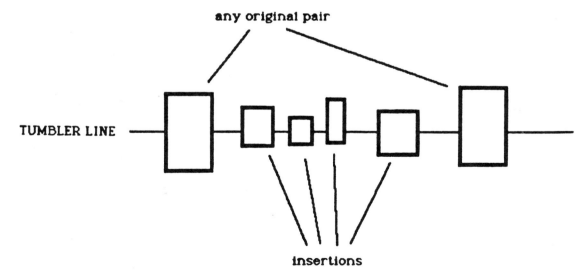

any original pair

TUMBLER LINE

insertions

LITERARY 4/19 MACHINES

The digit

.0.

is special; it is used as a divider between tumbler *fields*, discussed below.

FORKING

One digit can become several by a forking or branching process. This consists of creating successive new digits to the right; we call these "under" the previous digit.

For instance, if there is an item

.2.

it can branch into several more items, each of which is a daughter item. Thus

.2.1.   .2.2.   .2.3.   .2.4.   . . .

are successive items being placed under .2.

Similarly,

.2.4.6.

is the sixth item under

.2.4.

and

.2.4.6.312.

is the 312th item under the sixth item under the fourth item under .2.

The owner of a given item controls the allocation of the numbers under it. How these successive numbers are to be chosen depends on various technical factors and various choices by the owner.

FIELDS

A *field* is a series of non-zero digits which may have forked as described, or may have just one digit if there has been no forking. Some fields have more psychological meaning than others.

A series of digits (not necessarily a whole field) may together refer to a specific kind of object, such as a server node or a document. Their rules of reference and application vary.

Fields are separated by the major divider

.0.

(to be discussed). Typical examples of fields include:

1.3776.4.22.

.2001.2001.

.1.2.3.4.5.6.

THE MAJOR DIVIDER

The major divider between fields is

.0.

LITERARY 4/20 MACHINES

and so the zero digit is reserved for that purpose. This peculiar choice turns out to be arithmetically consistent with the rest of tumbler arithmetic, permitting a uniform arithmetic algorithm that passes along the entire tumbler.

THE TUMBLER LINE

The tumbler line is an abstraction representing the full tree-structure of the system. It is a linear, sequential ordering upon all of the addresses in the docuverse.

To put such a structure in a linear sequence is a puzzling problem. Consider even a small tree of the forking numbers we have discussed:

But now just put these tumblers in ascending order:

1
1.1
1.1.2
1.1.2.1
1.1.2.2
1.1.3
1.2
1.2.1
1.2.1.9
1.2.2
1.2.65
1.2.65.831
1.3
etc.

SMALL BRANCHING STRUCTURE
OF SIMPLE TUMBLERS

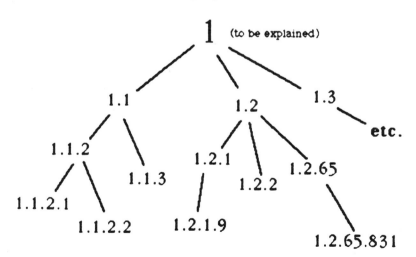

LITERARY 4/21 MACHINES

This simple ascending order of the tumblers generates the tumbler line of this particular structure:

1, 1.1, 1.1.2, 1.1.2.1, 1.1.2.2, 1.1.3, 1.2, 1.2.1, 1.2.1.9, 1.2.2, 1.2.65, 1.2.65.831, 1.3, etc.

In a sense the tumbler line is like the real line, i.e., the line of integers and all the numbers in between. But the tumbler line is a different kind of abstraction from the real line. The real line is the same under all circumstances. The tumbler line is an abstract representation of a particular tree.

The contents of the tumbler line are determined by the population of entities and relations on the tree it represents. Thus the tumbler line is not infinite in the same way as the real line; the tumbler line is a flat mapping of a particular tree, *finite but unlimited*.

APPROXIMATE HIERARCHY OF A TUMBLER ADDRESS

Thus the docuverse and its server nodes are mapped to a tree structure. The hierarchy is roughly as follows. We will deal with the exact specifics shortly.

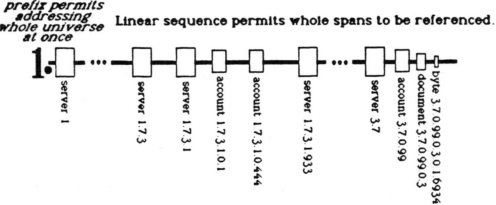

A WRITE-ONCE UNIVERSAL LINEAR ADDRESS SPACE

THE TUMBLER LINE

prefix permits addressing whole universe at once

Linear sequence permits whole spans to be referenced.

1.

server 1

server 1.7.3

server 1.7.3.1

account 1.7.3.1.0.1

account 1.7.3.1.0.444

server 1.7.3.1.933

server 3.7

account 3.7.0.99

document 3.7.0.99.0.3

byte 3.7.0.99.0.3.0.16934

LITERARY 4/22 MACHINES

Server Node	User Account (and possibly: /Subaccount /Department /etc.)	Document	Version	Contents: Individual Elements

In this diagram, an item to the right is necessarily under an item to the left. Each of these fields is a forkable integer, able to branch into a series of integer fields.

THE POPULATION OF TUMBLER-SPACE: ONLY CONTENTS ARE STORED

In the present implementation (XU.87.1), the only entities actually stored in tumbler-space are content bytes and links. While a number on the line may represent a document or an account, that doesn't mean there's an *object stored for it*. What's stored is the contents--bytes and links.

The docuverse is the *occupied* tumbler-space--as occupied by conceptually assigned positions, even if nothing represents them in storage.

Thus the address population of tumbler-space is also an abstraction, since *things may be addressed even though nothing is there to represent them in storage.* Consider what we may call "ghost elements:"

GHOST ELEMENTS, AND LINKS TO THEM

While servers, accounts and documents logically occupy positions on the developing tumbler line, no specific element need be stored in tumbler-space to correspond to them. Hence we may call them *ghost elements*.

GHOST ELEMENTS

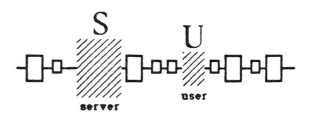

However, these elements are *virtually* present in tumbler-space, since *links may be made to them which embrace all the contents below them.*

It is possible to link to a node, or an account, even though there is nothing stored in the docuverse corresponding to them.

WHAT IT MEANS

A link to or search of an account or node will *find any of the documents under it.*

LITERARY 4/23 MACHINES

THE TWO FUNCTIONS OF THE TUMBLER

The tumbler has two principal functions: to represent addresses in the docuverse, and to represent *spans* of addresses, corresponding to tree structures within the storage of the system. Let us consider each of these in turn.

1. THE CANONICAL REPRESENTATION OF ADDRESSES

A tumbler address may automatically include server node, document, author, and position in document. Some addresses are shorter and leave out some of this information. However, *there are no addresses other than address tumblers.*

We say the representation of the address is "canonical" because in later implementations using the BEBE protocol (see "The Protocols", a Chapter 4) there will be copies of material distributed throughout the network--but still carrying (and found by) their original addresses.

Address tumblers remain valid no matter how much additional material has been added to the docuverse, even if the docuverse has grown enormously, much of it in spaces intercalated between the previous addresses. These changes in the address population do not affect an address tumbler.

2. THE CANONICAL REPRESENTATION OF SPANS AND SUBTREES.

SPANS AND SPAN-SETS

In this system we often need to designate a range of bytes, documents, servers or the like. We may want to make a link to this range, or search for all the documents in this range, or search for all the links that lie within this range (or overlap it).

Such a range we call a *span.*

A span in the tumbler line, represented by two tumblers, refers to a subtree of the entire docuverse, (or merely to a series of elements of the same type, which is a degenerate case of a subtree). Thus we may have spans of characters, spans of links, spans of documents, spans of versions, and spans covering large combinations of them-- including spans of servers with all their contents.

In fact, a tumbler-span may range in possible size from one byte to the whole docuverse on the whole network.

A tumbler-span is not a conventional number, and it does not designate the number of bytes contained. It does not designate a number of anything. It is *something else*, since it may include server nodes, links, and whatnot. Indeed, a span may also *usefully*

LITERARY 4/24 MACHINES

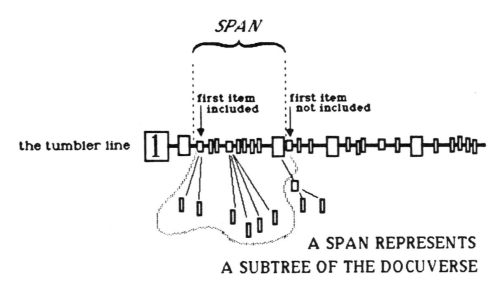

SPAN

first item
included

first item
not included

the tumbler line

**A SPAN REPRESENTS
A SUBTREE OF THE DOCUVERSE**

designate nothing at all, meaning a zone whose emptiness can be checked, or a zone which will have contents later. A span that contains nothing today may at a later time contain a million documents.

A span may be visualized as a zone hanging down from the tumbler line--what is called in computer parlance a *depth-first spanning tree*.

The first point of a span may designate a server, an account, a document or an element; so may the last point. There is no choice as to what lies between; this is implicit in the choice of first and last point.

Note: *if you want to designate a separated series of items exactly, including nothing else, you do this by a span-set, which is a series of spans.*

A tumbler-span is specified in two ways: by either a pair of address tumblers or by a difference tumbler which is packaged with an address tumbler. (Tumbler arithmetic is concerned with the conversion back and forth between these two forms.)

YOU CAN'T GET THERE FROM HERE

Starting from a given tumbler address, it may only be possible arithmetically to get to *some* places in the Docuverse--those notationally *after that address.**

_____

*Allowing negative and other additional modes of tumbler fields might correct this, but we have not explored the possibility.

LITERARY 4/25 MACHINES

Thus a tumbler-pair, beginning with an appropriate starting address, is necessary to specify every span. (There are other reasons for tumbler-pairs, as will be seen below.)

These have been some general principles. We will postpone tumbler arithmetic until our specific tumblers have been elucidated.

MAPPING OF THE XANADU™ TUMBLER-SPACE

For the Xanadu storage system and network, we have mapped the contemplated docuverse to the tumbler system.

A SYSTEM OF ASSIGNMENT AND INTERPRETATION

Given the tumbler concepts presented so far, mapping the Xanadu docuverse and literary system to the tumbler addressing method is a matter of assignment and interpretation. It has a few complications and subtleties.

The divisions have been carefully chosen because the tumbler system promotes in some ways a linking and searching hierarchy, and we endeavor to take best advantage of it, even though our materials are intrinsically non-hierarchical. (Whether to take advantage of any features not a part of our original virtuality design can be philosophically argued, but any method has certain directions of advantageous use, and we have endeavored to optimize the use of this one.)

THE FIELDS AND DIVIDERS

There are four major fields, each expandable indefinitely, with three major dividers between them. These fields are Server, User, Document and Contents. The following diagram will become progressively clearer.

TUMBLER ADDRESS MASTER DIAGRAM

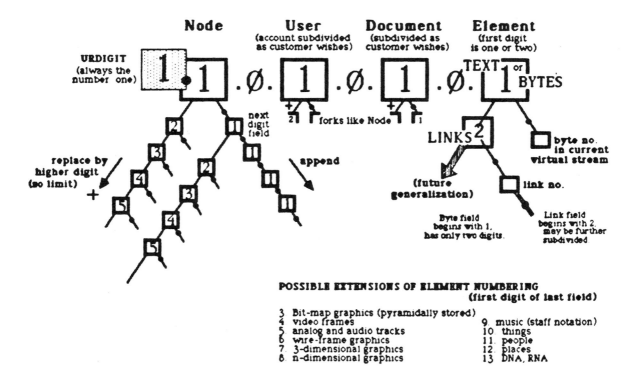

Node

User (account subdivided as customer wishes)

Document (subdivided as customer wishes)

Element (first digit is one or two)

URDIGIT (always the number one)

1.1 . Ø . 1 . Ø . 1 . Ø . 1

TEXT or BYTES

next digit field

replace by higher digit (so limit)

append

forks like Node

LINKS

(future generalization)

byte no. in current virtual stream

link no.

Byte field begins with 1, has only two digits.

Link field begins with 2, may be further subdivided

POSSIBLE EXTENSIONS OF ELEMENT NUMBERING
(first digit of last field)

3 Bit-map graphics (pyramidally stored)
4 video frames
5 analog and audio tracks
6 wire-frame graphics
7 3-dimensional graphics
8 n-dimensional graphics

9 music (staff notation)
10 things
11 people
12 places
13 DNA, RNA

LITERARY 4/27 MACHINES

A tumbler *address* may have at most three zero digits

.0.

These are interpreted as the major dividers, and have lexical significance as punctuation. There can be only three such zero-digits. (A *difference* tumbler may have any number of zeroes; see below.)

Here are some actual examples-- possible addresses of items on the network.

While this will initially refer to the physical device, it represents a logical division which may be mapped to subdevices or collections of devices in the future.

The server address always begins with the digit 1, since all other servers are descended from it. This may seem an unnecessary redundancy, but it permits referring to the entire docuverse by a "one" in the first position. (Discussed under "Request Sets," below.)

NODE 1.2368.792.6

USER 1.2368.792.6.0.6974.383.1988.352

DOCUMENT 1.2368.792.6.0.6974.383.1988.352.0.75

VERSION 1.2368.792.6.0.6974.383.1988.352.0.75.2

BYTE 1.2368.792.6.0.6974.383.1988.352.0.75.2.0.1.9287

LINK 1.2368.792.6.0.6974.383.1988.352.0.75.2.0.2.352

THE ITEMS IN THE DOCUVERSE

1. SERVER

A server is the node on which a document is stored. (This refers to its *canonical* storage, and not where extra copies may be put.)

The Server field may be continually subdivided, with new subfields indicating daughter servers.

2. USER

The User field of the tumbler keeps track of who or what is the owner of a document. For business use, we may call

LITERARY 4/28 MACHINES

this the Account, with such possible separate subdivisions as the Department, the Project and the Task. For personal use, it may be the Individual, his or her Area-of-Interest, and so on.

Typically, the user will have no control over the node address he, she or it is assigned; but once assigned a User account, the user will have full control over its subdivision forevermore. Hence it is important to understand what uses will do you the most good, whether you are a corporation or an individual.

The User field may be continually subdivided, with new subfields indicating daughter accounts, departments, interests and projects, or areas of record-keeping.

3. DOCUMENT

A document is the logical entity in which materials are stored. In the literary tradition, it has an owner, and may be quoted and linked-to by other documents--within certain rules intended to be fair.

The document number is the third field of the tumbler address.

The Document field of the tumbler may be continually subdivided, with new subfields in the tumbler indicating daughter documents and versions.

In a sense the version, or subdocument, number is only an accidental extension of the document number, and strictly implies no specific relationship of derivation. Its subdivisions are called "versions" by interpretation, but this reflects an important desirable feature of the system: the ability easily to make a link to *all versions of a document*.*

---

*While, in principle, the version and subdocument fields could contain unrelated stuff, we encourage using the version fields to designate actual versions and nothing else, so that links to "all the versions" are correct.

This convenient linking practice will work best if the document owner numbers the documents to reflect their actual development or association: by placing all the extensions of a document that he or she considers to be "versions" in successor fields of the main document number.

When there are several origins for a document, deciding which is the parent document is your choice. (There are other ways to represent and follow commonality, linkage and history, but this particular method is both convenient and elegant.)

Suggested good practice. If you have assigned a number to a document (say, 273), do not begin by injecting contents directly into it, but assign a version number at once (e.g. 273.1) to your first material, so as not to enshrine the initial input at a higher hierarchical level.

LITERARY 4/29 MACHINES

4. ELEMENTS

The fourth and final field of the Xanadu tumbler specifies the individual contents.

These are presently of two types, bytes and links.

4.A. BYTES

Bytes are designated by a 1 in the first position of the element field. Example:

N.0.U.0.D.V.0.1.1

The first byte of the document.

4.A.1 BYTE POSITION

The digit after the one indicates the byte position in the current ordering of bytes.

This is its *virtual stream address*.

Note that this order may be continually altered by editorial operations, but since the links are to the bytes themselves, any links to those bytes remain stably attached to them.

N.0.U.0.D.V.0.1.1

The first byte of the document, whether stored in the document's space or not.

N.0.U.0.D.V.0.1.799

The 799th byte of the document, whether stored in the document's space or not.

N.0.U.0.D.V.0.1.67890

The 67890th byte of the document, whether stored in the document's space or not.

BYTE-INCLUSIONS FROM ELSEWHERE

The bytes virtually present in the byte-storage of a document are not merely those bytes which have this document as their home, but *all* bytes which are used in this document by inclusion. While these bytes will be found by any byte-delivery request, they will actually be delivered from their home locations (or from copies elsewhere on the network). Such copies, wherever they may be, still retain the identity of their home locations, and are addressed as though they were there. See BEBE in "The Protocols," a Chapter 4.

4.A.2 SUBDIVISON OF BYTES?

While bytes could in principle be subdivided by the tumbler-forking process, no sensible interpretation of this idea has yet been found.

4.B LINKS

When the fourth field of a tumbler address begins with a 2, the address is that of a *link*.

4.B.1 LINK POSITIONS

The digit after the "2" in a link-address designates the link's serial position. Links are currently not rearrangeable, and thus are

LITERARY 4/30 MACHINES

stored in the order of their creation.

Examples:

N.0.U.0.D.V.0.2.1

(the first link of the document, stored in the document's space)

N.0.U.0.D.V.0.2.755

(the 755th link to which the document is home).

The *bytes* designated by tumbler addresses are in their *current* sequence, and may include as inclusions other bytes from anywhere else in the docuverse, assigned current virtual addresses within the document.

The *links* designated by a tumbler address are in their permanent order of arrival. A document includes *only the links*

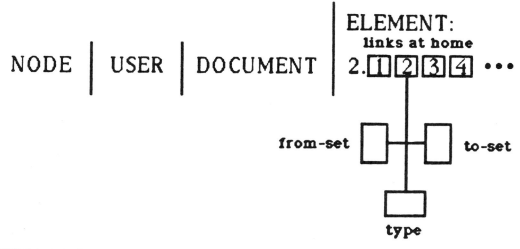

4.B.2 SUBDIVISION OF LINKS?

The subdivision of links by further digits (after "2" and the position) is a distinct possibility, and several possible uses have been discussed. However, such assignment has been postponed until the master link assignments are decided. (See section "Link Assignment" in "The Structure of Links," a Chapter 4.)

of which it is the home document. This poses no inconvenience in finding relevant links between specified items, since these links will be found wherever they may be.

However, links may be virtual copies of links in other documents. Thus a link may have a number of different documents as its home document. However, only one of these is its *native* document.

LITERARY 4/31 MACHINES

This addressing scheme for links designates the *logical ownership and control* of the links; what the links point to is a different matter. (See Links chapter.)

ADDRESS TUMBLERS AND DIFFERENCE TUMBLERS

As presently defined (XU.87.1), there are two types of tumblers: address tumblers, which represent addresses, and difference tumblers, which represent spans.

There are several important distinctions between address tumblers and difference tumblers, and the two are governed by different rules.

A difference tumbler cannot be used without a parent address tumbler, for various reasons to be explained.

1. MEANING OF ZEROES

These two types of tumblers must be distinguished because of the meaning of the zero.

An address tumbler is a long vector which refers to a specific server node, or account, or document, or version, or byte, or link, within our expandable tree-space. An address tumbler *has at most three zeroes*, interpreted as the major dividers between the Node field, the User field, the Document field and the Element field.

N.N. ... N.0.U.U. ... U.0.D.D. ... D.V. ... V.0.E.E

A difference tumbler always is defined in terms of an address tumbler, and designates a *span*. It may have as many zeroes as necessary. These represent both the same division-points as the zeroes in an address tumbler, and zeroes which are the result of subtraction, representing differences between the digits of the two address tumblers from which it is derived.

0.0.0.0.0.0.3781.652.0.0.736.9
typical difference tumbler

A difference tumbler always begins with one or more leading zeroes, except where it designates the entire docuverse, in which case it is 1.

2. STABILITY

As previously stated, an address tumbler remains valid forever. However, a difference tumbler is not stable in this way. It is fragile and does not remain valid unless carefully forced to.

3. NON-UNIQUENESS AND NON-TRANSPOSABILITY OF DIFFERENCE TUMBLERS

A difference tumbler cannot be meaningfully transposed elsewhere in the tumbler line. Moreover, even for a given location, *a difference tumbler has no meaning in isolation*. Suppose you wanted to refer to all the contents of server 1.2.3.4.5. Then your difference tumbler would be

0.0.0.0.1

LITERARY 4/32 MACHINES

However, it would be exactly the same difference tumbler if you wanted to refer to server 1.2.3.3.3.

This also means that the major dividers of the tumbler (between Server, User, Document and Element fields) cannot be recognized in the difference tumbler alone; there is no way to parse it.

4. BINDING OF DIFFERENCE TUMBLERS TO ADDRESS TUMBLERS

For the various above reasons, a difference tumbler must be packaged with an address tumbler, which specifies where the difference tumbler begins. Consequently every difference tumbler sent to the back end is preceded by an address tumbler.

TUMBLER OPERATIONS

Tumbler arithmetic is a consistent set of operations that does what we need and not much else. It is employed principally (at the front-end level) for finding spans and the ending positions of spans.

Tumbler arithmetic is a strange set of operations on whole tumblers. (Digits of the tumbler use integer addition and subtraction.) Tumbler arithmetic consists of a fundamental pair of operations:

the derivation of a difference tumbler, representing a span, from two address tumblers,

and the recalculation of the second address tumbler from the first address tumbler and the difference tumbler.

Calling the two address tumblers respectively START and AFTER, the valid mutual operations are:

Other enticing operations are not useful. For instance,

not unique
and not particularly useful

Tumbler addition is non-commutative (A+B does not equal B+A) and therefore there are two possible forms of subtraction. The one used for difference tumblers gives a unique answer. The other form, which we call "weak subtraction," gives a non-unique number and has no current use.

LITERARY 4/33 MACHINES

We will look at this again a little later.

PREPARATORY ALIGNMENT

Tumblers are squared up left-to-right, rather than right-to-left, as in conventional arithmetic.

Mechanics. For every leading zero in the second row, the corresponding integer is copied down from the first row. When a nonzero digit is encountered in the second row, an addition between the two rows is performed for that digit. All additional digits are copied down from the second row.

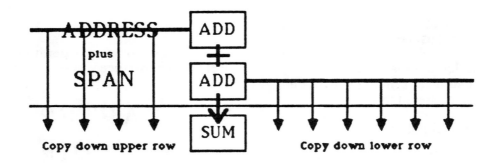

TUMBLER ADDITION

Tumbler addition has a tumbler *address* on top (the augend) and a tumbler *span* on the bottom (the addend).

The first tumbler represents the first element in the specified subtree; the second tumbler is a difference tumbler (bound to the address tumbler) representing the span; the result will represent the first element *after* the specified subtree.

EXAMPLES

Adding 300

```
  1 . 1 . 0 . 2 . 0 . 2 . 2 . 0 . 1 . 777
+ 0 . 0 . 0 . 0 . 0 . 0 . 0 . 0 . 0 . 300
  ─────────────────────────────────────────
  1 . 1 . 0 . 2 . 0 . 2 . 2 . 0 . 1 . 1077
```

LITERARY 4/34 MACHINES

HEAVIER EXAMPLE OF ADDITION

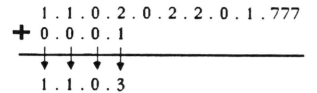

$$1 . 1 . 0 . 2 . 0 . 2 . 2 . 0 . 1 . 777$$
$$+ \; 0 . 0 . 0 . 1$$
$$1 . 1 . 0 . 3$$

INTERPRETATION OF TUMBLER ADDITION

Think of it as "stepping forward two chapters, three paragraphs."

There is no meaning to adding a chapter and going to the same point in the next chapter.

Similarly, when you add one chapter, think of it as going from mid-chapter to the beginning of the next chapter.

TUMBLER SUBTRACTION

Tumbler subtraction has an address on top (the minuend) and a smaller address on the bottom (the subtrahend). The result is a difference tumbler.

The first tumbler represents the first object in the specified subtree; the second tumbler represents the first element *after* the specified subtree; the result is a difference tumbler representing the intended span.

Mechanics. Starting at the left, and for every digit that is the same in both rows, subtraction yields a zero digit in the result.

When an actual difference is encountered in corresponding digits, the integers in that digit are subtracted. (The result cannot be negative; this means the subtrahend was larger than the minuend, which is illegal.) All additional digits are copied down from the top row.

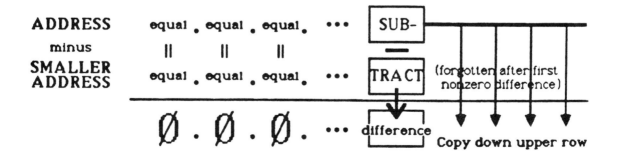

LITERARY 4/35 MACHINES

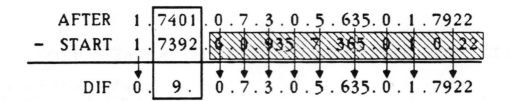

			AFTER	1 .	7401	. 0 . 7 . 3 . 0 . 5 . 635 . 0 . 1 . 7922
−			START	1 .	7392	. 6 . 0 . 935 . 7 . 365 . 0 . 1 . 0 . 22
			DIF	0 .	9 .	0 . 7 . 3 . 0 . 5 . 635 . 0 . 1 . 7922

INTERPRETATION OF TUMBLER SUBTRACTION

Think of tumbler subtraction as "stepping backward a chapter and three paragraphs," meaning stepping across a chapter boundary and then three paragraphs backward.

PARADOXES OF TUMBLER ARITHMETIC

1. Addition: *a range of addends gives the same answer.*

2. Subtraction: *a range of minuends gives the same answer.*

PARADOX OF ADDITION:
a range of addends give the same answer.

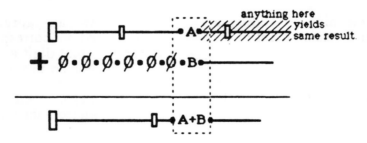

PARADOX OF SUBTRACTION:
a range of minuends give the same answer.

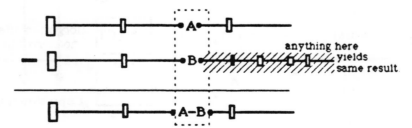

LITERARY 4/36 MACHINES

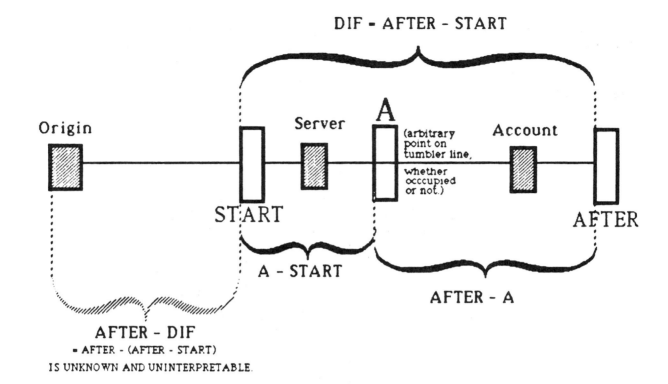

DIF - AFTER - START

Origin

Server

A

(arbitrary point on tumbler line, whether occupied or not.)

Account

START

AFTER

A - START

AFTER - A

AFTER - DIF
= AFTER - (AFTER - START)
IS UNKNOWN AND UNINTERPRETABLE.

These outlandish operations mystically complement each other, providing a useful numeration and arithmetic for all references within the system.

REQUEST SETS

A request set is a set of spans, or spanset, presented to the back end in the FEBE protocol. A request set may be a set of spans which is to be searched for documents or links, or to which a link is to be attached. The manipulation of request sets is an important aspect of what front-end functions do.

Understanding spans is a key to appropriate software design for handling request-sets. Let us start with the simplest spans, those which are one item wide.

LITERARY 4/37 MACHINES

1. SPANS ONE ITEM WIDE IN XANADU TUMBLERS

We have already discussed Spans in general. Here is an important payoff for our allocations: a digit of "one" may be used to designate all of a given version, all versions of a given document, all works of a given author, all documents in a given project, all documents on a given server--or the entire docuverse.

This is accomplished by leading zeroes and a "one" in the appropriate digit.

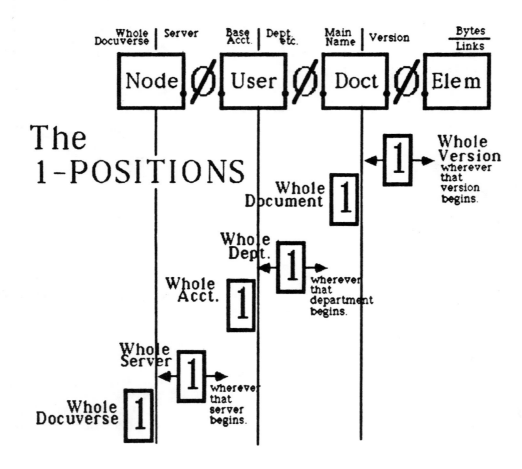

The 1-POSITIONS

LITERARY 4/38 MACHINES

2. OTHER REQUEST SETS

In stressing how easy it is to address large units and hierarchies of units with a single tumbler span, I do not want to give the impression that this is always what you want to do. In fact, any set of tumbler addresses may be covered exactly by a *series* of spans, or spanset, which is an acceptable argument to any of the linking and search commands.

We will not here get into the subtleties of how to specify spans, as that is a whole nother chapter. The arithmetic so far covers this issue grossly, enough for mathematicians, and most users will ordinarily be shielded from the inner details of such matters by their fromt-end applications.

TUMBLER FORMS IN XU.87.1

How a front-end application handles these numbers mechanically does not matter technically, provided that they are handled correctly.

To use the FEBE protocol, an address tumbler must be constructed as follows:

A first digit of 1.

Any number of ASCII integer digits (integers from zero to unlimited) separated by points.

No more than three zero digits, corresponding to the three major dividers.

No point at the beginning or end of a tumbler.

As a matter of interst to hackers and lovers of technical detail, the different tumbler implementations in XU.87.1 are as follows:

LITERARY 4/39 MACHINES

	Integer Digit Position	Minor Divider	Major Divider	Exponent (how leading zeroes of difference tumbler are specified)
FEBE.87.1 transmission tumblers and front-end protocol handler	ASCII string	Period	.0.	Integer
XU.87.1 back-end CPU	32-bit binary	Implied by binary divisions	32-bit Zero	Binary
XU.87.1 back-end disk storage	Humber	Implied by humber divisions	Humber Zero	Humber

ELEGANT OR SUPERHACK?

This is a curious, bizarre, powerul, consistent, non-obvious and hard-to-visualize system. It also has a certain quirkiness and charm. Call it a hack, yes; but it is definitely a superhack.

FEEL FREE

No proprietariety is asserted for humber and tumbler methods or for their names; use them freely. (Indeed, tumblers are a required part of any front-end application.) However, the group would not mind a little credit now and then.

While it went through many changes, and represents contributions by numerous members of the Xanadu troupe, the present form of tumbler was worked out by Mark Miller, with help from Roland King and Roger Gregory, in approximately June of 1980.

LITERARY 4/40 MACHINES

THE STRUCTURE OF LINKS
and THE MEANING OF SEARCHES

A Xanadu link is a connective unit, a package of connecting or marking information. It is owned by a user. It is put in by a user (or a front end), and thereafter maintained by the back end through the back end's inner indexing mechanisms.

The Xanadu link is a meta-virtual structure connecting parts of documents (which are themselves virtual structures). The link is used for information that connects, marks, represents alternative structure and points of view, and much more.

Xanadu links, and the methods by which we search through them, are a system of retrieval quite unlike any other in the world. Their potential use is so varied and promising that we are continually discerning new possibilities and subtleties. No simple generalization suffices; only by considering the link mechanism in detail is it possible to grasp the possibilities overall.

The link mechanism ties together the whole corpus of materials on the Xanadu system. There is essentially nothing in the Xanadu system except documents and their arbitrary links. For instance, there is no *system directory*; rather, we encourage the on-line publishing of directory documents by users. These will provide access to the documents they cite through links.

LOOKUP METHOD
Directory
(a document owned and published by someone)

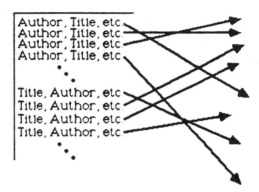

1. TECHNICAL MECHANISMS

WHERE LINKS ARE

The address of the link in a document is not where the link data is actually stored; rather, it is a *token* permitting the link to be referred to. (See "The Xanadu Document," a Chapter 4.) It may be referred to, at that address, by a tumbler span in the same way that spans of final data bytes are referred to. A tumbler-span of 1 pointing to that link refers to it alone. A broader tumbler span may refer to several links, the whole document, and so on up to the whole

LITERARY 4/41 MACHINES

docuverse. (See "Tumbling Through the Docuverse," a Chapter 4.)

Every link has an address in at least one document. These are its home documents, where it either originated or has been included by virtual copy. The *original* home document of a link is called its *native* document, the place it was created. (If this terminology seems confusing at first, consider that you yourself may have several homes but were only born in one place, your place of nativity.)

THE LINK AS A STRAP BETWEEN BYTES

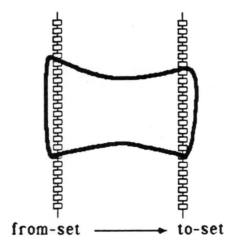

from-set ———→ to-set

LINKS MAY BE EDITED

Links may in principle be edited. (Not in XU.87.1.)

2. THE STRAP BETWEEN SPANS

A Xanadu link is not between *points*, but between *spans* of data.* Thus we may visualize it as a strap between bytes.

This has a crucial advantage: it means that *links can survive editing*. If any of the bytes are left to which a link is attached, that link remains on them. This also works for alternative versions in which part of each end has survived.

3. END-SETS

We see from above that one end of a link may be on a broken, discontiguous set of bytes. This illustrates the *endset:* a link may be to or from *an arbitrary set of bytes.* These may be anywhere in the docuverse.

4. DIRECTIONALITY

A link is typically directional. Thus it has a *from-set*, the bytes the link is "from," and a *to-set*, the bytes the link is "to". (What "from" and "to" mean depend on the specific case.)

---

*Presently only one-dimensional data is defined within the system, so that all spans are linear or sequential. As multidimensional data types are added, spans will become multidimensional.

SURVIVABILITY:

Links between bytes can survive deletions, insertions and rearrangements, if anything is left at each end.

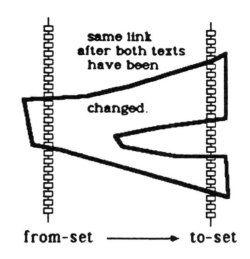

same link after both texts have been changed.

from-set ⟶ to-set

(Some types of links are intrinsically bidirectional. These are a special case.)

5. LINK TYPES

A link has a *type*. We can visualize this as a pointer from the link to a list of types off somewhere.

LINK TYPES GENERALIZED

Since the "from" and "to" of a link may point anywhere, so may the link type. Thus the link type is technically a *third endset* of the link, which we call a *three-set*.

The type may be specified by an arbitrary endset pointing anywhere in the docuverse.

WHAT IS A LINK TYPE?

Links are meant to be extensible for the arbitrary needs of any user. Thus the set of link types is open-ended, and indeed any user may define his or her link types for a particular purpose. This is done with a mechanism which is powerful and symmetrical.

6. THE GENERALIZATION OF ENDSETS

The from-set may be an arbitrary collection of spans, pointing anywhere in the docuverse. Similarly, the to-set may be an arbitrary collection of spans pointing anywhere in the docuverse. *We adopt the same convention for link types.* A link's

LITERARY 4/43 MACHINES

LINK ENDSETS

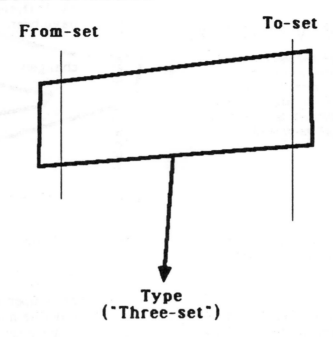

From-set

To-set

Type
(`Three-set`)

type is specified by *yet another end-set*, pointing anywhere in the docuverse. This is symmetrical with the other endsets.

Note that a link's type--the three-set--may be *several* pointers.

LINK SUBTYPES

A link subtype may be indicated by an additional span, or parameter, in the threeset. Thus the link may be found not only from its main type, but also from its subtype as well.

ARBITRARINESS OF A LINK'S TYPE

What the "type" designation points to is completely arbitrary. This is because of the way we will be searching for links. The search mechanism does not actually look at

LITERARY 4/44 MACHINES

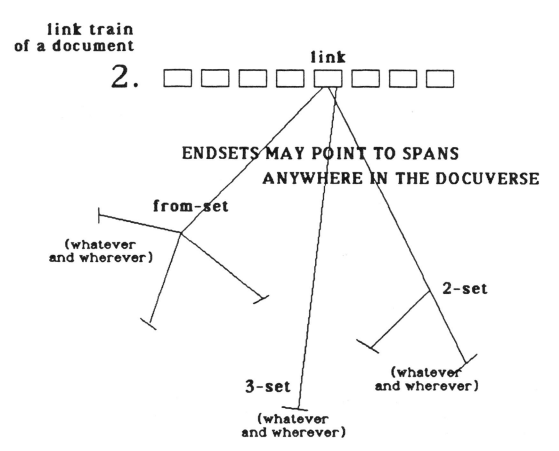

**link train
of a document**

2.

link

ENDSETS MAY POINT TO SPANS

ANYWHERE IN THE DOCUVERSE

from-set

(whatever
and wherever)

2-set

(whatever
and wherever)

3-set

(whatever
and wherever)

what is stored under the "type" it is searching for; it merely considers the type's address. It is the matching of the link-type address, rather than the actual contents of that address, that determine the search. (Searching will be discussed further below.)

Indeed, there is no need for the presence of elements at the addresses specified. Link types may be ghost elements, as explained in "Tumbling Through the Docuverse," a Chapter 4.

7. MAPPING A LINK TO TUMBLER SPACE

There is a universal address space, the tumbler line (again, see "Tumbling Through the Docuverse," a Chapter 4). We may visualize a link's endsets as mapping to it.

LITERARY 4/45 MACHINES

A LINK'S ENDSETS MAP TO THE TUMBLER LINE

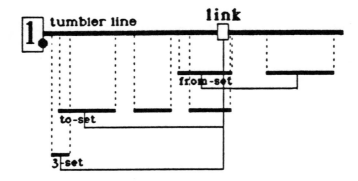

Another way of looking at it is to consider a square of tumbler lines, the Tumbler Square. A link's home (any home) is an element located on one side; and its three endsets map to the other sides.

LITERARY 4/46 MACHINES

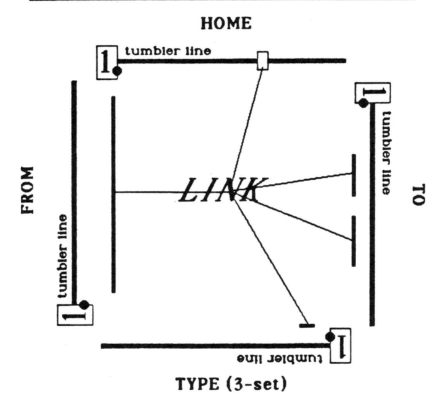

A LINK MAPS TO THE TUMBLER SQUARE

HOME

FROM

TO

TYPE (3-set)

LINK

tumbler line

LITERARY 4/47 MACHINES

THE ONE-SIDED LINK (e.g., paragraph)

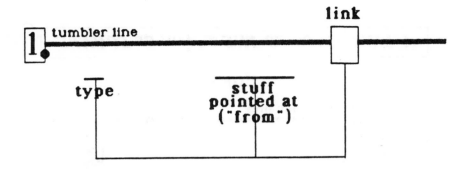

8. THE ONE-SIDED LINK

An important link type has only one side: it is matter being pointed to, but not by other matter. A paragraph designator is an example. For this we use the *one-sided link*.

Unfortunate terminological problem: since it has only one side, we use the first endset to designate the matter pointed at. To call this "from" is inane.*

---

*TERMINOLOGICAL PROBLEMS

Because of the generalized mechanism, the terms "from" and "to" seem to have become unnecessary anchors. Another confusion arises from the fact that a *one*-sided link has two endsets and a *two*-sided link has *three* endsets.

We hope to clean up these terminological matters soon.

If it has:	Link is:	But also:
three-set only	no-sided	monadic
three-set and "from-set"	one-sided	dyadic
three-set, from-set, two-set	two-sided	triadic

LITERARY 4/48 MACHINES

LINKS TO LINKS

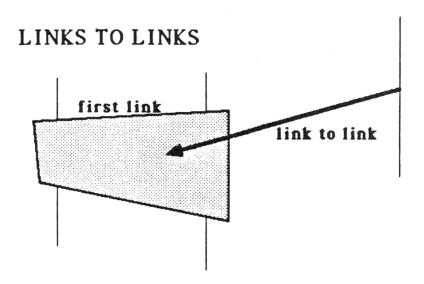

9. POINTERS TO LINKS

Because of the universality of tumbler-space, and the fact that links are located there as well as data, it becomes easy for a link to point at another link (or, indeed, to point at several).

The to-set of the link need simply point to the actual link address in the tumbler line, with a span of 1 to designate that unit only.

LITERARY 4/49 MACHINES

HOW A LINK-TO-LINK WORKS

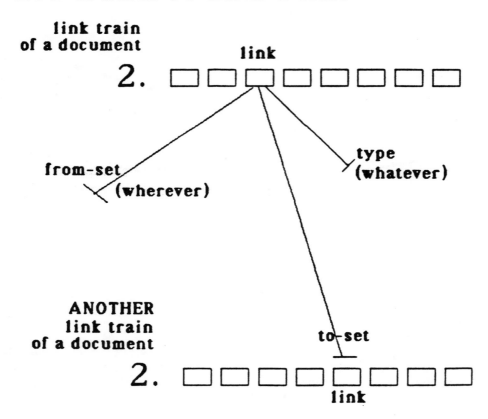

LITERARY 4/50 MACHINES

10. COMPOUND LINKS

Complex relational structures, such as the faceted link (discussed in Chapter 2), may be constructed with links to links. These use the two-sided link structure much like the CONS cell in LISP, and may be built into arbitrary compound links.

Note that this mechanism can be used for hierarchical link types, subtypes and supertypes. It is searchable for upper- and under-links, and all final data matter below; as well as for many other compound structures.

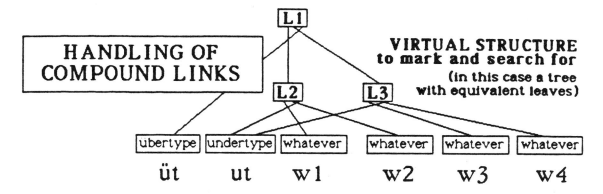

HANDLING OF COMPOUND LINKS

VIRTUAL STRUCTURE to mark and search for
(in this case a tree with equivalent leaves)

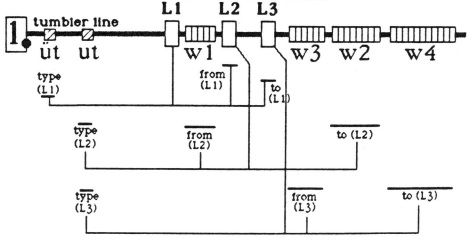

SAME STRUCTURE MAPPED TO TUMBLER-SPACE:

LITERARY 4/51 MACHINES

LINK ASSIGNMENT: THE MAPPING

Given this wealth of mechanism, an immense variety of links can be created; the generality is both disconcerting and exasperating. The problem is to map exactly those structures which are needed. This is a new paradigm: not just a system of mechanisms, but a way of thinking.

STANDARDS ISSUES

Because of this richness and complexity, we have not yet settled certain standards issues of the docuverse; especially, standardizing on a set of user link types.

The way to think of standardization is as an n-person game, among 1) those individuals and parts of our minds who want to do things in differing ways, for various reasons, 2) those who recognize a common interest in standardization, and 3) those who simply want to be understood.

An administrative problem is how to establish those link types which are most needed and distribute them to the user community. Presumably a canonical base set (with documentation) will migrate to user servers, though others may inhabit the docuverse anywhere.

Another standards issue: eventually we want to standardize links as a common data method for the incoming archival conversion of all data structures. But this is not, for obvious reasons, the first thing to be done.

Standardization of a working set of link types is now a high priority, but has less priority than getting up a robust demonstration node.

A TENTATIVE LISTING OF SOME LINK TYPES

Link types are open-ended, so this is the merest beginning. *This listing is provisional, to give the flavor of current thinking.*

METALINKS

These are links expected to apply to whole documents, whether from outside or from inside.

Title
Author
While the title and the author's name ordinarily reside inside a document (though not necessarily at the beginning), the "author" and "title" links will normally go from the author's name and the principal appearance of the title to the whole document.*

Document Supersession Link
This link indicates that one document or version supersedes another. It is the

---

*Note that the Author link can also be used from outside a document to claim that the author is *really someone else*.

canonical way to find out whether you are reading the latest version. A front-end request for supersession links is normally expected before starting to read a new document.

ORDINARY TEXT LINKS
(for sequential documents)

Correction Link
A correction may be supplied by anyone to anything by means of a *correction link*. This saves making a whole new alternative version.

Comment Link
This will be a connection between a set of material and a comment on that set of material, whether in the same document, a comment document or elsewhere.

Counterpart Link
The counterpart link shows that there are correspondences between two equivalent documents, sections or passages. (This has also been called a *collateral* or *correspondence* link. Note that a counterpart link will typically have a comment attached to it.

Translation Link
This will indicate that a document (or part of a document) has been translated. A second parameter in the type will indicate the language or dialect.

Heading Link
This is an internal heading or subtitle within the document. The front end will look for these for ordinary text formatting or outline browsing.

Paragraph Link
A paragraph link is a one-sided link which points at a whole paragraph. (Note that the front end must update the paragraph link whenever the paragraph is edited.*)

Note that the "paragraph" link type may be further qualified for different purposes by including a second parameter in the link-set after the initial address for plain paragraph.

The Quote-Link
A quotation is a piece of material which is a part of a document, yet which is *acknowledged* as having its origin elsewhere. This acknowledgment is a quote-link, showing the connection to the original and providing a bridge by which the user's front end may leap to the original.

Note that a quote-link is not the same as an *inclusion*, which is not ordinarily

---

*It would be possible to have instead a *beginning-of-paragraph* link, pointing only to the first character, but this would also have to be updated--whenever there were editorial changes at the beginning of the paragraph. Pointing at the whole paragraph makes more sense.

LITERARY 4/53 MACHINES

indicated to the user. While a front end may readily ask which portions of a document are inclusions, inclusions are not ordinarily flagged or shown unless a user requests it.

QUOTE-LINK

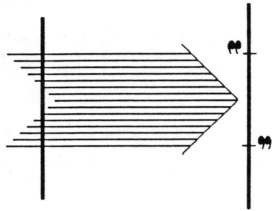

Since a quote-link indicates the author's acknowledgment of the origin of a piece of quoted material, the quote link becomes a form of meta-punctuation. Thus the quote-link is essentially an *annotation* of an inclusion.

Layout, Typography, Epigraphy Links
Pourable prose is not the only kind of text. Some kinds have significant layouts and typography on paper; the ability to specify layouts and typography for screens will also be important. Such layout instructions will be handled by layout links. However, as with all Xanadu usage, these layouts and arrangements may only be *recommendations*, and users will not be restricted to them in any way.

Footnote Link
The footnote link provides a break from sequence for an author not electing to use fuller hypertext structures.

HYPERTEXT LINKS

By "hypertext links' we mean links to make any possible arrangements for explorable materials. The possible types are legion.

Vanilla Jump-Link
This is a plain link from one place to another. The user may use it to follow a line of thought; then, as a front-end function, the user may jump back when satisfied.

Modal Jump-Links
These are jump-links which are distinguished in some way as to type.

Suggested-Threading Links
These are chainable links which propose a pathway through a corpus of material.

Expansion Links
These propose the expansion of text or graphics to another version or view.

The many possible forms and uses of hypertext will have to be explored elsewhere.

LITERARY LINKS

The literary links are those which extend beyond the sequential document into a universe of documents.

Citation Link

Like a footnote referring to a source, the citation link provides a jump or bridge to that source itself.

Alternative-Version Link

This informs the reader of a document that there is an alternative version. (Asking if there is such a link is a front-end function.)

Comment Document

This is a document commenting on another document.

Certification Links

These are links which certify and authenticate stored material. They may be applied to alternative versions proposed by the certifier or certifying agency.

Mail Link

"Mail" is material addressed to a user through a mail link. It is not *sent*, but merely lives where it is first put. The mail link connects any document to the user's space in an orderly fashion. Since links will be dated, the time of mailing is shown. The user "opens the mailbox" with a front-end request for items with a mail link more recent than the material already seen.

DISPLAY AND FRONT-END INSTRUCTIONS AND CONVENTIONS

It is desirable for documents to carry information on how to show and manipulate them--that is, general information for the front-end designer.

Instructions to front ends for display and manipulation may be in the form of text explanations or programs (in whatever language). Within the spirit of Xanadu linkage, this information should be carried as a link to the document; how is undecided.

REQUESTS

The fundamental operation of the Xanadu system is the *request*, usually a request for links (or their attached contents) fulfilling certain criteria. These criteria can become remarkably complex. The system is designed so that you can ask for certain types of links, and those pointing to and from certain places, with total flexibility.

Requests to the Xanadu system are made by programs in the user's front end through the FEBE protocol (see "The Protocols of Xanadu," a Chapter 4).

Consider a typical command, the one for finding the number of links of a certain type. The command (called for obscure reasons FINDNUMOFLINKSTOTHREE) requires four endsets:

the *home-set*, those spans of the

LITERARY 4/55 MACHINES

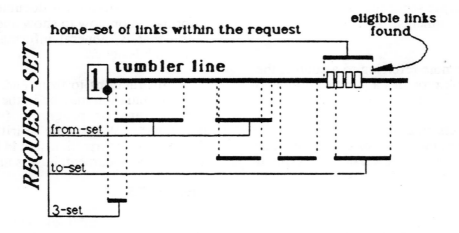

A REQUEST MAPS TO THE TUMBLER LINE

docuverse in which desired links are to be found;

the *from-set*, those spans of the docuverse wanted at the first side of the links;

the *to-set*, those spans of the docuverse wanted at the second side of the link;

the *three-set*, spans covering the *types* of link that are wanted in the request.

Taken all together, these are the *request-set* of the command.

It is instructive to note how a request-set maps to the tumbler line.

Another visualization uses the Tumbler Square.

LITERARY 4/56 MACHINES

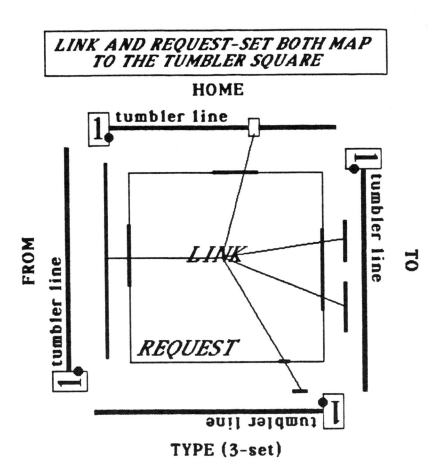

LINK AND REQUEST-SET BOTH MAP TO THE TUMBLER SQUARE

HOME

tumbler line

LINK

REQUEST

FROM

tumbler line

TO

tumbler line

tumbler line

TYPE (3-set)

LITERARY 4/57 MACHINES

SATISFACTION OF A REQUEST: A SYMMETRICAL METHOD

Why we generalized link type to three-set becomes clear when we see what the search mechanism does with it.

A link satisfies a search request if part of each type of endset satisfies a corresponding part of the request. To score as a hit, a link must satisfy *each* type of element of the request-set--HOME-SET, FROM-SET, TO-SET, THREE-SET.

The fundamental retrieval function:
The AND of the ORs

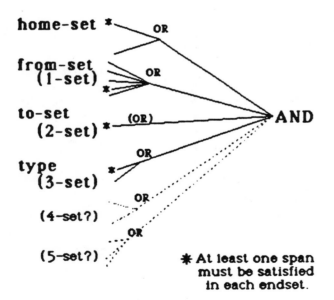

home-set *
from-set (1-set) *
to-set (2-set) *
type (3-set) *
(4-set?)
(5-set?)

OR
OR
(OR)
OR
OR
OR

AND

* At least one span
must be satisfied
in each endset.

(A link satisfies a request's home-set if its home, or one of its homes, is within the spans defining the home-set in the request.)

We may visualize request satisfaction as a Boolean function, the AND of ORs.

A target link must satisfy one span of a home-set OR another span of the home-set; one span of the from-set OR another; one OR another of the to-set; and one OR another of the three-set. In this fashion it must satisfy the home-set AND the from-set AND the to-set AND the three-set.

This overall method is powerful for many applications. It can find all the links *from* a given document, all the links *to* a given document, all the links of a given type, and so on.

GENERALIZATION TO ADDITIONAL ENDSETS

Because of the power of this method, possible extensions to additional endsets (4-set, 5-set...) have been considered. However, these will not be implemented until a clear use is known for such structures.

ANDing THE LINKS

It would be very nice if we could send a request to the back end for the AND of links, as in, "Show me all the material linked to by both an A link *and* a B link." (This is one of the ways to create a closed-world restricted context.)

LITERARY 4/58 MACHINES

ANDing THE LINKS
-- a front-end function

The back end does not support this and probably never can, for combinatorial reasons. However, *this can be handled in the front end.* If the front end can perform its own ANDing of request sets, the same effect can be obtained. (Hint: this foists the combinatorial difficulties into the user's resource-space.)

THE SEARCH MODEL IN THE BACK END

The way a user request is processed by the Xanadu back end is as follows.

The back end receives a command with a collection of request sets, and creates a large tumbler expression which then becomes the search model.

This expression is bound to the user's request and presented to the internal algorithms, which operate on the internal Xanadu data structures and yield the output address lists delivered by the typical command.*

*In later versions of the storage system, we expect the back end to combine the search models of different users to create a barrel-roll shared search model which repeatedly crosses the address space on behalf of all a server's users simultaneously, thus greatly improving performance over the pipelined successive-user search methods in the prototype.)

THE COST OF SEARCHES

Because of our unusual algorithms, link-search is deemed to be "free," and a great variety of searches may be performed with what we expect to be tolerable overhead.

THE QUANTITY OF LINKS NOT SATISFYING A REQUEST DOES NOT IN PRINCIPLE IMPEDE SEARCH ON OTHERS. That is, we anticipate soft-corridor expansion behavior (degradation between logarithmic and square root, as described in "The Only Way It Could Work," a Chapter 4); and thus it should be possible to navigate without obstruction *in a universe dense with junk.*

Thus the sophisticated user (or the sophisticated front end) will make link searches based on some fairly complicated link-filtering functions. So that, in principle, you can sift all the links to create and inhabit subworlds that only deal with parts of the docuverse.*

THE JUNK-LINK PROBLEM

Clearly, filtering out junk links in a universe full of them is a vital aspect of system performance. Note especially the use of the *home-set* in junk filtering functions. Control of incoming links by their *origin* is a key to eliminating garbage.

LINK FILTERS

Filtering links is a key aspect of front-end design. This is a separate study in itself.

---

*THE RESOURCE UNIT

However, clever users can ask for the moon and stars simultaneously. While early versions of the system will merely fetch what is asked for on a simple queuing basis, more sophisticated service algorithms will have to ration resources.

The Resource Unit (RU) then becomes a basic internal unit of software accounting, dividing the system's effort on your behalf. A standard customer gets one RU. (Priority customers might get more service by paying more.)

If the user's front end sends for an object, the search for it proceeds with a force of one RU. If two entities are called for simultaneously, each gets 1/2 RU and so on. RUs are divided as requests fan out.

It is easy to see why this is necessary. The request fanout can easily become astronomical, which is *all right;* the problem is to find an orderly basis for servicing MIRVed searches (Multiple Independent Reading Virtuality). The divisible Resource Unit keeps the overall Systems Effort equal to unity rather than inflating in combinatorial explosion.

LITERARY 4/60 MACHINES

THE PROTOCOLS OF XANADU

In computer parlance, "protocol" refers to the formal rules for interchange in some sort of communication system. The protocols of Xanadu are called FEBE and BEBE; there are also additional complications of various sorts.

Note that none of these commands are to be seen by the user. The user's concerns are to be seen on the screen; the complications of the protocol are to be handled invisibly by programs in the user's front-end machine, leaving the user free to think about other things.

Some of the commands as presently defined will obviously return avalanches of material. Further refinement of the protocol will specify handshaking methods for controlling this.

1. THE FEBE PROTOCOL

What the Xanadu storage and hypertext system does--and thus *is*--is defined by the commands to which it responds. These commands make up its user protocol, FEBE (Front End-Back End language).

The FEBE protocol is concerned mostly with the addresses necessary to find text and links and to follow them: of the 17 current commands in XU.87.1, only one command (RETRIEVEV) is concerned with delivery of the actual content fragments.

(Note: before proceeding further, the user should be familiar with the structure of links; see the Chapter 4 of that name.)

FEBE includes instructions for insertion in a document, deletion from a document, and rearrangements of unlimited size. These are comparatively simple.

However, the commands for links and commonality (material shared between documents and versions) are more esoteric, particularly since they have been generalized for the interconnection of broken lists of data.

FEBE commands are presently in verbose ASCII. They will be shortened eventually.

Here are some examples (given in simplified form for initial study). Note that the curious names have to do with the internal documentation. (There will be a formal presentation in full Backus-Naur form a little further on.)

FEBE SAMPLES IN SIMPLIFIED FORM

DELETEVSPAN (doc, span)
   deletes the span.

LITERARY 4/61 MACHINES

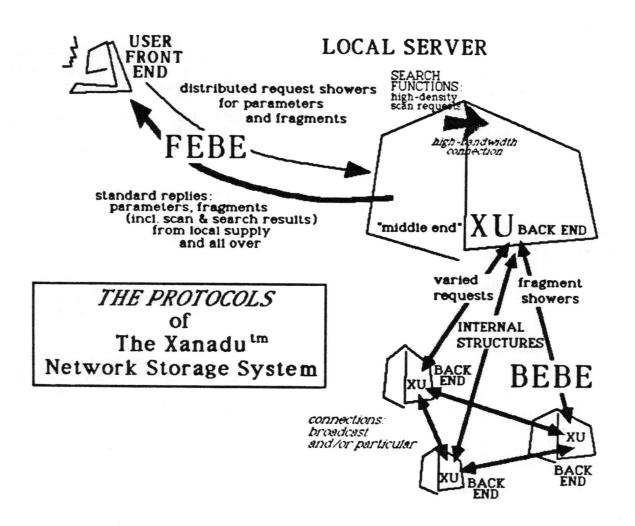

USER
FRONT
END

LOCAL SERVER

distributed request showers
for parameters
and fragments

SEARCH
FUNCTIONS:
high-density
scan requests

*high-bandwidth
connection*

FEBE

standard replies:
parameters, fragments
(incl. scan & search results)
from local supply
and all over

"middle end" XU BACK END

THE PROTOCOLS
of
The Xanadu ᵗᵐ
Network Storage System

varied
requests

fragment
showers

INTERNAL
STRUCTURES

BEBE

XU BACK
END

*connections:
broadcast
and/or particular*

XU BACK
END

XU
BACK
END

LITERARY 4/62 MACHINES

MAKELINK (doc, from-spanset, to-spanset, type)

The document must be specified because that determines the actual residence of the link--since a document may contain a link between two other documents.

FINDNUMFOFLINKSTOTHREE (home-set, from-set, to-set, type)

This returns the number of links of the specified type between the from-set and the to-set residing in the home-set.

If the home-set is the whole docuverse, the total number of all links is returned.

FINDLINKSFROMTOTHREE (home-set, from-set, to-set, type set)

This is the most powerful command. It finds all the links of the specified types connecting any bytes of the from-set to the to-set, provided that those links reside in the home-set.

If the home-set is the whole docuverse, all links between these two elements are returned.

FINDDOCSCONTAINING (spans)

This returns a list of all documents containing any of the material specified by the span addresses, regardless of where the native copies are located.

If you understand these examples, you are ready to look at the whole protocol. (Note that "type" is hereafter referred to as "three-set.")

FEBE 87.1 PROTOCOL IN BACKUS-NAUR FORM
(c) 1980, 1984, 1986, 1987 XOC, Inc.

The following is not guaranteed to be current; possible users should consult Project Xanadu or XOC, Inc.

This describes the current Xanadu front-end/ back-end interface language. It is in the form of a BNF for the language with annotations describing what the various pieces are for.

LITERARY 4/63 MACHINES

Formats for information exchanged between the back end and the front end:

<wdelim>   ::= '\n'

The newline character is used throughout the protocol as a general purpose delimiter.

Tumblers:

<tumbler>   ::= <texp> <tumblerdigit>* <wdelim>
<texp>   ::= <integer>
<tumblerdigit> ::= <tdelim> <integer>
<tdelim>   ::= '.'

Tumblers are denoted by period- separated strings of integers.

Addresses:

<doc id>   ::= <tumbler>
<doc-set>   ::= <ndocs> <doc id>*
<link id>   ::= <tumbler>
<doc vsa>   ::= <tumbler>
<span-set>   ::= <nspans> *
          ::= <tumbler> <tumbler>
<spec-set>   ::= <nspecs> <spec>*
<spec>   := { 's' <wdelim> } | { 'v' <wdelim> <vspec> }
                   /* v for vspec, s for span */
<vspec-set>   ::= <nvspecs> <vspec>*
<vspec>   ::= <doc id> <vspan-set>
<vspan-set>   ::= <nspans> <vspan>*
<vspan>   ::=
<ndocs>   ::= <integer> <wdelim>
<nspecs>   ::= <integer> <wdelim>
<nvspecs>   ::= <integer> <wdelim>
<nspans>   ::= <integer> <wdelim>

Addresses come in various flavors. A <doc id> is the V-stream

LITERARY 4/64 MACHINES

address of a document . A <link id> is the address of an atom which happens to be a link. A <doc vsa> is the address of an atom inside some document. A indicates a range of addresses and is denoted by a starting address tumbler and a length tumbler. <doc-set>s, <span-set>s, <spec>s, <spec-set>s, <vspec>s, <vspec-set>s, and <vspan>s are various sorts of collections of all of these.

Stuff:

```
<vstuffset>      ::= <nthings> <vthing>*
<vthing>         ::= <text> | <link id>
<text-set>       ::= <ntexts> <text>*
<ntexts>         ::= <integer> <wdelim>
<text>           ::= <textflag> <nchars> <char>* <wdelim>
<textflag>       ::= 't'
<nchars>         ::= <integer> <wdelim>
<nthings>        ::= <integer> <wdelim>
```

"Stuff" is the generic term for the various sorts of things that can be found in a document: data ("text") and links.

Link stuff:

```
<from-set>    ::= <spec-set>
<to-set>      ::= <spec-set>
<home-set>    ::= <spec-set>
<link-set>    ::= <nlinks> <link id>*
<nlinks>      ::= <integer> <wdelim>
```

Links are generally talked about in terms of their end-sets.

Calls to the back end:

```
CREATENEWDOCUMENT   ::=   <createdocrequest>

                    returns   <createdocrequest> <doc id>

<createdocrequest>      ::= '11' <wdelim>
```

LITERARY 4/65 MACHINES

This creates an empty document. It returns the id of the new document.

CREATENEWVERSION ::= <createversionrequest> <doc id>

               returns <createversionrequest> <doc id>

<createversionrequest> ::= '13' <wdelim>

This creates a new document with the contents of document <doc id>. It returns the id of the new document. The new document's id will indicate its ancestry.

INSERT   ::= <insertrequest> <doc id> <doc vsa> <text set>

         returns <insertrequest>

<insertrequest>::= '0' <wdelim>

This inserts <text set> in document <doc id> at <doc vsa>. The v-stream addresses of any following characters in the document are increased by the length of the inserted text.

DELETEVSPAN   ::= <deleterequest> <doc id>

          returns <deleterequest>

<deleterequest> ::= '12' <wdelim>

This removes the given span from the given document.

REARRANGE   ::= <rearrangerequest> <doc id> <cut set>

         returns <rearrangerequest>

LITERARY 4/66 MACHINES

```
<rearrangerequest>      ::=  '3' <wdelim>
<cut set>               ::=  <ncuts> <doc vsa>*
<ncuts>                 ::=  <integer> <wdelim>
                             /* ncuts = 3 or 4 */
```

The <cut set> consists of three or four v-addresses within the specified document. Rearrange transposes two regions of text. With three cuts, the two regions are from cut 1 to cut 2, and from cut 2 to cut 3, assuming cut 1 < cut 2 < cut 3. With four cuts, the regions are from cut 1 to cut 2, and from cut 3 to cut 4, here assuming cut 1 < cut 2 and cut 3 < cut 4.

```
COPY         ::=  <copyrequest> <doc id> <doc vsa> <spec set>

        returns  <copyrequest>

<copyrequest> ::= '2' <wdelim>
```

The material determined by <spec set> is copied to the document determined by <doc id> at the address determined by <doc vsa>.

```
APPEND          ::=  <appendrequest> <text set> <doc id>

        returns  <appendrequest>

<appendrequest>  ::=  '19' <wdelim>
```

This appends <text set> onto the end of the text space of the document <doc id>.

```
RETRIEVEV       ::=  <retrieverequest> <spec set>

        returns  <retrieverequest> <vstuffset>

<retrieverequest> ::=  '5' <wdelim>
```

This returns the material (text and links) determined by <spec set>.

LITERARY 4/67 MACHINES

```
RETRIEVEDOCVSPAN          ::=  <docvspanrequest> <doc id>

                          returns <docvspanrequest> <vspan>

<docvspanrequest>         ::=  '14' <wdelim>
```

This returns a span determining the origin and extent of the V-stream of document <doc id>.

```
RETRIEVEDOCVSPANSET  ::=  <docvspansetrequest> <doc id>

                     returns <docvspansetrequest> <vspanset>

<docvspansetrequest>      ::=  '1' <wdelim>
<vspanset>                ::=  <nspans> <vspan>*
```

This returns a span-set indicating both the number of characters of text and the number of links in document <doc id>.

```
MAKELINK             ::=  <makelinkrequest> <doc id> <doc vsa>

                          <from set> <to set> <three set>

                     returns <makelinkrequest> <link id>

<makelinkrequest>    ::=  '4' <wdelim>
```

This creates a link in document <doc id> from <from set> to <to set> connected to<three set>. It returns the id of the link made.

```
FINDLINKSFROMTOTHREE :=  <linksrequest> <home set>
                         <from set> <to set> <three set>

                     returns <linksrequest> <link set>

<linksrequest>            ::=  '7' <wdelim>
```

LITERARY 4/68 MACHINES

This returns a list of all links which are (1) in <home set>, (2) from all or any part of <from set>, and (3) to all or any part of <to set> and <three set>.

```
FINDNUMOFLINKSFROMTOTHREE   ::=  <nlinksrequest> <home set>
                                 <from set> <to set> <three set>

                            returns  <nlinksrequest> <nlinks>

<nlinksrequest>                  ::= '6' <wdelim>
```

This returns the number of links which are (1) in <home set>, (2) from all or any part of <from set>, and (3) to all or any part of <to set> and <three set>.

```
FINDNEXTNLINKSFROMTOTHREE   ::=  <nextnlinksrequest>
                                 <from set> <to set> <three set>
                                 <home set> <link id> <nlinks>

                            returns  <nextnlinksrequest> <linkset>

<nextnlinksrequest>              ::= '8' <wdelim>
```

This returns a list of all links which are (1) in the list determined by <from set>, <to set>, <three set>, and <home set> as in FINDLINKSFROMTOTHREE, (2) past the link given by <link id> on that list and, (3) no more than <nlinks> items past that link on that list.

```
RETRIEVEENDSET            ::=  <retrieveendsetsrequest> <spec set>

                          returns  <retrieveendsetsrequest>
                                   <from spec set> <to spec set>

<retrieveendsetsrequest>  ::=  '26' <wdelim>
<from spec set>           ::=  <spec set>
<to spec set>             ::=  <spec set>
```

LITERARY 4/69 MACHINES

This returns a list of all link end-sets that are in <spec set>.

SHOWRELATIONOF2VERSIONS ::= <showrelationrequest>
                            <spec set> <spec set>

                    returns <showrelationrequest>
                             <correspondence list>

<showrelationrequest>   ::= '10' <wdelim>
<correspondence list>   ::= <ncorresponences> <correspondence>*
<corresponence>   ::= <doc vsa> <doc vsa> <tumbler>
<ncorrespondences>   ::= <integer> <wdelim>

This returns a list of ordered pairs of the spans of the two spec-sets that correspond.

FINDDOCSCONTAINING   ::= <docscontainingrequest> <vspec set>

                    returns <docscontainingrequest> <doc set>

<docscontainingrequest>   ::= '22' <wdelim>

This returns a list of all documents containing any portion of the material included by <vspec set>.

THE BEBE PROTOCOL

BEBE (Back End-Back End) is the protocol for connecting nodes of the Xanadu network. It is still undergoing definition and will not be made public anytime soon. The BEBE protocol will use the back end's internal codes, structures and forms of numeration, which are presently proprietary.

The function of BEBE is to meld the contents of separate Xanadu servers into a single unified space. This is done basically in two ways.

A. THE FORWARDING SYSTEM

First, by the forwarding of requests as they fan out from users to servers able to

LITERARY 4/70 MACHINES

supply; and the pass-through of material that is returned to the requesting user in reply.

B. SUPREPRESENTATIONS AND CO-MODELLING

Material is moved between servers for a number of purposes:

1. for more rapid access to final material;

2. for more rapid access to needed material which indexes material on other servers;

3. for rebalance in keeping with demand;

4. for redundancy and backup purposes.

The method we plan to use is unusual.

SUBREPRESENTATION OF THE DOCUVERSE IN EACH NODE

Each server contains a map and a subset of the whole -- a microcosm that shrinks and grows.

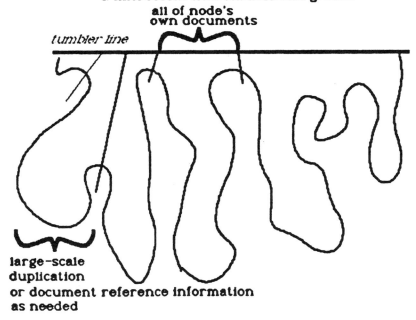

all of node's own documents

tumbler line

large-scale duplication or document reference information as needed

LITERARY 4/71 MACHINES

Each server contains a continuously valid model or subrepresentation of the entire docuverse and (because of tumbler addressing) a model of the entire network.

This model is maintained by copying selected portions of the data and internal structures between servers. Each server has a map, with samples, of the whole. Thus the different servers *model each other,* each assimilating material from the others as needed.

A server's network model, from the null case on up, is at all times unified and operational; whatever information moves between servers is assimilated at once to its overall structure, leaving each server in canonical operating condition with a slightly improved map of what is elsewhere. The contents can slosh back and forth dynamically.

Any resemblance to the Vulcanian mind-meld is intentional.

THE SEARCH PROBLEM AND MIDDLE-END FUNCTIONS

Many people, particularly those who are accustomed to the scanning model of text systems, have a hard time getting used to our link model, and insist that scanning should be part of the Xanadu back end.

We agree that scanning functions are necessary, but have a different place to put them.

Scanning functions are potentially very complex: for instance, the more sophisticated scanning functions employ conditionals and wild-card markers and ranges of conditional closeness. There is essentially no limit to the complexity of possible searches and scans.

Putting these in the Xanadu back end would only lead to trouble, considering that the maintenance of the existing data structures is already extremely complex. Moreover, managing complex searches all the way from the front end would use a great deal of channel capacity for their interchanges.

However, we agree that these functions are necessary, and so plan to add (after the back end functions are rugged and sufficient) a module which we call the *middle end.* In the single-user version this will be a software module, in the network version it may be another machine.

This middle end will parse user commands, and pass through directly the standard FEBE commands. Scanning and search commands (not presently determined) will be executed in the middle end, allowing for high-speed interchange with the back end, and not tying up communication lines.

Back-comparison, version comparison. Another function especially suited to middle-end implementation is the intercomparison of versions. To best prepare materials for Xanadu storage that were not created on the Xanadu system itself, to chart substantial commonalities between different versions and to allow for the later detailed intercomparison of their alternative versions, the keyed-in versions need to be compared for suitable compression to our unique storage. This can be an algorithmic process and is best suited to the middle end.

LITERARY 4/73 MACHINES

HOW THE NETWORK WORKS

How much work
would a network work
if a network would work nets?

The planned Xanadu network has two types of connections: the connections of individual users to storage nodes, or servers; and the connections *between and among* servers.

These two connections are quite different.

CONNECTION TO USERS

Connection to the users is through whatever convenient channel (telephone, local-area network, laser, fiber-optic, etc.) using standard ASCII at whatever transmission rate is convenient.

Users' workstations communicate to a Xanadu server through the FEBE protocol (discussed in "The Protocols of Xanadu," a Chapter 4).

THE REQUEST TRAIN AND ITS FAN-OUT

As required to refresh the screen or pursue whatever work is underway, the user's workstation requests a series of document fragments. These requests go into the user's local server and then, retransmitted by the user's local server, fan out to those

servers which can honor them. (Whether this is in broadcast mode or as specific requests to individual servers depends on various factors.)

RETURNING FRAGMENT SHOWERS

Inversely, the reply to a train of requests is a shower of returning fragments, funneled first into the user's local server and then retransmitted to the user's workstation.

While the return of these document fragments is actually the main consummation of the interchange, much of the interchange is concerned with numerical parameters of various sorts in answer to the many FEBE inquiries required to keep things going.

CONNECTION BETWEEN SERVERS

Connection between servers will be on high-bandwidth channels, such as satellite microwave. An entirely different protocol will be employed, which we call BEBE (Back End-Back End). The BEBE protocol is still undergoing definition.

The BEBE protocol consists of user requests forwarded between servers, and replies to them; and traffic concerned with

LITERARY 4/74 MACHINES

local subrepresentations of the network.

LOCAL SUBREPRESENTATIONS

Each server contains a partial map of the rest of the docuverse, in internal enfiladic forms. This map may be increased in any part of its resolution as required by network demand.

As demand for materials from certain parts of the network increases and decreases, that part becomes mapped in more and less detail in a given server. Thus much traffic is concerned with the moving of copies and subcopies between servers.

The distribution of subcopies will in many cases speed a reply to a user query, since the request can be serviced locally rather than from the home node of the fragment.

UNHEARD-FROM NODES

It is a truism that "computer networks are always broken." Meaning that on the average some nodes are disconnected or not working.

With this common-sense understanding, the network must have standard operating procedures to deal with such nonfunctional conditions. Thwarted requests will be forwarded to backup copies around the network, or, as a last resort, return a "not currently available" message.

LITERARY 4/75 MACHINES

NOTES ON FRONT ENDS

*Q. How many Xanadu people does it
take to change a lightbulb?*

A. None; that's a front-end function.

Front ends must do a great deal. The Xanadu group is prepared to maintain the part of the program for talking to the back end (the protocol-manager module), but that is only part of it. The front end must do a great deal more, as indicated throughout this book.

Furthermore, the front end must present *link-filtering functions* to the user and then to the back end.

People who program text systems are accustomed to doing certain things like maintaining textual data structures. Not so in the Xanadu system: the data structures are all maintained by the back-end server, following sequence and linkage information sent in

THE PARALLEL TEXTFACE^{tm}

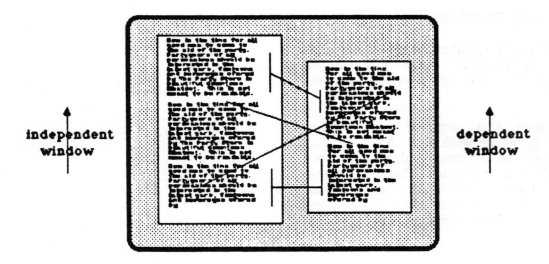

independent window

dependent window

LITERARY 4/76 MACHINES

from the front.

Thus the function of the front end is *presentation and manipulation*--showing the wealth of connections, or not showing it, according to the user's need.

Front ends may be done in any style. The popular pop-up windows, of the Xerox PARC school, are extremely limited in what they show easily. Another viewing paradigm is the Parallel Textface™, first presented in the book *Computer Lib*, where two texts can scroll side by side with links pointed out by dynamic lines displayed between them. (We may also call this *companionate scrolling*.)

In companionate scrolling, one window shows independent text, being scrolled by the user, and a *dependent* text

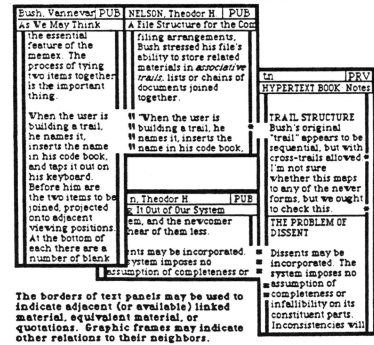

The QFRAME
A NO-NONSENSE SEMITILED
MULTIPANEL DISPLAY TECHNIQUE
for linked and related contents

The borders of text panels may be used to indicate adjacent (or available) linked material, equivalent material, or quotations. Graphic frames may indicate other relations to their neighbors.

LITERARY 4/77 MACHINES

which scrolls or breaks into sections derivatively.

For today's screen displays, I suggest a style of linkage and display that employs *connections between* windows to show connectivity and linkage.

Unlike the standard PARC (or "pop-up") windows, they are connected *at their boundaries* to other frames. I call such windows Qframes, because the frames themselves incorporate cues for understanding the connections of material inside the frame to materials outside.

These may also be used to show companionate scrolling, but they do not require the maintenance of a lot of diagonal lines on the screen.

THE CURRENT VERSION:
IMPLEMENTATION 87.1

In the current version, XU.87.1, the following aspects of our designs are not yet implemented. (Most are explained in various Chapters Four.) It may be several years before they are all in.

Settled conventions of major link types.

Private documents. (Currently all documents are visible to all users.)

Editable and rearrangeable links.

Time-coding on bytes, and sieving of links by time.

Provision for linkable data structures of other types: graphics (other than as byte streams)--bit maps, wire frames, 3D objects. Other forms of addressing: provision for movie frames, video frames, video scan-lines, music, sound tracks, persons, places, things, DNA, etc.

Accounting and royalty.

Front-end display instructions to be attached to documents.

Certain obvious FEBE extensions, for which full information is already available at the back end:

SHOW ORIGIN/HOME DOCUMENT OF SPAN

SHOW DELETIONS

SHOW A DOCUMENT'S ORIGINAL INPUT IN CHRONOLOGICAL ORDER

Search resource units as a method of rationing user demands.

Historical backtrack and its corresponding FEBE extensions.

4-sets, 5-sets ... n-sets supported in link storage and search.

Middle-end search and scanning functions.

Multiple-server methods and the BEBE protocol (still undergoing definition).

LITERARY 4/79 MACHINES

CHAPTERS FIVE

LITERARY 5/1 MACHINES

DEVELOPMENT PLAN

(This section was called BUSINESS PLAN in earlier and quite different versions, but it was never like a conventional business plan, so the title is changed somewhat.)

Our position is anomalous. We have managed to reach the prototype stage of a very big project with no outside capital. We would *like* backing, but all the potential backers so far have wanted the system to be something *else*, which did not provide much basis for discussion. The system is what it is.

We are especially interested in finding development partners who have need of our storage, linkage and retrieval methods. We are prepared to supply the back end for experimental purposes to interested firms at a negotiable price. A non-disclosure agreement is required.

IMMEDIATE APPLICATIONS

Among the immediate technical applications of the Xanadu system are:

Write-Once Memory Management

The cross-indexing of large document bases (esp. legal)

Technical documentation of very large engineering projects

Boilerplate text management in large-scale text applications

Version management in large bases of multi-version computer programs

Use as a document server for office local-area networks.

NEXT DEVELOPMENT STEPS

1. BACK END

The prototype is now at the end of a telephone; our immediate goal is to make this robust and add various key features. (Listed in "The Current Version," a Chapter 4.)

Performance figures are presently without meaning; the system will be slow for some time because speeding up the system comes later. The clean implementation of the basic package of features has first priority.

2. FRONT ENDS

Simple front ends are under development for the Macintosh, Amiga and PC. However, we presently wish to avoid the front-end business, and invite developers to produce application software for any purposes on the Xanadu system. We are pursuing discussions with several interested companies.

LITERARY 5/2 MACHINES

We are prepared to supply application and front-end developers with the source code for the resident protocol manager. Support, of course, costs extra.

3. THE PERSONAL MARKET

We are looking to supply a version of the Xanadu back end to the personal market, running on the Macintosh family with a megabyte or more, in 1988 or '89. We expect there to be front ends from other vendors by that time.

TOWARD THE LICENSABLE PACKAGE

The ruggedized back-end program needs more added to make it the licensable public-access utility. Royalty accounting and numerous other features must be added. However, it is probably only about two man-years further along than the single-user back end.

REAL SPEEDUP

The system will not be fast to begin with, but it should get faster from software improvement even as it gets larger. At a later time, parallel hardware in the servers (such as Transputer clusters) can be used to crank things up still further. Network distance (in various metrics) will always be a speed limit, but we can expect available network transmission facilities to improve for some time to come.

TOP-DOWN MARKETING

We believe we have a large constituency waiting on this product with a sense of immediacy. This represents, at the outset, the elite of knowledge workers--high hackerdom and scientists who recognize their own information control needs and will understand at once the potential of xanalogical storage and delivery for their programs, research notes, electronic mail, etc. We expect servicing this potential user base, at the apex of the user pyramid, to take all our effort for some time.

CREDIBILITY

In some ways our public relations have been too good: the long-term plan has seemed quixotic and fanciful, and people have not bothered to find out the actual structure of what we are building.

However, now that the hypertext concept has gotten widespread acceptance and hypertext products are doing well on the market, people are taking another look at the Xanadu system to find out what makes the Xanadu system different from other hypertext products.

LITERARY 5/3 MACHINES

THE TRADEMARKS

The following are the trade and service marks of the system described in this book, by which we distinguish our information services and products from others.

Note that our principal product is herewith offered in interstate commerce (though not for the first time): the Back-End Code Module is presently available to businesses and research institutions for a negotiable price under non-disclosure agreement.

GENERICS

Every trademark needs to refer to a non-trademarked description, as in "Mc-Donald's *hamburger restaurants*."

Just as Xerox faced a problem, when it brought out its first copier, as to the appropriate generic term (and came up with "xerography"), our generic product descriptions include the following:

computer program
computer system
hypertext system
electronic literary system
electronic literature
storage manager
network storage manager
write-once memory manager
distributed storage system
hypertext server

hypermedia server
hypertext network
hypermedia network
hypernet
electronic publishing method
xanalogical storage

PRINCIPAL TRADEMARKS

"X A N A D U™" to denote all our information services and products.

"XU™" as an abbreviated form of "Xanadu."

XU.87.1™, XU.87.2™, ...XU.88.1™, ... XU.99.1™, ... XU.00.1™, etc. to designate different versions of the system in different years.

"Xanadu Stand™" and "Silver-Stand™" to denote the stations at which service will be provided.

FRONT-END DESIGNS

"Parallel Textface™"

"Qframe™"

"Xanadu FREND™" as an authorized and approved FRont-END program or console.

LITERARY 5/4 MACHINES

SLOGANS

"Lightning Literature™"
"The World of You™"
"The Wings of Mind™"
"Anything Instantly™"
"All Roads Lead to Xanadu™"
"You'll Want It All Later™"
"The Magic Place of Literary Memory™"
"The Living Web of Literature™"
"That Great Computer in the Sky™"
"True Hypertext™"
"Keepers of the Flame™"
"Hypertext Forever™"
"If the Links Are on the Bytes, It Gives You the World™"

CARTOON CHARACTERS

ROSEBUD™
PORLOCK™
XAN MAN™
XANIMALS™
The MARGINALIEN™
THE HOBGOBLIN OF LITTLE MINDS™.

MISCELLANEOUS TRADEMARKS AND SERVICE MARKS

"XANAMAIL^{sm}" to denote personal message services.

"XANACARE^{sm}" to denote arrangements for guaranteed long-term storage.

"XANADOODLE™" for computer graphic systems.

"HYPERCORPS^{sm}" for an advanced steward brigade.

THE SYMBOL

And finally that X-ternal device, The Eternal Flaming X in all its variants.

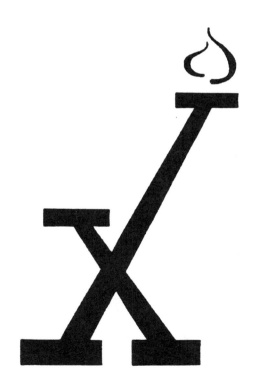

LITERARY 5/5 MACHINES

THE SILVERSTANDS™

The Xanadu hypertext network is a utility every person and company will need for their own purposes, and most usage will be from home or office, but the system also needs a community identity. This scenario is a marriage of Star Trek and McDonald's hamburger restaurants.

The Xanadu stations, or SilverStands, will be the local outposts of the network, parlors with a homey futuristic atmosphere, staffed by an attentive crew in perky uniforms. Besides being an actual storage and transmission depot, the SilverStand will serve as an induction and training office, a "drop-in center," a place for advertising, promotion, public relations, goodwill. Transactions occurring there will include the opening of accounts and the processing of publications.

Your local Xanadu stand is where you'll start your account and learn to use the system (even if you plan to be an at-home or office user). A cheery young person in futuristic garb will sit you down at a screen, and show you through an area of material of interest to *you*--text and/or pictures. Then, at the moment of Xanadu Shock, when you *get it*, when you cry "Holy ----!"--the kid grasps your forearm and says, "Mr. Jones, Welcome to Xanadu!"

The stand is the local port, what you dial up to from your home computer; it is where you sign publication chits and change your password.

You may hold business meetings there, or drop by to explore hyper-art while you have lunch. (You order food from your screen, and a Conductor (or "bystander") brings your food on a cart. Gracious.) The raucous, brainless atmosphere of the videogame parlor is not here. People typically come for an hour or more, relax and concentrate here, often in pairs.

There are no coin slots. Add-fare devices, like those in the D.C. Metro, recharge your use of the machines. Xanadu credit cards allow services to be charged.

The Xanadu Station is not impersonal; people stand face-to-face, without counters between. It is installed throughout with quality video monitors and doubleseats. You may rent a computer or bring in your own personal computer or what have you, with your own encoding devices embedded to taste.

There is a comparatively noisy social area near the front where the true Xanies hang out, with high-power flight-simulator-class equipment. Quieter carrels are to be found in the rest of the building.

THE BUILDINGS

The buildings are designed for expansion. The foundations are over-built;

LITERARY 5/6 MACHINES

the central area will be permanent; the rest will be built from a modular hexagonal building-kit system with furniture and monitors built into wall panels.

Looked at from above, the layout is an arrangement of hexagons; the building expands as a system of hexagonal vertical tubes, divided horizontally into carrels and roomettes. The outer angles of the castle-like exterior will therefore be pleatings. They will be faced with semisilvered twin glass, allowing external view without bringing in too much light. The building will expand simply by adding uprights and interchanging panels.

A geodesic dome, starting as a very small arc over the center, grows and is rearranged as the whole configuration expands. There is a large central room with a cone-shape of terraces under the dome, growing with it. On the terraces are café and lounge areas, as well as more and more screen areas. As the building grows with new palisades of hexagonal tubes, the cone of shared space grows in the center, under the growing dome.

Every stand has of course its main feeder machines (big Vaxen, Perkin-Elmers, RISCs, 68000 multiprocessors, or whatever is cost-effective at a given time). They may be visible through glass, starkly lit. But the disks and communication gear don't have to be seen, and are probably underground to save space.

OUTFITS

As at McDonald's, personnel wear crisp uniforms that change periodically. The motif is silver, but with other colors changing seasonally; there are a changing variety of tasteful accessories.

MISCELLANEOUS SERVICES

Printout, picture digitization, output to videotape, and many other I/O services are available.

THE HIGH PROFILE

For recognizability and access, Xanadu stands will be (among other places) in residential neighborhoods, near universities and theme parks, and along Interstates. While hours will presumably vary, round-the-clock accessibility to a diverse constituency will be an important criterion for location.

LITERARY 5/7 MACHINES

PRELIMINARY NOTES ON THE FRANCHISE

The licensing package for a Xanadu™ storage vendor will be a complete service and business system.

We foresee that the principal growth of the network will be through *franchised owner-operated neighborhood stands*, closely comparable to McDonald's hamburger restaurants. There will be licensing of nodes on other bases, but the Xanadu hypertext network will be created principally out of such franchised stands.*

What we hope to offer at the outset will be the opportunity to participate in an experiment, a preliminary arrangement to begin cash flow with demonstrable, feasible services.

FROM INITIAL SETUP TO FULL STAND

At the beginning only, we will offer provisional licenses to preliminary Xanadu stations with as few as eight modem lines.

---

*We are heartened by the number of prospective licensees who have talked to us, and we hope at some time soon to be able to write preliminary and experimental licenses for the public operation of the system, but we have at all times emphasized, and must continue to emphasize, the speculative character of these discussions.

We are instructed by legal counsel to emphasize that THIS IS NOT AN OFFER TO LICENSE XANADU STATIONS or in any way to franchise this system, nor is anyone prepared at the present time to undertake such an offer. Such an offer will be made only to qualified individuals showing financial and technical capability and a reasonable amount of business and technical sophistication, at such time as Xanadu back-end software appears ready for the purpose and we have taken appropriate legal steps. This is a speculative discussion of what may be a possible method for building the system, with the understanding that no guarantees can be made for this experimental software, and that our plans for the future growth of the system are speculative and impossible to verify except by building it.

No public-access electronic storage service has ever been offered before, except as an outgrowth of conventional time-sharing, and such a venture would be considered high-risk by any sane business person. There is no guarantee of any business whatever, of the feasibility of the plan, or even of salvage value for the equipment.

While we envision this as potentially a source of great income, there is no guarantee and no precedent for the business we envision. The following is preliminary, tentative, imaginative and fictitious, and presented only for the reader's intellectual stimulation.

LITERARY 5/8 MACHINES

The initial investment for early licensees will be quite low, on the order of $50,000 for computer equipment (plus other facilities as required). This is expected to cover an eight-line file server with disks and modems. In addition, there will be operating expenses for a location and telephone installation, as well as space, electricity, etc. As the system matures, however, the cost of a Xanadu stand will rise to approximately the cost of a McDonald's stand (about one million dollars exclusive of equipment).

The license will be offered on a basis quite like McDonald's: the licensee must be an individual of suitable character, knowledge and attitude, who presents a certain amount of capital. The licensee will be trained at Xanadu Central, and *must personally work in the Xanadu station.*

The licensee must be healthy and vigorous (age between 30 and 40 would seem appropriate), able to work long hours and cope with uncertain circumstances; with a clean credit rating; of sufficient means to be able to lose a substantial part of the investment if it doesn't work out.

The licensee must hire personnel and operate the business according to practices and standards developed by Xanadu Central.

There will be no territorial exclusive, but on an informal basis we will endeavor at the outset to distribute licenses geographically by area codes.

Preliminary spreadsheet estimates suggest a net income per franchise of about a thousand dollars a day within one year, assuming continual reinvestment of proceeds in storage, processors and lines as required by demand.

Licensee is required to maintain and upgrade equipment as appropriate to the volume of business. (This is one reason for the importance of a good credit rating.)

The preliminary stations will not be interconnected at first. However, since every part is a component of the anticipated system, the licensee is expected to make continual adaptations and upgrades as successive versions of our software and technical arrangements are fielded. When working interconnection methods become rugged, the licensee will be required to install appropriate high-bandwidth communication gear, including leased lines if necessary, to provide the connection between nodes necessary for the full Xanadu system.

Xanadu stands will evolve from relatively computerish and undecorated setups to fancier mall-like arrangements with meeting rooms, dining terraces, atriums and the like. Financial incentives will be provided to encourage licensees to move upward in the quality and size of their installations.

A single Xanadu stand should in principle be able to grow to about a thousand

LITERARY 5/9 MACHINES

outside lines, and two hundred inside users, but maintain at the same time a homey futuristic atmosphere.

Xanadu Central expects to supply a complete operational package for all phases of the business. This includes the service (storage, retrieval, communication, front ends), account maintenance and billing, customer credit system, method for rental of front-end machines and discounted sale of approved front-end machines and programs, printout services, scanning services, high-quality graphics output, motion picture output, etc.

Uniforms, promotional materials, architecture and software will all be supplied or prescribed by Xanadu Central.

On-the-job training for Xanadu conductors will take place in the stand. Additional training at Xanadu Central will be required for promotion of conductors to the Hypercorps, whose members will circulate among Xanadu stations to promote the generalist subculture and sophisticated use of the system.

LITERARY 5/10 MACHINES

PROJECTED COSTS OF NETWORK USAGE, 1990
--AND WHAT THEY GO TOWARDS

These are some estimated costs of using the Xanadu network during its start-up phase. Note that while an objective is to lower prices as fast as possible, in fact this means keeping demand within the growing network's ability to serve. That means lowering prices at a rate which will keep demand from swamping the network.

	Estimated cost to user
1. STORAGE THIS FIGURE IS SET BY THE STORAGE VENDOR.	
One-time charge (including redundant storage at one other server)	$ 20/meg (.02/kb)
Additional redundancy, per server	$ 5/meg
Annual maintenance, per server	$ 1/meg (.10 kb)
2. CONNECT TIME THIS FIGURE IS SET BY THE STORAGE VENDOR.	
Prime time	$ 5/hour
Off-time (typical)	$ 2/hour
3. BYTE DELIVERY CHARGE THIS FIGURE IS SET BY THE STORAGE VENDOR.	
	.00001/byte typical

1/1000 of a cent per byte works out to about five cents for a thousand words, or a dollar for twenty thousand words.

LITERARY 5/11 MACHINES

4. AUTHOR'S FUND/AUTHOR'S OR OWNER'S ROYALTY

This is charged in addition to the byte-delivery charge whenever bytes are shipped from a network server to a user.

Surcharge per byte   .000001/byte

Royalty is measured in *nibs*. A nib is the royalty or author's reserve charged per byte.

This surcharge is fixed by Xanadu Central and may change annually with six months' advance notice. (The figure is selected for public satisfaction, as the Xanadu enterprises get no part of it.)

This fee accumulates to the cash register of the given document; when the network charges incurred by that document have been offset, the remainder becomes the author's profit.

When bytes are taken from an unpublished document (one in the public domain), this surcharge is added to the Author's Fund, an escrow account whose purpose is the charitable funding of worthy causes within the network. These causes can include the costs of input and proofreading of non-owned documents, subsidies to struggling writers and artists, and other worthy purposes.

5. CONNECTION TO LOCAL STORAGE VENDOR

THIS FIGURE IS SET BY THE COMMUNICATION VENDOR (e.g., telephone company) and method of connection chosen (e.g., telephone line, high-bandwidth digital line, laser, etc.).

6. PUBLICATION FEE $ 5. per document

This is a one-time fee charged for the registration of a document to be published. It covers registration cost and conversion of the document to the published state, installation of cash register, registration on-site of claim to document ownership (not to be confused with official copyright registration, but carrying some evidential value), etc.

LITERARY 5/12 MACHINES

ROYALTIES IN THE XANADU
PUBLISHING METHOD

When you put a quarter in the jukebox you are paying royalties to songwriter, singer, musicians and agents. This method (worked out by ASCAP, the American Society of Composers and Performers), permits an immense amount of commercial traffic by handling the matter of royalty automatically on a fixed-fee basis.

(See earlier discussion in Chapter Two.)

Similarly, our method is simple, implementable, and allows free quotation and collaging of materials among documents.

Each published document has a *cash register*. This is a system-maintained counter which increments whenever bytes or links are delivered out of the document. The cash register has no size limit. It is in the user's system area, along with passwords and accounting information.

The publishing user may query the cash register of his, her or its document at any time. Users wishing to keep detailed time-accounting information--finding peak hours of usage, say, or the effect of a public event upon readership--may query it as often as they like, even dedicating a leased line to the purpose, but the system does not bother with such details.

Royalty is fixed per byte delivered.

The unit of royalty is the *nib* (as in "his nibs, the king").

BYTE ROYALTY

The level at which to set the byte royalty is a delicate issue. As a starting point, we want to set it at about the same level per byte as that received by the author of a paperback book.

LINK ROYALTY

A basis for link royalty is not yet established. It may be a fixed number of nibs per link, though this may not be counted for links within a document (such as paragraphs and text attributes).

AUTHOR'S FUND

Royalties are collected for all delivery of materials to the network. If the material delivered is *owned and published*, these fees are rebated to the publisher; otherwise they accumulate in the Author's Fund, to be used for worthy purposes related to the promotion of scholarship and creativity, and are administered by an appropriate governing body.

One way to think of it is that *all* royalty is taken in by the Author's Fund, and that individual copyright-holders are rewarded if their material is used.

LITERARY 5/13 MACHINES

FINE PRINT: THE CONTRACTS

The following proposed three contracts provide a tripod of legal relationships, indicating roughly the planned legal structure of operations for the proposed network. These constitute a tentative sketch and have not been extensively analyzed by counsel.

The three proposed relationships outlined are beween Project Xanadu and the Xanadu licensee or "storage vendor;" between the Xanadu licensee and the customer as private user; and between the licensee and the customer when the customer proceeds to publish something, i.e., becomes a "publisher." The publishing agreement is between user and storage vendor much as a car-rental agreement is between user and franchisee.

Inflation. Escalator clauses for inflation have been left out for clarity.

Grateful acknowledgment is made to Robert A. Heinlein for instruction in contractual design.

Between Project Xanadu and the Storage Vendor:

XANADU™ STORAGE VENDOR CONTRACT

This is an agreement between Project Xanadu and _____ ("Storage Vendor"), for provision of service based on the experimental software developed by Project Xanadu and XOC, Inc.

In return for Storage Vendor's participation in the Xanadu™ storage system and/or network, Project Xanadu agrees to furnish Storage Vendor with one executable copy of Xanadu™ storage and delivery software (the "Back-End Object Code"), for use on machines at Storage Vendor's premises at _____. This copy will be replaced by Project Xanadu from time to time by updated and changed versions of the Back-End Object Code, as developed by Project Xanadu or other parties.

In return for membership and participation in the Xanadu storage network, Storage Vendor agrees to use software furnished by Project Xanadu without modification. Storage Vendor agrees to honor requests for material from customers connected to servers operated by other Xanadu-licensed storage vendors, and accept material for storage from other Xanadu-licensed vendors within the network under prevailing arrangements for request and fulfillment of storage rental performed by Back-End Storage Code.

Storage Vendor agrees to engage in best efforts for the preservation and privacy of all customer material, and not to breach the confidence of any customer, examining customers' stored materials

LITERARY 5/14 MACHINES

only as required for the orderly maintenance of the system; and not to spy for any private persons, corporations or agencies of any government upon the private materials of any customers, nor discuss such private materials with anyone. Storage Vendor agrees to keep equipment in good working order, keep premises neat and clean, and take all necessary steps to assure continued, orderly and attractive service.

Non-disclosure agreement. Storage Vendor agrees to be bound by non-disclosure agreement with respect to all trade secrets of Project Xanadu, including but not limited to access to the Back-End Object Code, knowledge of internal operating principles which are not known in the general literature, use of unique terminology confidential to the Xanadu system, and plans for future development of the system.

Promotion of system; non-competition with customers. Storage Vendor agrees to promote the usage of Xanadu™ networking services, endeavoring to facilitate the use of the system by all orderly customers, favoring no partisan points of view or class of customer; and not to engage in the publishing of works competing with those of customers except as a private individual and customer.

Fees. Storage Vendor agrees to pay Project Xanadu an annual fee for every byte stored (at the annualized rate of $.00000_____ per byte). Storage Vendor further agrees to pay Project Xanadu a fee for every byte shipped to a customer (at the rate of $.00000_____ per byte).

Stand. If Storage Vendor operates a drop-in public-access user station for public relations and user instruction ("Xanadu Stand"), Storage Vendor agrees

to maintain such premises according to the marketing and maintenance guidelines of Project Xanadu, adhering to such standards as Project Xanadu will change from time to time, hiring personnel and organizing all aspects of the Xanadu Stand as specified by the standards supplied by Project Xanadu and altered by Project Xanadu from time to time.

Storage vendor further agrees to undertake no capital expansion except under the supervision and with the approval of Project Xanadu.

To encourage the building, staffing and maintenance of Xanadu Stands, Project Xanadu agrees to reduce the above fees by a proportion of _____% per year for each dollar spent in expansion.

Disclaimers. Storage Vendor acknowledges that the feasibility of the storage and publishing plans being undertaken by Project Xanadu have not been proven; that this enterprise is being undertaken at Storage Vendor's own risk; and that the software's local or large-scale operation or various of its announced intentions may prove infeasible. Storage Vendor acknowledges that the software field is a peculiar and unreliable art, and further acknowledges that the Xanadu storage-and- delivery software is experimental and under continuing development and modification; and that its reliability for the intact preservation and delivery of customer's information cannot be established now or at any foreseeable time; that aspects of the software which appear to work correctly at one time may not work correctly at a later time, circumstance, or state of development; that the endeavor to provide the contemplated services may be proven impossible or may never work; and that in no case will Storage Vendor seek damages from Project Xanadu for failures of the system to meet its

LITERARY 5/15 MACHINES

imaginative specification.

Cancellation of agreement. In the event of unsatisfactory performance by Storage Vendor, Project Xanadu may cancel this agreement at any time.

Storage Vendor may cancel this agreement for any reason upon _____ days' notice. Upon notice of cancellation, Storage Vendor will arrange for the orderly transition of all customer-stored materials to other Xanadu locations, and destroy all copies of customer materials thereon, and remove any Xanadu insignia from equipment owned by Storage Vendor. Storage Vendor will return all signs, promotional materials, uniforms, and other objects particular to the Xanadu enterprise, not allowing them to pass into other hands. In the event of such cancellation, Storage Vendor agrees not to go into the vending of computer storage (except in conjunction with conventional time-sharing services allowing the execution of customer programs in popular computer languages) for a period of five years except to residents of the state of Arkansas.

Between Vendor and User:

AGREEMENT FOR XANADU™
STORAGE AND DELIVERY SERVICES

This is an agreement between _____ ("User") and _____ ("Storage Vendor"), a licensee of the Xanadu™ storage system and publishing method ("The System"), for the long-term storage of data belonging to User, and for the delivery of copies and partial copies of that data on demand.

Storage Vendor's responsibility. In return for User's storage and other fees, Storage Vendor agrees to endeavor with best effort to store User's material safely, to transmit requested portions of it on demand to User and other persons permitted access to the material by User. Storage Vendor agrees to exert best efforts to maintain confidentiality of User's materials with the exception of such transmission, employing the experimental methods and software under development by, and from time to time modified by, Project Xanadu, XOC, Inc., and associated parties.

Storage of improper material. User agrees not to store material copyrighted by others or unlawfully in User's possession. User agrees to be responsible for all damages, direct and consequential, due to contents of material User makes wrongfully available on the network, including but not limited to damages resulting from libel, violation of privacy, violation of copyright, and violation of trade secret.

Rule of Law. User agrees to abide by all national, state and local laws in the use of The System, whether now in effect or later enacted. User acknowledges also that User may be liable for criminal charges resulting from making material

LITERARY 5/16 MACHINES

unlawfully available on the network, including but not limited to the improper disclosure of military secrets, dissemination of criminal knowledge, violation of the Trading With Enemies Acts, and such other laws as may from time to time come into effect.

Experimental nature of system. User acknowledges that all services are being performed by unproven software furnished by Project Xanadu, that the software field is a peculiar and unreliable art, and further acknowledges that the Xanadu storage-and-delivery software is experimental and under continuing development and modification; that the reliability and feasibility of these services has not been proven, that the reliability of such software for the intact preservation and delivery of User's information cannot be established now or at any foreseeable time; that aspects of the software which appear to work correctly at one time may not work correctly at a later time, circumstance, or state of development.

User acknowledges that Storage Vendor makes no guarantee as to the safety of material stored on any part of the network. Consequently User agrees that any damage, loss or alteration to User's data, failure to deliver it as requested, or unauthorized disclosure to other parties, will be wholly at User's risk, and Storage Vendor shall not be responsible for damages greater than what User has paid Storage Vendor for the storage of the lost or damaged portions, or for damages greater than the royalties proven to have been omitted. User agrees to hold harmless both Storage Vendor and Project Xanadu for any other damages, direct or consequential, resulting from unsatisfactory performance of The System, or the Storage Vendor's operation of it.

Safety measures by User for User's privacy. Vendor will make a best-effort attempt to safeguard material stored by User, by means of recommended application of experimental software furnished by Project Xanadu and XOC, Inc. However, User acknowledges that methods and precautions for privacy are rarely foolproof, and that use and consequences of such precautions and methods are at User's own risk. User further acknowledges that material stored as private on The System, though seemingly unseen by others, may be as public as if posted on a tree or bulletin board. User acknowledges that many forms of spying or accident may reveal contents of User's material to other parties. Considering such risks, if User still desires to store private material, User agrees to exercise diligence in the encryption of all materials User considers private; but User acknowledges that no such methods have been proven safe or reliable.

Unverified character of material on the network; liability for contents rests with users. User acknowedges that all material on the network is stored by users under similar arrangements to User's own, without verification or assurance of truth, authenticity, accuracy, usefulness or other beneficial character of such materials. User agrees that User will be the judge of such usefulness for User's purposes on an ongoing basis, and that no liability is assumed by Storage Vendor or Project Xanadu for any attributes, including truth, accuracy or usefulness, of material furnished by other users on the network.

User acknowledges that responsibility for the accuracy of material on the network rests with those users furnishing and publishing it; that liability for the consequences of inaccurate material rests with those users who furnish or publish it and represent it

LITERARY 5/17 MACHINES

to be correct and usable.

User agrees to be responsible for all damages, direct or consequential, due to actionable results of material furnished or published by User on the network, and to hold harmless Project Xanadu and XOC, Inc. for such damages.

Accurate reception. User acknowledges that due to possible unreliability of the software, unreliability and vulnerability of transmission systems, and myriad possibilities for intrusion and malicious mischief by unseen parties throughout the universe, all storage, and transmission of contents and links, and attempts to deliver such material, are at User's risk. User further acknowledges and accepts that Storage Vendor makes no guarantee as to the correctness or authenticity of any material received from other Users.

Refraining from harmful practices. User agrees to refrain from practices harmful to The System or to the interests of other users of The System, especially but not limited to crashing all or part of The System, or spying on, invading and/or altering others' private files; User further agrees to be responsible for all damages due to any such improper action on the part of User.

Resale and royalty. User agrees not to re-sell by transmission or access, any contents of The System without remanding to each provider of any works so sold a standard royalty (Nib) for every copy of every byte so sold, according to the standard Xanadu royalty mechanism.

Disclaimers. Storage Vendor acknowledges that the feasibility of the storage and publishing plans being undertaken by Project Xanadu have not been proven; that this enterprise is being undertaken at User's own risk; and that the software's local or large-scale operation or various of its announced intentions may prove infeasible. User acknowledges that the software field is a peculiar and unreliable art, and further acknowledges that the Xanadu storage-and-delivery software is experimental and under continuing development and modification; and that its reliability for the intact preservation and delivery of User's information cannot be established now or at any foreseeable time; that aspects of the software which appear to work correctly at one time may not work correctly at a later time, circumstance, or state of development; that the endeavor to provide the contemplated services may be proven impossible or may never work; and that in no case will User seek damages from Project Xanadu for failures of The System to meet its imaginative specification. Failure on the part of the User to adhere to this agreement may result in the termination by the Storage Vendor and/or Project Xanadu of any or all services provided by the Storage Vendor and/or Project Xanadu to the User.

(The following is to be printed on a multipart form like a credit-card charge slip, and must be filled out by the user and presented to the storage vendor for every work published.)

LITERARY 5/18 MACHINES

XANADU™ PUBLICATION CONTRACT

I hereby publish the Work entitled _____ (Xanadu document ID _____.0._____.0._____), according to the agreement printed on the back of this form. I declare that I am the owner of publication rights to this document, and that my possession or use or publication of its contents, and the consequent use of these contents by others, does not violate any laws or rights of others.

(Signature) _____, Publisher

(Xanadu User ID _____.0._____)

(Date) _____

Accepted,

(Signature) _____,
          Storage Vendor/Repository Printer

(Xauadu Server ID _____)

(Date) _____

(Full contract, printed on back, enumerates rights and duties of Publisher and Storage Vendor.)

BACK OF FORM:

This is the full agreement, as executed on the other side of this form, between parties identified as "Publisher" and "Storage Vendor/Repository Printer," as named on the other side of this form, regarding the "Work" identified on the other side of this form.

Publisher warrants that the Work is Publisher's intellectual property; that he, she or it is the sole owner of the Work, or, if not the sole owner, licensed to publish and distribute it by all others having rights in it. Publisher further warrants that the Work and its public accessibility do not violate national security, libel, trade secret or other rights of intellectual property, or the legal privacy of others; and that the Work's public accessibility does not violate any other rights, contractual obligations, or laws. Publisher further warrants that publication of the Work does not damage national security. Publisher further agrees to indemnify and hold harmless Storage Vendor/Repository Printer, Project Xanadu and XOC, Inc. from all damage due to any contents of the Work which are illegal or tortious, or lead to civil action by any parties.

Duties of Storage Vendor/Repository Printer. Storage Vendor/Repository Printer is functioning in the role of warehouser, printer and delivery service for the the Work. In return for the various fees of the system, Storage Vendor/Repository Printer agrees to store, with due diligence, one copy of the Work (the "Original") by electronic and/or magnetic means, and to furnish portions of the Work as rapidly as possible to any user operating properly within the rules of Xanadu™ storage and networking. Storage Vendor/Repository Printer further agrees to honor all requests for copies and partial copies of the work by users throughout the Xanadu network, employing experimental software furnished by Project Xanadu

LITERARY 5/19 MACHINES

and XOC, Inc., sending out such copies electronically to Xanadu-licensed customers or other Xanadu-licensed storage vendors, and will remand to Publisher a royalty fee for each byte so copied from the Work on each occasion of delivery of said byte to a customer. The royalty amount (Nib) will be fixed by Project Xanadu, and may be modified from time to time, but shall not be less than .00000_____ cent per byte.

Storage Vendor/Repository Printer agrees to furnish paper printing services of parts of the Work to all orderly Xanadu-licensed customers upon request, and any linked or related material as requested, forwarding standard royalties to Publisher for each byte so printed.

Storage Vendor/Repository Printer will delegate to other storage vendors _____ copies of the Work for safety, at prevailing rates of these storage vendors, this storage to be paid for by Publisher.

Storage Vendor/Repository Printer will present to receiving equipment the copyright status of all fragments transmitted from the Work, as represented by Publisher according to means provided within the Xanadu system, and Storage Vendor/Repository Printer will print copyright notices in association with all copyrighted fragments printed on paper. Storage Vendor/Repository Printer will further present to receiving equipment the trademark status of all trademarks from the Work, as represented by Publisher according to means provided within the Xanadu system.

Fees to Storage Vendor/Repository Printer. Publisher agrees to pay Storage Vendor/Repository Printer a publication registration fee of $_____ for the transfer of this work to Published status. The

cost to Publisher of publication will consist entirely of the said publication fee; all other charges will remain the same. These will consist of storage fees (as provided in Repository Printer's fee schedule) to be paid by Publisher, and byte-delivery charges to be paid by users requesting portions of the Work, in either printed or screen form.

Distribution costs. All costs of distribution will be borne by users according to standard fee schedules of Storage Vendor/Repository Printer and the Xanadu network.

Royalty. Operating royalty rules of Project Xanadu will be observed. Storage Vendor/Repository Printer will forward a royalty of one Nib to Publisher each time a byte of the Work is delivered to a final user connected anywhere to the Xanadu network, accounting of such Nibs to take place within systems of transactions provided by the Back-End Object Code. Royalties will be paid to Publisher's account and used to offset storage costs or paid separately if requested by Publisher and if storage costs have been paid.

Copies kept by users. Publisher acknowledges that users may keep copies of the material delivered to users through an approved Xanadu vendor, but may not distribute or resell such copies without the forwarding to Publisher of the standard royalty fees. Publisher acknowledges, however, that no means for enforcement of this provision is possible within the Xanadu network unless violating users re-store copies of the material on the Xanadu network at a later time for resale and this resale comes to the attention of Publisher.

Publisher agrees to permit any and all use of the Work by any users of the system, including

LITERARY 5/20 MACHINES

linkage to the Work or inclusion by virtual copy or quote-link of portions of the Work in other documents, provided that said royalty is collected and paid to Publisher for each delivery to a final user of material from the Work. Publisher acknowledges that if a private copy of portions or all of the Work is made and kept by a user in some other storage form, royalty will only be collected at the time the first copy is delivered to that user. A user's perpetual re-use of such a properly-purchased copy shall be deemed by Publisher to be fair use.

Publisher agrees to identify all trademarks and copyrighted material within the Work by means provided within the Xanadu system, so that identity of trademarks and copyrighted materials can be transmitted to users in association with each fragment transmitted, and printed on printouts of such fragments, and presented on screens in association with such fragments.

Damages. Publisher agrees to be responsible for, and hold Storage Vendor/Repository Printer, Project Xanadu and XOC, Inc. harmless from, any damages, direct or consequential, resulting from availability of the Work.

Removal by court order. Publisher acknowledges that the Work may be summarily removed from storage and publication on court order.

Withdrawal. Publisher may withdraw the Work from publication on one year's notice. Publisher agrees that there will be a withdrawal fee of $_____, to cover the posting of withdrawal notices and Repository Printer's exertions to withdraw. While Publisher may publish the Work by any other means simultaneously with Xanadu publication, Publisher agrees not to withdraw it from Xanadu

publishing without withdrawing it also from any other form of on-line publishing for a period of _____ months.

Publisher's claim to ownership. It is understood that Publisher's claim to ownership is not established by this agreement, and that this agreement does not constitute legal copyright registration (though this claim and this act of publication may contribute to the copyrighted status of the Work), and Publisher agrees take all appropriate steps for protection of Publisher's right in the Work.

LITERARY 5/21 MACHINES

MAIN PUBLICATIONS ABOUT THE XANADU™ STORAGE AND PUBLISHING SYSTEM BY OTHERS

K. Eric Drexler, *Engines of Creation: Challenges and Choices of the Last Technological Revolution.* Anchor/Doubleday, 1986. Especially pages 220-30.

Howard Rheingold, *Tools for Thought: The People and Ideas behind the* Next *Computer Revolution.* Simon and Schuster, 1985. Especially 24, 295-305.

Clifford Barney, "The Prophet from Xanadu." *PC World* vol. 1 #3 (undated, ca. June 1983), 292 ff.

BY TED NELSON

BOOKS.

Literary Machines, 1981; Edition 87.1, 1987. Published by the author.

Computer Lib, 1974, numerous reprintings. Published by the author. Second edition from Microsoft Press, 1987.

ARTICLES.

"The Tyranny of the File." *Datamation*, 15 December 1986.

"A Vision of the Future." *Publishers Weekly*, 23 Nov 1986.

"Computopia Now!" in Steve Ditlea (ed.), *Digital Deli* (Workman Publishing, 1984), 349-51.

"A New Home for the Mind," *Datamation*, March 1982.

"The Magicians, the Snark and the Camel." *Creative Computing*, December 1981.

"Replacing the Printed Word." Proc. IFIP 80 (S.H. Lavington, ed., *Information Processing 80*, North-Holland Publishing Co., 1980, 1013-1023).

"Interactive Systems and the Design of Virtuality." (In two parts.) *Creative Computing*, Nov and Dec 1980.

"A Dream for Irving Snerd." *Creative Computing*, ca. July 1977.

"Data Realms and Magic Windows." Proceedings of ACPA-5 (1975 meeting of the Assn. of Computer Programmers and Analysts).

"Electronic Publishing and Electronic Literature." In DeLand (ed.), *Information Technology in Health Science Education*, Plenum Press, 1978.

(With Tom DeFanti and Dan Sandin), "Computer Graphics as a Way of Life." In proc. Siggraph conference, 1974.

"A Conceptual Framework for Man-Machine Everything," Proc. National Joint Computer Conference, 1973.

LITERARY 6/1 MACHINES

"As We Will Think," Proc. Online 72 Conference, Brunel U., Uxbridge England.

"Computopia and Cybercrud," in Levien (ed.), *Computers in Instruction*, The Rand Corporation, 1974.

"Las Vegas Confrontation Sit-Out: A CAI Radical's View from Solitary," SIGCUE Newsletter, 1971.

"Barnum-Tronics," Swarthmore College Alumni Bulletin, December 1970.

"No More Teacher's Dirty Looks," *Computer Decisions*, September 1970. Partially reprinted in *Electric Media* by Les Brown and Sema Marks (Harcourt, 1974); fully reprinted in *Computer Lib*.

(With Steven Carmody, et al.), "A Hypertext Editing System for the 360," in Faiman and Nievergelt (eds.), *Pertinent Concepts in Computer Graphics*, U. Illinois Press, 1969.

"Getting It Out of Our System," in Schecter, *Information Retrieval: a Critical View*, Thompson Books, 1967.

"Stretchtext." Unpublished paper on stretchable hypertext form, 1966.

"Hypertext Notes." Ten brief essays on hypertext forms, ca. 1966. (Circulated in manuscript.)

"New Media and Creativity Systems." Graphical brochure intended to expound computer graphics and related concepts, ca. 1966.

"Suggestion for an On-Line Braille Display," Proc. Society for Information Display, Fall 1965.

"The Hypertext." Proc. World Documentation Federation, 1965.

"A File Structure for the Complex, the Changing and the Indeterminate." Proc. Association for Computing Machinery, 1965.

LITERARY 6/2 MACHINES

THANKS FROM THE AUTHOR

My gratitude to Lauren Sarno is inexpressible. She has served tirelessly as editor, literary agent, diplomat, artwork translator, pasteup artist and cheerleader. She has helped clarify the writing and temper its vehemence. Mainly she got the book out.

Many thanks to David Rabinowitz for the use of his laser printer in preparing the book.

My special thanks also to Steve Witham, who helped greatly on every edition of this book. It was only he that could work my old copier correctly, on which all the original copies were made, and only he that really understood how to make the PC and Macintosh work.

My very special thanks to Laura McLaughlin and Sean Harmon for their hospitality during different phases of this project.

Special thanks also to Robert W. Fiddler, whose sage advice has kept me out of a lot of trouble.

Thanks to my son, Erik Nelson, for suggesting the chapter title "Civilization and Its Disk-Contents."

Let me acknowledge here, too, my special indebtedness to my late grandparents, Mr. and Mrs. Theodor Holm, whose encouragement and help sustained me and this work through the years.

FRIENDS AND ASSOCIATES OF THE PROJECT

The following individuals are not merely friends of the group, but have specifically given help, encouragement, support, hospitality, or friendship to the project itself in one or more of its phases and branches.

We think this list is reasonably complete, but memory flags in reviewing many hundreds of events and many thousands of miles, so apologies in advance to that special person who may have been omitted.

Steve André
Glen Babecki
Tom Barnard
Roz Barnett
Bunty Barus
Carl Barus
Alan Boyd
Jacob Brackman
Sandy Brown
James Burke
Mike Butler
Stella Calvert
D.J. Cone
Stanley Cooke
John Copeland
Mark Crandall
Pat Crepeau
Hugh Daniel
Richard deVore
Tom Dinnella
Steve Ditlea
Steve Dompier

LITERARY 6/3 MACHINES

Rich Dutcher
Esther Dyson
Steve Eberbach
Doug Engelbart
Jonathan Fagin
Anne Fallon
Robert W. Fiddler
Harry Garland
Graham Gibbard
Edward Tesla Gregory
Anna Gruda
Eric Gullichsen
Paul Gumerman
Scott Guthery
Robert Haavind
Sean Harmon
Charles S. Harris
Judith Harris
Bevier Hasbrouck
Dennis Hayes
Dick Heiser
Richard Hill
Sheila Hill
Danny Hillis
Starr Roxanne Hiltz
Emil Hirsch
Mike Hirsch
Peter Hirschberg
Jean Parke Holm
Theodor Holm
Catherine Ikam
Peter Z. Ingerman
Herb Johnson
William Jovanovich
Mitch Kapor
Amy Karash
Alan Kay
Skip King

Art Kleiner
Gene Klotz
Elliot Klugman
Nat Kuhn
Timothy Leary
Mike Lecuyer
Debra Levin
Bob Levine
Ginny Levine
John R. Levine
Margy Levine
Faye Levine
Ann Lewin
Mary Jo Lewis
A. Sheldon Liederkranz
Joseph I. Lipson
Leon Loeb
Jeffrey Lord
Bob Lovell
Sue Lovell
John Mauchly
Mike McClary
Laura McLaughlin
Sheila McKenzie
Ann Miller
David C. Miller
Margaret Minsky
Marvin Minsky
Calvin Mooers
Chip Morningstar
Cameron Moseley
Jim Moses
Erika Muhlenberg
Maria Nekam
Erik Nelson
John Nelson
Peter Nelson
Janie Noble

Tim Oren
Gail Pergamit
Chris Peterson
Jan Peugh
Jonathan V. Post
Bob Radford
Laura Raettig
Naomi Reynolds
Suzanne Ropiequet
Bill Richard
Phil Salin
Lauren Sarno
Dennis Schmidt
Jonathan Schmidt
Steve Senzig
Charlie Smith
Dan Smith
Nancy Smith
Olga Smyth
Jean-Pierre Soisson
Barbara Staudt
Dave Staudt
Deborah Stone
L. Joseph Stone
Johan Strandberg
Ull Strandberg
Geo Swan
Paul Terrell
Les Tietz
Murray Turoff
Peter Vellenga
John Verity
Bob Wallace
Bryan Wanty
Lauren Wedeles
Mike Westgate
Steve Witham
David Woodcock
Maggie Woodcock
Leor Zolman

LITERARY 6/4 MACHINES

EPILOG

FATE ACCOMPLI

This is a Caper story--a beckoning dream at the far edge of possibility that has been too good to let go of, and just too far away to reach, for half my life. The intrepid little group of co-conspirators--my comedy burglar team--has gotten far closer to this dream than any sane person could have thought possible.

Though everything has seemed to block our way, on balance the Fates have been very much with us: laying down a trail of crumbs, as it were, through a very strange forest to a very unusual place. We propose to build a palace here and let you all inside.

Whether the ground will hold, what beasts and trolls may assail us here, all remain to be ascertained. We have done our best and will continue to do so.

We bring banners. We have held to ideals created long ago, in different times and places, the very best ideals we could find. We have carried these banners unstained to this new place, we now plant them and hope to see them floating in the wind. But it is dark and quiet and lonely here, and not yet dawn.

Now it is for you the reader to examine this place and say where, if anywhere, you would rather be. We hope you share our sense of urgency and of history. The choices are fewer than you might have thought, and perhaps they need to be made quickly. Good luck to you, and to us all.

LITERARY 6/6 MACHINES

About The Author

Ted Nelson is a rogue intellectual, social critic, and designer: especially, a designer of interactive computer systems for our world of tomorrow. He has been designing computer text systems on his own since 1960, and may thus be considered one of the inventors of word processing. Douglas Engelbart, the original inventor of word processing, gives Nelson equal credit for the discovery of the text link, and full credit for the invention of the hypertext concept.

Nelson holds degrees from Swarthmore and Harvard, and has taught, consulted and lectured variously. He was the editor of *Creative Computing* magazine in 1980 and 1981. His book *Computer Lib* is often cited as an "underground classic."

A dynamic orator, he was an invited speaker at the Eighth World Computer Congress, giving his talk "Replacing the Printed Word," on which this book is based, in Tokyo and Melbourne.

Nelson's ideas have a wide underground following in the computer field. His maverick point of view stresses the art and conceptual integration of screen graphics and other responding environments, and an apocalyptic and millenarian view of a new Golden Age — a changed and better life to come at tomorrow's computer screens (completely unlike today's).

This is a report on his religion and his life's work, the Xanadu Hypertext System, a scheme for instantaneous publishing and archiving with very broad implications — designed for "children, researchers and heads of state."

ORDERING INFORMATION

Books by Theodor Holm Nelson

[ ] Literary Machines $19.95

[ ] Computer Lib, Original Edition. $15.95

[ ] Computer Lib, Revised and Updated Edition $18.95

For Additional Copies

Title	Price	Quantity	Amt. Enclosed

Shipping: $2.00/first book; $1.00/each additional book:

Total Amount Enclosed:

Ship to:

Name _____

Address _____

City/State/Zip _____

Telephone: _____

Standard retail discounts available on volume purchases. Please inquire.

Make check or money order payable to:

The Distributors, 702 S. Michigan Street, South Bend, IN 46618

ORDERING INFORMATION

Books by Theodor Holm Nelson

[ ] Literary Machines $19.95

[ ] Computer Lib, Original Edition. $15.95

[ ] Computer Lib, Revised and Updated Edition $18.95

For Additional Copies

Title	Price	Quantity	Amt. Enclosed

Shipping: $2.00/first book; $1.00/each additional book:

Total Amount Enclosed:

Ship to:

Name _____

Address _____

City/State/Zip _____

Telephone: _____

Standard retail discounts available on volume purchases. Please inquire.

Make check or money order payable to:

The Distributors, 702 S. Michigan Street, South Bend, IN 46618